MW01502611

INTRODUCTION TO THE LAW OF TORTS

Thomas B. Alleman
Frances B. Whiteside

Copyright © 2001
All rights reserved.
Pearson Publications Company
Dallas, Texas

Website: Pearsonpub-legal.com

ISBN: 0-929563-54-9

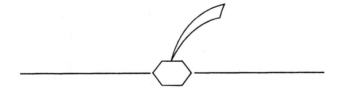

Introduction to the Law of Torts is designed as a textbook for classroom use. The information contained herein is intended only for educational and informational purposes.

ACKNOWLEDGMENTS

The authors wish to thank all those who contributed to this textbook during its preparation, especially Kathryn Myers, Ben H. Wilcox, A. McDonald, Reginia Judge, and Lance Cooper in the final editing stage.

Thomas B. Alleman, Esq.
Frances B. Whiteside

For Sarah, Virginia and Sam....and specially for Susan...

Thomas B. Alleman, Esq.

TABLE OF CONTENTS

Introduction
The Study of Law and This Book

Chapter One
Torts, Contracts, and Crimes:
What They Are and What They Aren't

Chapter Two
The First Torts: Trespass,
Assault, Battery, and Conversion

Chapter Three
**Seems Reasonable to Me: The Idea
of Ordinary Care and Negligence**

Chapter Four
**Reality Check: Establishing the
Standard of Care in the Courtroom**

Chapter Five
No Cause for Alarm: The Concept
of Causation in the Law of Torts

Chapter Six
"Dee-Fense, Dee-Fense":
Defenses to Claims of Negligence

Chapter Seven
The Special Duties
of Landowners

Chapter Eight
What's It Worth to You?
Compensatory Damages in Tort Cases

Chapter Nine
"Ooooh...Gross!": Aggravated Negligence,
Fault, and Punitive Damages

Chapter Ten
Tort Liability for Defective Products

Chapter Eleven
**Sticks and Stones: The Law of
Defamation, Libel, and Slander**

Chapter Twelve
**"I Want To Be Alone": Torts
Involving Privacy and Seclusion**

Chapter Sixteen
The Role of Insurance in the Law of Toxic Torts

Chapter Seventeen
A Few Closing Thoughts

THE STUDY OF LAW
AND THIS BOOK

In this book and others that you may read during your education, you will be the victim of a gentle deception. It is easy to assume that the purpose of reading case excerpts is to glean the legal principles they present and understand the thinking that goes into concepts like negligence, strict liability, defamation, and many others. Your instructors will encourage this by giving you cases to brief in which you will place portions of case holdings into relatively neat pigeonholes.

The problem with this approach is that it overlooks the most important part of a case: the facts. All case law is fact driven. As Justice Oliver Wendell Holmes remarked, "The life of the law has not been logic: it has been experience."[*] In other words, legal principle rarely emerges from abstract study. It generally arises when two people are having a dispute, and they seek a neutral arbiter to resolve it. The law has the same roots as a parent resolving a dispute between two children — the need for peace among disputants and for predictable rules to resolve disputes.

Admittedly, this is oversimplification, but it still catches a great deal of the common law legal process. Think about it. Someone files a lawsuit in which one alleges that another (or others) has done wrong. That person asks the court for some kind of remedy. The defendants can file a response asserting their defenses. Ultimately, with or without discovery or other proceedings, the parties present their evidence to the court or jury. Based upon what is presented (or not presented) in the trial, the judge fashions jury instructions that embody the law applicable to the situation existing between the parties.

---

[*] O. W. Holmes, Jr., *The Common Law* 1 (Howe ed., 1963)

What if there is no jury instruction that precisely meets the needs of a particular case? Then the court *creates* one. The parties often have a voice in this process, and some intensely practical judges allow the parties to put forward the instructions they want, reasoning that the parties will have to defend the jury charge on appeal. At some point, though, the judge gives instructions to the jury on the law. It is this moment — essentially the judge's *reaction* to the factual evidence in the case and his or her decision as to what rules should apply[*] — that embodies more than any other the process by which the law evolves.

If the trial judge gives a new instruction, one that goes beyond or in a different direction from prior law, the change in law is immediate. An appellate court may choose not to permit the change. But in doing so, the appellate court generally must consider what the trial court did and why it did it. Lawyers and judges, being who they are, cannot consider anything without commenting about it, and comments lead to opinions, which you get to read!

Conversely, if the judge refuses a party's request for an instruction or theory, that party can ask the appellate court to require the trial judge to give the requested instruction. Again, this requires the appellate court to consider the merits of permitting the change, and in doing so, it still must consider what the trial court did and why it did it. This process goes on thousands of times every day, and it is the vehicle by which our common law expands. Still, it does not quite explain why you should focus on facts.

The importance of the facts in each case becomes clearer when we add another goal: predictability. People benefit by knowing in advance the likely outcome of doing or not doing something. Just as children learn not to do something because they see other kids go to "time out" or be spanked, grown-ups and businesses can look at what has happened to others with similar problems and predict what will happen if they try it.

---

[*] If you are familiar with the trial process, you can see that it does not change much from case to case. Plaintiff goes first. Defendant follows. Plaintiff rebuts. The rules of evidence do not vary greatly from case to case. In other words, the process of a trial is, for most purposes, a constant.

Where do they look? To court decisions that have the same or similar facts as their own situation, of course.

The common law encourages this reflection and comparison through a principle known as *stare decisis*. In Latin, it literally means "to stand by things decided," but idiomatically it can be translated as, "Copy!" Courts applying principles of *stare decisis* do so to honor and follow their older decisions. When presented with disputes that are substantively similar to a matter already decided, courts honoring *stare decisis* use the same substantive legal principles they used in deciding the prior case. What is the glue that binds earlier decisions to current case law? It is the facts of the case, because they form the basis for the dispute's substance.

That is why you should always focus on the facts as a primary basis for your study of legal issues. It all boils down to this process:

> My case involves a particular kind of factual dispute or claim. When the court last dealt with this kind of dispute, it applied the following rules: [fill in this space with your proposed court's rules.] As a result, [fill in the blank] happened. This is why the court said it was doing what it did: [fill in the blank with the prior court's basis/justification/reasoning.] Because courts act consistently, [fill in the blank] is likely to happen here. This is why we will win.

But now comes the fun part and the reason legal professionals always will have work: disputes are not always identical. Whichever side of a dispute we are on, our job is to take some aspect of it and emphasize (or de-emphasize) it so that a court will apply rules or decisions favorable to us. Sometimes this is hard. When a court has used the same rules to decide rear-end collision cases 1,000 times, you can comfortably predict that your chance of getting a different principle applied is very small unless you have a titanic difference between your case and prior cases to show the judge. On the other hand, your chances may be better in new areas of law or in situations where existing rules have been criticized by courts in other states or legal scholars. Your chances might also improve because of changing technology or shifts in society's stance on a particular issue (such as slavery).

Learning how to turn small differences into big ones, or vice versa, is a key to success as a legal professional. Sometimes a legal principle will be ripe for change, but much more often, you and the others on your team will rely upon differences in facts to make a more favorable case for your client.

There are two ways to go about developing facts. One is simply to collect more than the other parties involved in the case by discovery and by investigation. The other is to appreciate the importance of what you have better than your opponents.

Hands-on investigation is a crucial part of the legal business, but sadly, it is one that many young professionals view as less and less important. Even with all the modern investigatory aids, it remains essential that someone go and see. Here is an example. In a toxic tort case, suppose that a plaintiff's expert opines that poisonous vapors came into residential units through separate air conditioners located in each unit. The only problem was that the units did not have separate air conditioners; each building had a large chilled water unit. End of theory. End of expert. OOPS....

Investigation means go look and see. Interview. Dig. Find. This is not to minimize the importance of the discovery process. Quite the contrary. All the same, those who stay in their offices hoping that the facts will come to them are likely to be disappointed.

In an information age, superior appreciation and bigger piles should not be confused. In a recent mass toxic tort case, the parties marked well over *10,000* exhibits. Some of these were documents that experts needed as foundation for their testimony, but most were not. Of the 10,000, the parties used about 300 exhibits at trial. Of the 300, as demonstrated by the way the parties used them, only 40 were truly important. Big stacks of exhibits do not necessarily mean big evidence.

Many legal professionals tout the use of sophisticated database programs as a remedy for this. It must be said that developments in scanning and search engine technology bring closer the day when everything can be put in one database and searched word by word. But regardless of how sophisticated our computers are, someone still has to create the database and then read and appreciate the significance of what is there. In some cases, knowing who did or did not receive a key piece of paper can be vital. Sometimes it is important to understand ·how a particular medical test is done. Recreating an accident by animation or even with toy cars may be important. In one case, for instance, an attorney who was also an architect illustrated the stresses on a building's roof by making a model of the crucial joint from cardboard and a toilet paper tube. To paraphrase John Le Carre, the facts are the body of a case. You try on theories like suits of clothes.

Why, then, do we study the legal cases? Knowing what kinds of evidence must be presented in a courtroom to make a case that a jury can hear helps you know what facts to look for. If we say — and we will — that the plaintiff must prove the existence of a duty, this means that the plaintiff's team must come up with facts that would allow such a relationship to be created. Doctor-patient, attorney-client, architect-customer, and the driver on a public street are all examples of a relationship. We prove them by adducing facts showing existence of the relationship:

Q: When did you first see Dr. Smith?
A: August 7.

Q: Why did you go to see Dr. Smith?
A: I was having pains in my chest.

Q: Did Dr. Smith treat you?
A: Yes. He gave me a stress test, and some x-rays and....

Here we leave our humble example, because the relationship has been established. On August 7, Dr. Smith treated our witness, and a doctor-patient relationship came into being.

This kind of thing can happen with a document, as in this example:

Q: Did you ever ask the Smith law firm to represent you?
A: I did.

Q: Would you please identify Exhibit 3 for us?
A: It's my copy of my retainer agreement with the Smith law firm.

Q: What's the date on that document?
A: August 7.

Q: Is your signature on it?
A: Right there.

Q: Does another person's signature appear on that document?
A: Yes. Mr. Smith's name is right there.

Q: Your honor, Plaintiff offers Exhibit 3....

Here the plaintiff establishes the duty by introducing the written contract between lawyer and client. Although the issues can be mind-bogglingly complex, you can get the general idea from these short examples.

A Note About the Case Excerpts

As you read the case excerpts in this book, think about the kinds of evidence the parties in the case used to establish their points. Were they effective? Were they creative? Were they persuasive? Did they work? What did the court want? We use excerpts of cases to give you an idea of what kinds of evidence to put on, and to show you the beginnings of this process of evaluation and comparison that are at the core of *stare decisis*. So, that is what this is all about.

In choosing excerpts for this book, we tried to select cases that illustrate majority rules and developing trends in the law. However, the state in which you live may not apply the majority rule. Your state may have a statute that supersedes the common law. At times, you may find that your

state has not yet taken a position on a certain point of law. Therefore, check your own state law carefully to determine your state's law on the areas that we discuss in this book.

With the exception of important historical cases, we have tried to select decisions that are as recent as possible on a given point and from as many states as possible in the hope that this will provide the student with the most current trends in legal thinking. We certainly have not intended to slight any particular jurisdiction and its courts by omission of cases.

Chapter One

TORTS, CONTRACTS, AND CRIMES: WHAT THEY ARE AND WHAT THEY AREN'T

Much of what happens in the practice of law involves classification. From the most general to what sometimes seems to be the unbelievably minute, lawyers classify everything from behavior to remedies. Lawyers do this so that they can give advice concerning what someone's conduct should be and to determine what kinds of relief are available to a person or business harmed by another person's breach of an obligation. As a legal professional, you will also participate in this classification process.

At the most general level, the law divides the obligations assumed by individuals and businesses into three categories: **tort, contract,** and **criminal.**

Associated with each of these classifications are different forms of **duty, intent,** and **damage** (or **remedy),** which are themselves subject to classification and are more or less directly traceable to the nature of the relationship and obligations involved.

Tort Obligations — A Study in Contrasts

You'll soon see that contract law and criminal law are discussed in this chapter. Why is that? There are several reasons.

First, and most obviously, you can understand torts better by understanding how they differ from the other forms of obligation imposed by the law. Contrasting the concepts of contract, tort, and crime helps you to understand each better, just as it is easier to understand the differences between retrievers, beagles, and terriers by looking at them next to each other.

Second, these classifications do not always coexist comfortably with each other. There have been, and will continue to be, efforts to turn certain kinds of breaches of contract into torts. Thus, knowing where the edges of each concept are helps the analyst determine if, when, and how the concepts should overlap.

Third, each of these areas of obligation carries with it different historical baggage. Understanding the very different histories of contract, tort, criminal, and property law is essential to comprehend not only what these fields of law mean today, but what they might also mean in the future.[1]

Promises and Contracts

Perhaps the oldest form of obligation is that which one person voluntarily undertakes toward another. Whether one describes this as a covenant, promise, or even an oath, it involves some obligation or duty voluntarily assumed by one person and owed to another.

These obligations are marked by the fact that they are **negotiated**, **voluntarily assumed**, and **individual**. As we will soon see, the fact that these promises or contracts are negotiated is the first situation in which the general rule carries with it a body of exceptions.

Contract. An agreement that is
enforceable or recognizable at law.

A duty arising in contract requires the passage of consideration between the parties. A **duty** is a legal or moral obligation. **Consideration** is simply an exchange of something ("my rookie cards for your 1957 Mickey Mantle card").

Less often, consideration can be **detriment** or **forbearance**, as when someone agrees to put off collecting a debt in return for some action or promise by the debtor. In any case, the idea of consideration is essential to the notion that a contract is a bargained-for exchange.

Why does the law require people to keep their promises? In commercial transactions, enforcement of promises to sell or buy goods or services is necessary to ensure the predictability and stability of the marketplace.[2] But the same values of predictability and stability permeate virtually every relationship in society. Holding everyone to his or her promises gives the promises more value because it makes the person receiving the promise (the promisee) more likely to accept one.

An analogy to this is paper money, which for many years was backed by the government's promise that the bill could be redeemed in equal value for gold or silver. The idea that the intrinsically worthless slip of paper was backed by the government's precious metal reserves gave the public confidence in paper money. Here, the idea that a promise can be enforced in a court of law gives confidence.

Freedom to Bargain

Much is, however, to be gained by giving people the **freedom to bargain** with as few limitations as possible. This freedom encourages individuals and businesses to take on risky or unusual obligations, which in turn can benefit society. To do this, the courts will permit parties to enter into contracts of almost any kind, so long as their object is not illegal or in violation of a strongly-held public policy.[3]

Redress

A second way in which the law encourages people to enter into contracts is by permitting a party aggrieved by another person's breach to obtain **redress** in court without having to prove that the breach was intentional, malicious, or done with any other particular level of intent. Obviously, it often is easier to show that someone breached a promise than it is to show that the promise was breached with a particular intention or state of mind. The idea that it is relatively easy to get help when a promise is not performed gives incentive to enter into agreements.

Limiting Consequences

The third way that courts encourage people and businesses to enter into contracts is by **limiting the adverse consequences** that can arise from **breach of contract**. Imagine a situation in which a company fails to live up to its obligation to supply a small part crucial for the operation of a factory. As a result, the factory is idle too long, substantial production is lost, and the company goes into bankruptcy.

What should the supplier in our example above be required to pay? There are two approaches that can be taken in answering this question. The first is to award the bankrupt company a sum of money that represents the value of its injury, which in this case is something like the difference between being a viable, on-going business on the one hand and a bankrupt hulk on the other. The other is to award a sum of money that represents the value of the promise — in this case, the value of the part that was not delivered on time.

The term *status quo ante* means the position the parties were in before the contract was entered into. This provides the difference in value of what was promised and what was received.

The next question to be answered is, if you were the parts supplier, would you make the deal to supply the part for the factory if you knew going in that you might be liable for all the consequences of your failure to install it in time? Courts have historically taken the position that people and businesses would not be prone to enter into contracts if they faced the likelihood of being forced to be responsible for more than what they had promised to do.

The reason for this is that it would be almost impossible to determine in advance (and negotiate a price for) the consequences of how a breached promise could affect another person's business.

The Essential Characteristics of Contractual Duties:

- personal obligation
- reached after negotiation
- in return for consideration
- that can be enforced in court without having to prove why someone did not keep his or her promise
- with relief generally limited to the value of the promise.

A Look at Legal History

We will take a brief historical sojourn here to begin our analysis of what constitutes a tort obligation. In 1881, Oliver Wendell Holmes delivered lectures later published as *The Common Law*,[4] one of the most important American legal compilations of its time.

Mr. Holmes had a great deal to say on property, contracts, and many other subjects, but little to say about torts. There was very little he could say because the law of torts, as we presently understand it, was then in its infancy. Modern tort concepts are children of the 20th century, especially of its final 50 years.

A tort is a civil wrong, other than a breach of contract, which has caused harm to person or property or some business interest.

Where do torts come from? As Holmes noted, they certainly have moral antecedents.[5] The Sermon on the Mount and the Golden Rule are as close to the basis of modern tort law as could be found in one place. But the more likely basis for imposing obligations in tort comes from the transition of Anglo-American society from agrarian to industrial and commercial during the 19th century.

In small frontier villages and market communities based upon semi-barter economies, every transaction was likely to be face-to-face and negotiated. People saw and knew each other more intimately; goods and services tended to be provided locally. In such worlds, a law of contracts — a law of negotiated obligations running from individual to individual

— and a criminal law that involved the individual's relationship with government would be more than enough to handle almost any problem that could have been expected. Disputes could be handled by contract law or criminal law.

As society changed, relationships no longer depended as much on face-to-face contract or negotiation. People no longer dealt directly with the manufacturer of the products they used or the home they lived in. Rules that depended on privity no longer worked so well when, say, the user of a potentially defective product was in Great Falls and the manufacturer was in Harrisburg.

In *The Common Law*, Holmes would write on this issue as follows:

> [W]hen A assaults or slanders his neighbor, or converts his neighbor's property, he does a harm which he has never consented to bear, and if the law makes him pay for it, the reason for doing so must be found in some general view of the conduct which every one may fairly expect and demand from every other, whether that other has agreed to it or not. Such a general view is very hard to find....[6]

Holmes also described the other principle that had to be accounted for before a cogent theory of torts could evolve:

> The general principle of our law is that loss from accident must lie where it falls, and this principle is not affected by the fact that a human being is the instrument of misfortune. But relative to a given human being anything is accident which he could not fairly have been expected to contemplate and therefore to avoid.... No case or principle can be found ... subjecting an individual to liability for an act done without fault on his part.... All the cases concede that an injury arising from an inevitable accident, or, which in law or reason is the same thing, from an act that ordinary human care and

foresight are unable to guard against, is but the
misfortune of the sufferer, and lays no foundation for
legal responsibility.[7]

This view of the field undoubtedly was correct. Our modern view of a
tort, which is an obligation owed by all members of society to each
other, comes not from some "Eureka!" moment in which a scholar such
as Holmes or a judge dug down and found a new notion. It arose instead
as judges and scholars struggled to figure out a standard or rule by which
it could be determined just *what* ordinary human care and foresight
ought to be able to guard against.

Remember that this struggle took place against a background of several
hundred years' worth of cases and commentaries. Tort law arose slowly,
in part at least, because the procedural system in existence until the late
19th century made it virtually impossible to fit tort claims within a series
of pigeonholes (forms of action) allowed by the courts.[8]

These historical struggles still pervade the law of torts today. They also
give us three of the key distinguishing factors that always mark the
distinction between tort and contract obligations.

Distinguishing Factors of Torts

There are three distinguishing factors of torts:

1. Tort obligations are not personal. They arise instead, as Holmes
    put it, out of some general view of the conduct that everyone
    should fairly expect and demand from everyone else.
2. Tort obligations are not negotiated. The obligations arise
    whether "that other," who we soon will refer to as the
    tortfeasor, has agreed to it or not.
3. Nowhere in this process do we see any reference, hint, clue, or
    inference that there is in a tort obligation some analogue to the
    concept of consideration in contract obligations. There is not,
    except to the extent that getting to live in society somehow
    supplies it.

Unlike breach of a contract, breach of a tort obligation permits the injured party to recover damages and relief equal to the value of the injury. Since one cannot negotiate an obligation that arises in tort, there is no compelling reason to limit the value of recoverable damages to the value of the promise rather than the value of the injury. This is expressed most often as the difference in value of the injured property or person before and after the tort.

Suffice it to say, for present purposes, that — unlike the situation existing in contracts — breach of a tort obligation permits the injured party to recover damages equal to the value of the injury.

Blameworthiness

Now, we turn to the word we have been skirting, the "B" word inherent in torts: **blameworthiness**. Modern history to the contrary notwithstanding, it is still the case that tort liability arises when an individual's conduct falls culpably below some minimum level. In most situations, tort obligations carry with them inherent gradations of blameworthiness or fault, ranging from the inevitable accident — the idea most troubling to Holmes and his contemporaries — to vengeful, spiteful conduct intended to harm another.

In some cases, a certain level of fault is necessary before a court will find that a tort has occurred. In others, a higher level of blameworthiness will entitle the plaintiff to powerful kinds of relief (*i.e.*, a larger damage award). In virtually every case, we will look for blameworthiness and other facts that will support imputing liability to someone.

To summarize once again, tort obligations are:

- general obligations imposed on all society
- without negotiation
- without return promises or other consideration being given in exchange
- concepts of blameworthiness or fault are central elements

- the relief generally corresponds to the value of the injury inflicted.

Criminal Law

The third of the great divisions of obligation we discuss in this chapter is criminal.

Crime. An act that violates the penal law of the local, state, or federal government.

Stories of criminals and criminal punishment abound in everything from the Bible to Grecian mythology, and criminal laws may be found in all manner of ancient codes and legal compilations. The Code of Hammurabi and the Ten Commandments each contain principles we easily recognize today as being criminal in nature.

The obligation in criminal law is of an individual to a sovereign, rather than to other individuals as a group (tort law) or to a particular individual (contract law).

The foundation of criminal law is in the prerogative of keeping the peace. This prerogative resides in the sovereign authority, whether it is a monarch who rules by divine right or a popularly elected constitutional democracy. This was once known as the king's peace,[9] and it was the king or other sovereign to which the duty was owed to obey criminal law. As head guy[10] of the kingdom, the king not only was the person to whom the duty was owed, but he was also the person who judged what constituted breaches of that peace.

This resulted in rather rigidly defined rules governing what constituted breaches of the peace, what punishments could be imposed for what breaches and, most important, how the king or his officers would hear the complaints. The reason courts evolved was simple and very practical. The king had lots to do and could not spend all day every day hearing every criminal case that came along.

Intent

For people studying torts, the most important result of all this was the concept of **intent**, something that will permeate much of what we discuss in this textbook.[11] It can range at one end from entirely innocent activity that somehow causes harm to another (here we are at Holmes' inevitable accident again) to conduct designed from the outset to kill or destroy indiscriminately.

Intent. The state of mind accompanying an act.

The various degrees of criminal intent ordinarily involve some kind of active conduct or design rather than mere omission, though the latter could give rise to liability in tort. This is not to say that active intent to cause harm cannot be the basis of tort liability, because it certainly can. However, in criminal law active intent is usually necessary, while in tort law it is less likely to be.

Other kinds of intent involve harm inflicted for beneficial reasons. Consider the idea of an emergency amputation performed to rescue a victim trapped under the rubble. Such an amputation was performed during the aftermath of the collapse of the skywalks at the Hyatt hotel in Kansas City in 1981, and it figured in the civil lawsuits that followed in the wake of that disaster.

Finally, there is the issue of justification, or an excuse for doing harm. Self-defense is an example of justification.

Similarities in Tort Law and Criminal Law

Having gotten this far, we can see that there are many similarities between criminal obligation to the sovereign and tort obligation to others. Both are imposed on everyone, and they do not arise voluntarily or by negotiation. No consideration passes to the person who obeys the law, except to the extent that living in society is consideration (*quid pro quo*). At the same time, however, only the king or sovereign can extract punishment or redress for violations of criminal law, and the right to choose the punishment also lies exclusively with the sovereign, who may punish without regard to the interest of the victim.[12]

And, of course, the nature of the relief afforded is different, because it is imposed upon the wrongdoer based upon the perceived degree of the wrong, which is not necessarily the same thing as the degree of the injury, without any requirement that the victim's interest be satisfied.

Summarizing, criminal and tort law have the following characteristics:

- general obligation imposed on all society
- without negotiation
- with return promises or other consideration being given in exchange
- concepts of the perpetrator's intent are central elements
- punishment of the perpetrator, which can only be imposed by the sovereign, is central, rather than relief for the victim.

A Summary of Contract, Tort, and Crime Elements

Elements of a Contract	*Elements of a Tort*	*Elements of a Crime*
Personal obligations	General obligations imposed on all society	General obligations imposed on all society
Reached after negotiation	Without negotiation	Without negotiation
In return for something (consideration)	Without promises or consideration being given in exchange	Without promises or consideration being given in exchange
Which can be enforced in court without proving why someone did not keep his or her promise	In which concepts of blameworthiness or fault are central elements	In which concepts of the perpetrator's intent are central elements

Elements of a Contract	*Elements of a Tort*	*Elements of a Crime*
With relief generally limited to the value of the promise or consideration.	With relief according to the value of the injury or harm inflicted	Relief of which is punishment of the perpetrator by the sovereign

When Worlds Collide: What Happens
When Contracts, Torts, and Crimes Meet

Much of the time it will not be difficult to distinguish between torts, crimes, and contracts, but there are moments when the areas overlap, or when someone tries to make them overlap. Examples can include situations in which someone pleads that another "negligently breached a contract," or cases in which a defendant is acquitted of criminal charges, but still faces tort liability. The O. J. Simpson case is an excellent example of a matter that was tried in both civil and criminal court. These situations turn up enough that they justify some discussion before moving on to the substance of various torts.

Traditionally, courts have been extremely reluctant to permit parties to assert causes of action in tort for pure breaches of contract. Most courts have justified this refusal by saying that turning contract obligations into tort obligations would have the effect of swallowing up the whole idea of contractual obligation, because large damage awards could be imposed regardless of what the contracting parties had agreed to do. Nevertheless, in many situations courts have held that a party's conduct may constitute a tort and a contractual breach.

The rule is usually stated in these terms:

> A breach of contract may be said to be a material failure of performance of a duty arising under or imposed by agreement. A tort, on the other hand, is a violation of a duty imposed by law, a wrong independent of contract. Torts can, of course, be committed by parties to a contract. The question to be determined here is whether

the acts or omissions complained of constitute a
violation of duties imposed by law, without regard to
whether a contract is present, or of duties arising by
virtue of the alleged express agreement between the
parties.[13]

In other words, parties to a contract can expressly or impliedly agree to
assume obligations that would also be a tort. If the tort obligation exists
independently of the contract, the injured party may be able to pursue
relief under either concept.

In practice, it is difficult to tell when a court is likely to pick contract or
tort as a sole vehicle for providing relief to injured parties. How a
plaintiff chooses to proceed may have a significant impact on this issue.
So, too, may the facts. For example, in one case, a patient entered into a
contract with a hospital to provide medical care and was injured by
malpractice. The court found the obligation to provide competent
medical care to be one of tort, something that makes perfect sense when
one considers what the "value of the promise" to provide competent
care was (the value of being healed properly), and the general interest in
ensuring that everyone gets competent medical care without having to
negotiate for it.[14]

By contrast, until very recently, courts were quite reluctant to impose
tort obligations upon the designers and builders of buildings, since,
unlike medical care, the negotiated needs of the parties were much more
particular and the likelihood of harm from variation in design much
less.[15]

Suffice it to say for now that there are often situations in which parties
seek relief in both tort and contract (civil and criminal as well). The
situations in which it can be obtained are less frequent, and more or less
dependent upon the particular circumstances that exist in each case. The
keys in any given case will be the extent to which the purported tort
obligation can be separated from the specific terms of a negotiated
agreement and the extent to which the court believes that the obligation

in issue should or already does exist and should be general in nature. The question at its heart is truly one of independence.

At the other end of the spectrum, why is it that a person can be acquitted of criminal charges and still be liable in tort? In part, this question arises from a misunderstanding of the concept of double jeopardy, a constitutional limitation on the number of times an individual may be tried for the same criminal offense. However, it also depends to some extent on a misperception of the effect of a jury's finding of acquittal. Both of these problems can be solved by remembering the different objectives of tort and criminal law.

Remember that criminal obligations flow only from individual to sovereign, while tort obligations flow independently from individual to individual. The goals of each area or system are independent from each other; as noted above, the idea that criminal law embodies some obligation to the victim is both recent and revolutionary. To put the matter a little differently, the law views the sovereign as the only real victim of a breach of criminal obligation, no matter who was shot, stabbed, hurt, stolen from or otherwise involved. Criminal law exists to protect and vindicate this interest and none other. Victims can sue for breach of tort obligations. The two interests overlap at the edges sometimes, but truly are independent in operation.

Moral of the story: by long usage, the obligations embodied in contract law, tort law, and criminal law are independent, and much time and thought has gone into keeping them that way. Holmes's famous aphorism applies with full force here. The life in these distinct obligations comes not from logic, but experience. Experience — yours included — will help shape them still further.

Key Words and Phrases

blameworthiness
breach
consideration
contract

crime
damage
duty
injury
intent
privity of contract
public policy
quid pro quo
redress   •
remedy
status quo ante
tort
tort obligations
tortfeasor
writ

Review Questions

1. What three inducements or assurances are used by the law to encourage individuals and entities to contract with each other?

2. What are the elements of a contract?

3. What does the term "*status quo ante*" mean?

4. What are the three key distinguishing factors that mark the differences between tort and contract obligations?

5. Who is a tortfeasor?

6. What are the elements of a tort?

7. What is the obligation in criminal law?

8. What are the elements of criminal law?

---

[1] In this book, we do not address much from the field of property law, the other great classification in law, even though it has substantial impact on some areas of tort law and on basic concepts of legal and moral philosophy such as personal autonomy and how we conceive of ourselves in relation to one another. The concept of ownership directly and indirectly impacts how we compute damages and provide remedies.

[2] *See, e.g., Freeman Mills, Inc. v. Belcher Oil Co.*, 11 Cal.4th 85, 97, 900 P. 2d 669, 676, 44 Cal.Rptr.2d 420, 427 (1995).

[3] *See, e.g., Judwin Properties, Inc. v. U.S. Fire Ins. Co.*, 973 F.2d 432 (5th Cir. 1992).

[4] O. W. Holmes, Jr., *The Common Law* (Howe ed. 1963)

[5] *Id.* at 65.

[6] *Id.* at 63.

[7] *Id.* at 76. [Internal quotations omitted.]

[8] *Id.* at 63–64.

[9] Or the queen's peace, depending upon who was on the throne. *See* Stephen, *A History of the Criminal Law of England*, at 184–185.

[10] The author's highly technical phrase meaning "top dog" or "big kahuna."

[11] This system had other effects that have permeated our law, one of which was the forms of writ—that is, the kinds of cases that could be reviewed and the kinds of relief that could be granted. The basic rule was that a person's claim would not be heard if it did not fit within one of the writ forms that the royal court could issue. The persistence of this form of jurisprudence well into the 19th century substantially limited the growth of tort law, and certainly it limited for many years the growth of concepts such as negligence.

[12] As an example of the depth of this distinction, it has only been within the last 20 to 25 years that criminal law has taken account of a victim's rights or the idea that a perpetrator should be compelled to make some form of restitution. This is

another example of how criminal law is oriented toward maintaining the "king's peace" rather than redressing the harm caused to individuals.

[13] *Malone v. University of Kansas Medical Center*, 220 Kan. 371, 374, 552 P.2d 885, 888 (1976).

[14] *Id.*

[15] *See, generally, Chubb Group of Ins. Companies v. C.F. Murphy & Associates, Inc.*, 656 S.W.2d 766 (Mo. Ct. App. 1983).

Chapter Two

THE FIRST TORTS:
TRESPASS, ASSAULT,
BATTERY, AND CONVERSION

This book will not say much about the basic legal concept of ownership or, more generally put, of possession.[1] For the purposes of this textbook, it is enough to say that much of the early history of the common law focused on who could own what, in what way, for how long, and how they could dispose of it.

Forms of ownership and possession became the subjects of much arcane study, most of which still has enough importance to bedevil you in your courses on real and personal property.

So, why bring up the importance of possession? The first recognizable torts arose from the concept of **possession**. Courts of old devoted much time to declaring what property rights people had. It became obvious that those rights were not worth much unless the courts, which bestowed rights of possession, also protected those rights from encroachment or attack.

What could be protected? Property, obviously, both real estate and personal items or goods, could be, and was, protected. Courts also began to protect self-possession, that is, the right to be free from unwarranted personal contact while living on one's property or anywhere else.[2]

These concepts spawned obligations whose breaches are known respectively as **trespass**, **battery**, and **assault**. These three torts share a common and ancient origin, which is worth recounting in summary form.

History

In the history of the common law, there is perhaps no right older than a person's right to be free from unwarranted personal contact. As early as the middle of the 13th century, English law, through the writ of *trespass vi et armis* (Latin for "with force and arms"), provided a method of monetary recovery for impermissible contacts with the person. Originally, recovery depended upon there having been some act of violence, but at a very early time the action required only a "slight" force and did not depend upon whether the touching was done intentionally, negligently, or even accidentally. By the 14th century, it was held that trespass would lie for any attempted "battery" that had failed to take place.

The modern law of battery grew out of a criminal action designed primarily to protect the king's peace. Nonetheless, the element of personal indignity always was given considerable weight. Indeed, as the action developed, the wrong prevented was thought primarily to be in the violation of the person or the "breaking of the close."[3] It is this interest in the physical security of the person and the integrity of the body upon which the modern tort of battery is premised.[4]

These are ancient torts; in a historical sense, they are the first torts. But before we start delving into the study of these obligations, let us pause for a moment to examine the elements of a tort and how they affect the substance of the law.

A Brief Digression: The Elements of a Cause of Action

An **element** of a cause of action is a factual proposition or inference that a judge or jury hearing a case must be able to draw from the evidence. These propositions or inferences are often described as **ultimate facts**.

> ***Element.*** A constituent part of a claim
> that must be proved for the claim to succeed.

You will notice that we constantly refer to the "elements" of a particular tort, but this term is used not only with torts but also with other causes of action ranging from crimes to contracts. Elements, often interchangeable from tort to contract or crime, are the basic building blocks of litigation.

A more practical approach is to think about them as elements or components of proof or evidence that must be presented during a trial to have the court grant the relief or request.

Another way to think about it is as the outline of a jury charge or jury instructions (*i.e.*, questions that the jury answers during deliberations). During trial, the plaintiff must prove several elements to get a favorable ruling, but a defendant may also have elements of his or her own to prove during the trial. As an example, let us look at a standard jury instruction used in Alabama, which rather conveniently lists the elements of a claim for trespass, something we are about to study:

Alabama Pattern Civil Jury Instructions 31.72

Trespass — Real Property — Burden of Proof

The plaintiff has the burden of proof to satisfy you reasonably from the evidence:

(1) that the plaintiff had title to or owned the land, or
(2) that the plaintiff was in possession of the land, or
(3) that the plaintiff was in possession of the land by adverse possession, and
(4) that the defendant ... intentionally, and with force, trespassed on the plaintiff's land without the plaintiff's consent [force is implied by the law in every trespass to land, if a person crosses another's land, however peaceably or thoughtlessly]; and
(5) the plaintiff was damaged by the defendant's entry.

The plaintiff here is obligated to produce evidence on at least three separate issues.

When the plaintiff comes forward with evidence on every element of a cause of action, he or she has made a *prima facie* case or "showing," entitling him or her to have a jury decide whether relief should be granted. If the plaintiff fails to make a *prima facie* case on any of the required elements, he or she has failed to prove a cause of action and is not entitled to have a jury deliberate on the outcome.

Notice, of course, that it does not say "entitled to win" in the last paragraph — and with good reason. A *prima facie* case is simply the admission ticket to having a jury make a decision on a claim. It declares that the plaintiff has supplied enough facts to entitle him or her to a jury finding, not that the plaintiff is entitled to get what he or she wants from the jury.

There are several reasons for this. Even if no one but the plaintiff puts on any evidence, the jury may simply disbelieve whatever evidence is offered to support one or more of the elements of the plaintiff's cause of action. So, merely stating that the plaintiff has made a *prima facie* case is not a commentary on the strength of a case.

Second, the defense team is entitled to put on its case — the defendant's version of what happened — to persuade the jury that a different view of the evidence is the correct one. This may result in an adverse result against the plaintiff.

Finally, the defendant may also present an affirmative defense, which is simply a legal basis or theory by which it can avoid liability. Self-defense is one of these.

What makes these defenses "affirmative" is that the party asserting them must come forward with proof of the elements that comprise the defense. The party asserting an affirmative defense must show evidence of each element of that defense. In other words, the defendant must do something other than simply trying to negate the plaintiff's case.

In any event, from now on, be aware that we will frequently be referring to the elements — components of evidence — that establish tort obligations, the defenses to those obligations, and the relief a court can provide in ruling on breaches of those obligations.

Elements Necessary for Plaintiff to Prove a Trespass Action

- Plaintiff had title to or owned the land.
- Plaintiff was in possession of the land.
- Plaintiff possessed the land by adverse possession.

- Defendant intentionally and with force, without the right to do so, regardless of whether the conduct was peaceable or thoughtless, trespassed on plaintiff's land without the plaintiff's consent.
- Plaintiff was damaged by defendant's entry (trespass).

Possible Elements for Defendant to Defend a Claim of Trespass

- Plaintiff failed to make a *prima facie* case in that
  1. defendant did not go onto the land
  2. plaintiff did not have possession of the land
  3. plaintiff had no beneficial use of the land entered by defendant
  4. defendant had no intention to intrude or trespass on plaintiff's land, and the intrusion was accidental or non-volitional
  5. defendant did not cause the intrusion (if someone else was the intruder).

- Defendant has a defense to plaintiff's claim in that
  1. plaintiff consented to defendant's trespass
  2. defendant had the privilege to enter because of necessity, to abate a nuisance, or to retake possession of the land by force.

Back to Work: Trespass Torts

As we saw earlier in this chapter, the concept of trespass is extremely old as legal ideas go. It is, in fact, so old that it has evolved significantly and spawned a series of torts, including conversion, battery, and assault, which we will discuss later in this chapter. In the meantime, however, it is appropriate to see what has become of trespass itself.

Trespass. A wrongful act committed against another, especially unauthorized entry onto another's land.

Remembering that a trespass arose whenever there was entry onto someone else's land or interference with someone's person, we can guess how the old judges classified the forms of trespass to land.

As you think about daily life, you will see a number of common situations where trespass to land retains its vitality. The homeowner who builds a shed that crosses a neighbor's property line has committed a trespass to land. So has the dog owner whose favorite puppy gets into someone else's rose bushes. These do not seem difficult to resolve, except perhaps to the neighbors. Modern judges still find the tort of trespass to land relevant to pressing issues, and a quick search reveals that trespass to land is very relevant. Consider this case.

Mock v. Potlach Corp.
786 F.Supp. 1545
United States District Court
District of Idaho
1992

Ryan, Chief Judge:

* * * *

The plaintiffs reside on real property approximately 1,800 feet directly north and across the Clearwater River from the Potlach plant in Lewiston, Idaho. They have made their home on this property since 1971.

This dispute first began when Potlach installed a new steam-driven turbine electrical generator in late 1990 and early 1991. Potlach maintains that because of the high speed of the turbine and its mechanical design, a particle of any size would cause substantial damage to the turbine blades. Consequently, the connection pipes which conduct steam to the turbine had to be cleaned by forcing high-pressure steam through the pipes.

This cleaning process was performed periodically in late 1990 and 1991.... The plaintiffs complain that the noise level increased dramatically at the plant, to the point that they were being subjected to noise more than 100 decibels at times. The plaintiffs further allege that the increased noise levels still occur periodically, and that not all of the increased noise comes from the cleaning of the turbine pipes.

The plaintiffs brought suit based on ... trespass.

* * * *

The traditional common law requirements for recovery for trespass to land include (1) an invasion (2) which interferes with the right of exclusive possession of the land, and (3) which is a direct result of some act committed by the defendant. Historically, an invasion must constitute an interference with possession in order to be actionable as trespass. This requirement still persists today, and forms the basis of the distinction between the tort of trespass and the tort of private nuisance. The tort of trespass applies to wrongful interference with the right of exclusive possession of real property, while the tort of private nuisance applies to wrongful interference with the use and enjoyment of real property.

Generally, an interference with the exclusive right of possession involves an entry onto the land. An entry may take the form of the defendant personally intruding on the land, causing another to intrude on the land, or causing some tangible thing to intrude on the land....

* * * *

The plaintiffs argue that the noise created by Potlach constitutes a "force" entering upon the land. The plaintiffs offer no authority for their position.... Therefore, the court feels compelled to look elsewhere to determine if there is any support for the proposition that noise can constitute an "entry."

* * * *

The modern trend relating to actions in trespass can be summarized as follows. If there is a direct and tangible invasion of another's property, there is an infringement of the right of exclusive possession, and the law will presume damages. On the other hand, if the invasion is indirect and intangible (such as noise, odors, light, smoke, etc.), the proper remedy lies in an action for nuisance, based on interference with the right of use and enjoyment of the land. However, if the intangible invasion causes substantial damage to the plaintiff's property, the damage will be considered to be an infringement on the plaintiff's right to exclusive possession, and an action for trespass may be brought.

The right of exclusive possession described in the case above is the right to have the land in the first place. The right of use and enjoyment is the right to do what you want with your land once you are in possession.

This leaves us with a lot to think about. First, we find ourselves pondering the difference between trespass, the old tort, which is the focus of this chapter, and **nuisance**, its much younger sibling. We will return to nuisance in a subsequent chapter. Suffice it to say for now, the two live in a state of uneasy truce because it is difficult at best to decide where the right to possess a piece of land ends and where the right to enjoy it begins.

The second issue here (also discussed in a later chapter) is the extent to which modern environmental problems can create remedies in the older, more traditional world of torts, which generally did not recognize the idea that environmental interference was wrong and actionable.

Having stated these caveats, Judge Ryan's decision in *Mock* does suggest that trespass retains a significant role today in cases involving pollution cleanup and land uses, among other modern problems. It also suggests that the form of obligation at issue would be at least vaguely recognizable to the judges of older times.

These, then, are the elements of trespass to land, a senior citizen in the world of torts that has not lost its relevance or vitality even after 700 years:

- an invasion
- that interferes with the right of exclusive possession of the land
- which is a direct result of some act committed by the defendant.

Conversion: Trespass to Personal Property Hundreds of Years Later

Now that we have seen that an interference with the right of exclusive possession of land constitutes a form of trespass, is there also an obligation not to interfere with someone else's personal property? The answer is yes.

In old common law terms, trespass to personal property (also known as "chattels") arose whenever the defendant interfered with the plaintiff's right to possess a piece of property other than real property.[5] This could occur when the defendant prevented the plaintiff from getting to his or her property (such as a herd of animals), when the defendant damaged or injured the property, or when the defendant took it for his or her own.

Elements of Trespass to Chattels

- Plaintiff owns the chattel/personal property (*i.e.*, tangible or intangible property other than land or things attached to land).
- Plaintiff is in immediate possession of the chattel, or plaintiff is entitled to immediate possession of the chattel.
- Defendant intends to take possession of plaintiff's chattel.
- Defendant does take possession of plaintiff's chattel.
- Except for defendant's actions, plaintiff would still have possession of the chattel, and defendant was a substantial factor or reason for causing plaintiff to lose possession of the chattel.

As time went on, this idea of interfering with another person's right to possess personal property merged with the idea of theft, a criminal law concept, to create a different tort: **conversion.**

Conversion. The wrongful interference with or possession of another's property.

Elements of Conversion

A charge for conversion must allege the following elements:

- an unauthorized and wrongful assumption for control, dominion, or ownership by a defendant over a plaintiff's personal property
- plaintiff's right in the property and that the person who takes it does not have such a right
- plaintiff's right to the immediate possession of the property, absolutely and unconditionally

- a demand for possession of the property that was refused by the defendant.[6]

This excerpt would be relatively easy to decipher by judges from the 18th century. But since this is the 21st century, a word of explanation is in order.

The second and third of the elements contained in the above excerpt tell you that the person suing must have a right to "immediate possession" of the property — in other words, to hold it and keep it. The defendant must not have such a right, which is a rough translation of the first element into real-people-ese. If the defendant does have a right to possess the property now, conversion cannot exist. You cannot take what you already own.

Finally, to prove conversion you must ordinarily prove that you asked for the property back and were turned down. In some cases, this requirement need not be met but, surprisingly, it still can play a role in whether the plaintiff will succeed on a claim of conversion.

Reducing all of this still further, to have conversion of your property, you have to possess it now, and the person who takes it must not have such a right. You have to ask for it back before you can sue. Then, if all of these elements are met, you are entitled to the fair market value of the converted property.

Can Money Be Converted?

A final question on conversion, but one that is important: can money be converted? The answer, somewhat contrary to logic, is "no," unless the money can be identified as a "specific fund."

Think of it this way. If I borrow money and sign a note, the note is a form of contract, an agreement to pay back the money of specified terms. My right to the money comes about only by virtue of signing the contract ("giving the note"). My failure to pay is a breach of the contract, whether it is an IOU on scrap paper or a complex loan with a multivolume commercial-loan facility.

Turning my contractual breach into the tort of conversion would violate the line of demarcation we have discussed between tort and contract obligations, which courts do not like to do. Hence, failing to pay something you owe is not conversion.

Trespass to chattels does not involve any *taking* and *keeping* of another person's property. Conversion does.

On the other hand, if I come to your house and steal a rare coin, I have taken something that counts as a "specific fund," an identifiable and discrete piece of property that can be described as such. The same would be true if I broke into your piggy bank and took the money there or if I went to your safe deposit box and took the money there. In each case, there can be conversion, because the fund is identifiable as such.

Another way to think about this distinction is by visualizing how the defendant got the money. In our hypothetical debt situation, the defendant legally got possession of the money or at least came into possession of it with some right to have it; there was no wrongful taking. In the case of the rare coin, the initial taking was wrong. Hence, conversion becomes possible.

The Difference Between Trespass to Chattels and Conversion

The difference between **trespass to chattels**, or *trespass vi et armis*, and conversion lies in the fact that trespass does not involve any taking and keeping of another person's property. The kid who paints graffiti on the side of a truck in New York City has committed a trespass to chattels. The kid who steals the same truck has committed conversion, regardless of whether he paints graffiti on it first.

The damages for trespass to chattels are limited to recovery of the harm and injury caused by the defendant. A good example of this would be the repair costs or the cost of renting a substitute. Further, if hatred or malice by defendant was proven, the plaintiff might possibly recover punitive (*i.e.*, additional) damages as well.

The damages recoverable by a plaintiff in a conversion action are slightly different. A conversion plaintiff can recover the full fair-market value of the chattel at the time of conversion. The actual result is that the defendant is forced to buy it, even if the defendant offers to return it in its original condition.

Defenses to conversion are generally the same as those for trespass to chattels.

Assault and Battery: Descendant of Trespass to Person

The other descendants of ancient trespass are a pair of torts involving interference with a person's right to be free from unwanted personal contact. These two torts, known as battery and assault, respectively, are very much alive and well today, as the following excerpt shows.

Rivera v. Puerto Rican Home Attendants Services, Inc.
930 F. Supp. 124
United States District Court
Southern District of New York
1996

Kaplan, J.:

* * * *

The amended complaint ... added assault and battery as theories of recovery.... In Ms. Rivera's case, the complaints alleged that in March 1995, Mr. Hernandez on the last night of a conference "asked her to dance and in the course of the dance held her improperly close." When she pulled away, he "threatened" that she would have to "suffer the consequences" if she did not come to work the next day. As for Ms. Fernandez, the complaints alleged that on November 10, 1994, Mr. Nunez "put his arms around her and made clear that he sought sexual favors from her." When she reminded him that she did not want to be involved with office colleagues or superiors, he became "angry with her."

Defendants claim that assault and battery theories require allegations of a "grievous affront" and an "intent to injure".... This argument mischaracterizes the law.... [A]n assault is "an intentional placing of another person in fear of imminent harmful or offensive contact." A battery is "an intentional wrongful physical contact with another person without consent." [Citation omitted.] The terms "assault" and "battery" do not in any way depend upon "the degree of violence" because the law "totally prohibits the first and lowest stage, since every individual's person is sacred and no other has the right to touch it."

Contrary to defendants' suggestion, [the] law does not make intent to cause physical injury an element of the torts of assault and battery. [Citations omitted.] Rather, the intent requisite to an assault ... is the intent to inflict personal injury or to arouse apprehension of harmful or offensive bodily contact. [Citations omitted.] To prove battery, the required intent is merely that the defendant intentionally made bodily contact and that the intended contact was itself offensive or without consent.

Here, the facts alleged ... state claims for battery.... Each plaintiff clearly alleged that the individual defendants deliberately touched them and that the intended physical contact was offensive and unwelcome, thereby stating a claim for battery....

Whether the allegations state a claim for assault is a closer question. There is no express allegation that either plaintiff was placed in apprehension of harmful or offensive bodily contact or of personal injury. However, Ms. Rivera alleges that she pulled away from Mr. Hernandez and was threatened with retaliation, while Ms. Fernandez alleges that she met with Mr. Nunez' anger after rejecting his embrace and advances. These circumstances could give rise to the apprehension necessary to an assault.

This excerpt suggests how timely the concepts of assault and battery remain today, and it gives us insight into the elements of each tort. We can confirm our understanding by examining a jury instruction given to a jury in assessing the sufficiency of a plaintiff's evidence:

Iowa Civil Jury Instruction 1900.2

An assault is committed when a person does: (1) an act intended to put another in fear of physical pain or injury; [or] (2) an act intended to put another in fear of physical contact which a reasonable person would deem insulting or offensive; and the victim reasonably believes that the act may be carried out immediately.

Iowa Civil Jury Instruction 1900.4

A battery is committed when a person intentionally does: (1) an act resulting in bodily contact causing physical pain or injury [; or] (2) an act resulting in bodily contact a reasonable person would deem insulting or offensive.[7]

Assault or battery may exist even if there is no intent to injure by the conduct.

From the case excerpt quoted above and these jury instructions, you should note a number of important points. First, the person committing the assault or the battery need only intend to do the act that constitutes the assault or battery. Second, like the defendants in *Rivera* above, who may in their own minds only have been out for a "good time," it is only necessary that the defendant intend to do the act itself. Assault or battery may exist even if there is no intent to injure by the conduct.

The next issue is whether the victim must be aware that the offensive touching or encroachment has taken place at the time it happens.[8] The answer to this question has long since been settled as "no."[9] Battery provides the obvious reason for this rule. Consider the physician who engages in inappropriate touching while the patient is under anesthesia.[10]

These torts are designed to protect the sanctity of the individual and his or her property, not merely the perception of security. Requiring an immediate or, at least, contemporaneous awareness of the invasion would create a tremendous loophole in this protection. It would be especially hard upon those least able to remember or complain — those who are sick, injured, insane, or drugged.

Damages

The third item of importance has to do with damages. Unlike torts, we soon will discuss, the plaintiff who brings a cause of action for trespass, battery, or assault need not prove any damages to prevail. In such situations, the court can award what are called nominal damages (usually one dollar) to the plaintiff who proves trespass, assault, or battery. To obtain large damage awards, the plaintiff must come forward with evidence of a larger injury. Then the measure of damages is equal to a dollar award representing the jury's impression of the injury's value.

Nominal Damages

What good does an award of nominal damages do for a plaintiff? The legal answer, of course, is, "it depends." For example, as we shall soon discuss, one defense to a claim that you trespassed upon another person's land could obviously be that you own the property itself, so it is not wrong for you to be there.

In fact, for many years before the development of accurate land surveys and descriptions, courts and litigants used trespass for just this purpose. The suit was called **trespass to quiet title**. If the purpose of the case was to establish who owned the property, an award of one dollar was more than enough to show that the plaintiff was in fact the owner. Here, then, nominal damages could, and often did, serve an important role.

Relief by Injunction

The idea of nominal damages can be confusing because plaintiffs ordinarily ask for, and expect to receive, a great deal more than one dollar if they win. The plaintiff may also expect some alternative form of relief in addition to damages, usually in the form of an injunction. An **injunction** is a prohibitive writ forbidding a party to do some act.

All of which leads to the discussion usually held about this time in every class in torts, which goes something like this:

> Disgruntled Serious Student ("DSS"): Professor Shlabotnik, you told us in class that any unwanted touching, no matter how slight would be sufficient to be a battery, right?
>
> Bemused Professor Shlabotnik ("BPS"): Right.
>
> DSS: So, if I touch you as lightly as a feather right now, and you do not want me to, that is still a battery, right?

BPS: Right again.

DSS: But that is just not fair. That means that anyone I touch could ... well ... sue me!

BPS: Yup.

[Sounds of student stomping off.][11]

In fact, our disgruntled student is quite right. By consistently referring to "unwanted touching," courts leave open the idea that any touching can be actionable, no matter how innocuous in theory. So why are courts not flooded with "unwanted touching" battery cases? There are several reasons, all of which bear upon the difference between studying in the classroom and dealing with the practicalities of the principle in the real world.

First and most important, having the right to do something does not make doing it mandatory. Putting the matter differently, each of us experiences many situations on a daily basis where we are touched, prodded, bumped, jostled, or generally in contact with another. Each of these may give us a right to sue, but we rarely think about it. We have no need or inclination to exercise our theoretical rights. We just do not want or need to, and so we do not. In other words, we use restraint.

Second, even if we were prone to sue, and some people are, most of us would not do so because the costs and aggravation far outweigh any possible benefits. Because in most of these situations the benefit is a favorable ruling and one dollar, it is easy to see why so few people take the plunge. In a related vein, it is difficult to interest most attorneys, who also have families to feed and mortgages to pay, to handle a case with such a minuscule financial benefit.

Finally, most of those people who have not been scared off already generally give up when they consider that their chances of winning the dollar are not that high anyway. In addition to proving who did the touching, the plaintiff also has to prove that the touch was offensive and that the defendant intended to do it. These elements are not as easy to prove as they appear.

Moral of story and vital principle bearing upon our business: having the right to do something does not make it the right thing to do.

Defenses to Trespass, Battery, and Assault

What are the defenses to these torts? As we have seen, each has some which are unique, but there are several that apply to all of them.

Lack of intent, if proven, is a defense to trespass and battery. Likewise, a **privilege** may give the defendant some overriding right to do whatever he did. **Self-defense** or **consent** are also defenses to battery and assault.

The first defense is what we can call **lack of intent**. In other words, as our friend DSS has inadvertently reminded us, it is possible for a wind to carry you onto another person's property, or for you to touch someone (think of that crowded elevator) without having any intent to do so. This lack of intent, if proven, is a defense to trespass and battery. Other defenses are privilege, which is some overriding right that permits the defendant to do what happened, and self-defense, which can be a defense to battery or assault.

The last major defense to all of these torts is **consent**. The idea of consent is both easy and difficult to understand, so it is worth a brief excerpt.

Hogan v. Tavzel
660 So.2d 350
District Court of Appeals of Florida
Fifth District
1995

W. Sharp, Judge:

* * * *

Hogan and Tavzel were married for 15 years but encountered marital problems, which caused them to separate. During a period of attempted reconciliation between October 1989 and January 1990, Tavzel infected Hogan with genital warts. He knew of his condition but failed to warn Hogan or take any precaution against infecting her.... Hogan brought this suit in 1993....

Tavzel moved to dismiss. The trial court ... dismissed the battery count because he found that consensual sexual intercourse fails as a matter of law to establish the element of unconsented to touching which is required to sustain the tort of battery....

* * * *

We ... turn our attention to ... dismissal of the battery count.... A case similar to the one presented here is *Kathleen K. v. Robert B.*, 150 Cal. App. 3d 992, 198 Cal. Rptr. 273 (2d Dist. 1984). There a cause of action in battery was approved when one partner contracted genital herpes from the other partner. The facts indicated that the infecting partner had represented that he was free from any sexually infectious disease, and the infected partner would not have engaged in sexual relations if she had been aware of the risk of infection. The court held that one party's consent to sexual intercourse is vitiated by the partner's fraudulent concealment of the risk of infection with venereal disease (whether or not the partners are married to each other).

* * * *

Hogan's consent, if without the knowledge that Tavzel was infected with a sexually transmitted disease, was the equivalent of no consent, and would not be a defense to the battery charge if successfully proven.

If I let you come onto my land or touch me or take my property after full and honest disclosure, and I have consented, you are free from liability. But my consent must be based upon full knowledge of the facts. With trespass or conversion, battery, or assault, if the defendant obtains my permission by hiding the truth, there is no consent, and therefore no defense.

Key Words and Phrases

adverse possession
affirmative defense
assault
battery
cause of action
caveats
consent
conversion
damages
element(s)
immediate possession
injunction
intent
nominal damages
nuisance
possession
prima facie
privilege
punitive damages
quiet title
self-defense
specific fund
trespass
trespass to chattels
trespass vi et armis

Review Questions

1. What elements must a plaintiff prove to prevail on a cause of action for trespass on real property?

2. What affirmative defenses are there for a claim for trespass on real property?

3. Discuss with your colleagues in class the point at which tolerated, although unwanted, touching crosses the gray line into assault or battery. Take a scenario of a bus or subway car, a form of public transportation that is regularly crowded at certain times of the day. Add the element of the regular riders who board from the same bus stop or station at the same time every day. Could a reasonable complaint arise from this situation, or is the scenario simply an accepted risk of urban life in the 21st century?

4. What are ways in which an owner can protect real property from trespass if the owner does not reside full-time on the real property? Think not only of standard ways (a sign) but also of more creative ways.

---

[1] This is because there are forms of possession other than ownership — renting or leasing, for example.

[2] If you doubt this idea, think about slavery or serfdom, both involved the sale or giving of ownership of a person — a self — to another.

[3] Here the "breaking of the close" is an invasion of privacy on land.

[4] *Davis v. Hubbard*, 506 F.Supp. 915, 930 (N.D. Ohio 1980) discusses trespass and battery in context of involuntary administration of psychotropic medication to patients at state mental hospital.

[5] *See Whited v. Fields*, 582 F. Supp. 1444 (W.D. Va. 1984), which discusses development of the doctrine in context of whether firing of employees constituted such a situation.

[6] *Fonda v. General Casualty Co. Of Ill.*, 279 Ill. App. 3d 894, 899, 665 N.E.2d 439, 442, 216 Ill. Dec. 379, 382 (1996).

[7] *See Greenland v. Fairtron Corp.*, 500 N.W.2d 36 (Iowa 1993).

[8] Assault doesn't count here, because you can't be put in apprehension of something by someone without that person literally being "in your face."

[9] *Vosburg v. Putney*, 80 Wis. 523, 50 N.W. 403 (1891).

[10] *See, e.g., Haug v. State Farm First Cas. Co.*, 481 N.W.2d 393 (Minn. App. 1992).

[11] Well, *I* didn't stomp.

Chapter Three

SEEMS REASONABLE TO ME: THE IDEA OF ORDINARY CARE AND NEGLIGENCE

As you think about the four kinds of obligations we have just discussed, it should be somewhat apparent that the scope of assault, battery, trespass, and conversion is somewhat limited. Most of us go for days without violating someone else's property, intentionally touching someone improperly, making someone apprehensive, or taking what doesn't belong to us. Thus, while these torts are useful in some situations, they are not general in scope. They do not provide general guidelines for behavior or establish convenient standards with which to measure our obligations to one another.

There are several ways to broaden the scope of what we have studied already. The first is to proceed on a situation-by-situation basis, creating new obligations that extend only to relatively small groups of situations. The other is to seek for some relatively general formula that can be applied in most, if not all, situations.

As we shall see, lawyers and judges have taken both approaches. We will return to certain categories of obligation that developed over time in response to relatively specific needs or relationships. But for the last 150 years or so, the "action" has been in trying to find and develop a general standard of obligation that could be applied in all kinds of situations without having to think too hard about special rules or principles.

In this chapter we examine how this process took place and meet the central figure of an ongoing drama: the **reasonable person**, an individual we shall soon meet.

The Search for a Standard

At the beginning of the 19th century, American courts could call upon various forms of trespass to provide relief to people injured by the conduct of another. Although they were still in their rookie seasons as discrete torts,[1] assault and battery existed in appropriate circumstances to provide redress to those physically injured by another person's conduct.

There were still problems, however. On the one hand, as we have seen, trespass, battery, and assault all involve a volitional element, some intent to do the act that causes the injury, even if not the injury that flows from it. Thus, they do not work well in cases of **omission**, that is, in situations where someone fails to do something that he or she should (hit the brakes in time, for example) and thus lacks any intent to do any act. They therefore don't provide much help with many situations that we instinctively feel ought to be redressed.

At the other end of the spectrum, the worry of our poor old Disgruntled Serious Student from the last chapter is a serious one that cannot be pushed aside so easily. If *any* touching or encroachment is actionable, it is difficult not to provide some kind of relief even in cases where we instinctively feel that we ought not to do so. Better and more specific methods of providing redress ought to be available.

These questions emerged against the background of the ongoing Industrial Revolution, which itself created new ways for people and businesses to exist and interact. The changes in human and business relationships (look at the factory houses in Lowell and Manchester and the long production lines) begat equally fundamental changes in almost everything else.

Enter Chief Justice Lemuel Shaw of Massachusetts, not alone, of course, but as an object lesson of how courts of the day solved the problem. Oliver Wendell Holmes venerated Shaw as "the greatest magistrate this country has produced,"[2] so what Shaw did with our problem is worth a bit of time.

The case was *Brown v. Kendall,*[3] and the facts were simple. Kendall, the defendant, was trying to separate two fighting dogs. As he raised his stick over his shoulder to strike the battling mutts, it hit Brown, who was coming up behind, in the eye. Brown sued for trespass and battery.

As we have seen, if Chief Justice Shaw had stuck to the existing law, Brown would have recovered damages from Kendall because all of the elements of a battery were satisfied. There clearly had been an injurious touching. Kendall had intended to strike something, so his act was volitional and therefore intentional enough. Brown certainly had not consented. It should have been open and shut.

But it wasn't. Shaw, it seems, was mindful of the problems the law faced, and chose a different path. Let Holmes tell the story:

> The case was stronger for the plaintiff than if the defendant had been acting in self-defense; but the court held that, although the defendant was bound by no duty to separate the dogs, yet, if he was doing a lawful act he was not liable unless he was wanting in the care which men of ordinary prudence would use under the same circumstances, and that the burden was on the plaintiff to prove the want of such care.[4]

Let's repeat the important phrase and savor its implications:

> [H]e was not liable unless he was wanting in such care as men of ordinary prudence would use under the circumstances....

The first gold nugget in this phrase is the idea that there is nothing specific about it. **Ordinary prudence** can vary from minute to minute and situation to situation and is tied to "the circumstances" — the actual situation in which the actor finds himself or herself. Applying our new idea to Brown and Kendall, Kendall was obligated merely to do what persons of ordinary prudence would have done in separating two fighting dogs. If he did, he was not liable. Under the circumstances, he had not breached an obligation he owed.

More generally, no longer are we defining standards or obligations by touching or putting someone in apprehension or breaking the close. In fact, we no longer have to set forth any specific thing that can or cannot be done. We only have to compare the defendant's conduct against "persons of ordinary prudence in the same circumstances." That is about as general an algorithm as one can find.

The second thing to note about this standard is that it is objective rather than subjective, and uniform rather than individualized. If the defendant does not live up to what persons of ordinary prudence would have done, it matters not that he or she acted out of the most beneficent of motives or even that he or she believed that he or she was using the highest degree of care or very best judgment. Mother Teresa or Saddam Hussein, the standard is the same.

The third principle to draw from this is that the standard is fact-based and therefore jury-friendly. It is not at all difficult to picture twelve jurors asking themselves, "What would I have done?" or arguing, "There but for the grace of God go I," in deciding whether the defendant had discharged his or her obligations. In most situations, no judge need intervene except, as we will see, to read a simple instruction or definition.

Finally, the idea of comparison implicit in this standard imparts a standard of fault or blameworthiness that is morally and intrinsically easier to apply than the somewhat artificial ideas of volitional activity and defense that were more ordinary in the concepts of trespass and battery.

Looking at Brown and Kendall, we can see how this was so. Kendall's action — trying to separate fighting dogs — had obvious social value, and so it is difficult to fault him for trying it. Note that this is effectively what imposing liability for battery would have done.

In more philosophical terms — fans of John Stuart Mill, watch out — figuring out how much care people of ordinary prudence would have used in the circumstances, implicitly and instinctively, requires some measuring of the value or worth of what the defendant was doing. The more useful it was, the less likely for blame to be imposed casually.

The utter simplicity of this concept, and its ability to be applied so broadly, swept all before it, so much so that by the time of *The Common Law*, Holmes would concede that the idea of fault or blameworthiness as a basis for liability was "the general notion upon which liability ... is founded." Holmes was right. This concept is called **negligence**, or **blameworthy conduct**, by this uniform, objective standard.

> *Negligence.* The failure to exercise the care
> that a reasonable person would have exercised
> under similar circumstances.

Who Is the Reasonable Person?

So, who is this guy? Who is often referred to as the "reasonable man," the human embodiment of the standard of reasonable care? A.P. Herbert, a legal scholar whose reputation lives on largely because of this quote, wrote on this question:

> He is ... one who invariably looks where he is going,
> and is careful to examine the immediate foreground
> before he executes a leap or bound; who neither star-
> gazes nor is lost in meditation when approaching
> trapdoors or the margin of a dock ... who never mounts
> a moving omnibus and does not alight from any car
> while the train is in motion ... and will inform himself
> of the history and habits of a dog before administering a
> caress ... who never drives his ball until those in front
> of him have definitely vacated the putting green which
> is his own objective; who never from one year's end to
> another makes an excessive demand upon his wife, his

neighbors, his servants, his ox, or his ass; ... who never
swears, gambles or loses his temper; who uses nothing
except in moderation, and even while he flogs his child
is meditating only on the golden mean.[5]

He is, in short, someone Mark Twain was willing to go to hell to avoid
and who we wouldn't like very much.

But in this humorous concept are a couple of points worth pondering.
They form the basis for the limitations upon our standard. Herbert's
description of the "reasonable man," the standard against which we all
are judged, is not "reasonable," but "perfect," and therefore guaranteed
to result in a verdict for plaintiff every time — because after all, who
among us ever can be perfect? Are we therefore condemned to an
unending series of slam-dunks? Are all tort defense professionals
condemned to pushing the big rock up the hill like Sisyphus?

Again, we are rescued by a bit of old Yankee wisdom:

> The standards of the law are standards of general
> application. The law takes no account of the infinite
> varieties of temperament, intellect, and education which
> make the internal character of a given act so different in
> different men. It does not attempt to see men as God
> sees them.... [W]hen men live in society a certain
> average of conduct, a sacrifice of individual peculiarities
> going beyond a certain point, is necessary to the general
> welfare. If, for instance, a man is born hasty and
> awkward, is always having accidents and hurting
> himself or his neighbors, no doubt his congenital defects
> will be allowed for in the courts of Heaven, but his slips
> are no less troublesome to his neighbors than if they
> spring from guilty neglect. His neighbors, accordingly
> require him, at his proper peril, to come up to their
> standard, and the courts which they establish decline to
> take his personal equation into account.

The rule that the law does, in general, determine liability by blameworthiness, is subject to the limitation that minute differences of character are not allowed for. The law considers, in other words, what would be blameworthy in the average man, the man of ordinary intelligence and prudence, and determines liability by that. If we fall below the level in those gifts, it is our misfortune; so much as that we must behave at his peril.... But he who is just intelligent and prudent does not act at his peril, in theory of law. On the contrary, it is only when he fails to exercise the foresight of which he is capable, or exercises it with evil intent, that he is answerable for the consequences.[6]

As Holmes reminds us, then, the reasonable man or reasonable care standard properly applied is not one of perfection, but a floor. Perfection is fine and, in some situations, it may be reasonable. But the core of the standard is not one of ceilings but of floors, and thus of the idea that some mistakes are permissible.

But these quotations don't really answer the problem on the floor, which is what we should take into account in deciding whether someone's conduct is reasonable.

The follow-up question is this: How much is reasonable to anticipate? To find out how courts have struggled with this question, let us turn back the clock to 1928 and take a ride on the railroad.

Palsgraf v. Long Island Railroad Co.
248 N.Y. 339, 162 N.E. 9
New York Court of Appeals
1928

Cardozo, C.J.:

> Plaintiff was standing on a platform of defendant's railroad after buying a ticket to go to Rockaway Beach. A train stopped at the station, bound for another place. Two men ran forward to catch it. One of the men reached the platform of the car without mishap, though the train was already moving. The other man, carrying a package, jumped aboard the car, but seemed unsteady as if about to fall. A guard on the car, who had held the door open, reached forward to help him in, and another guard on the platform pushed him from behind. In this act, the package was dislodged, and fell upon the rails. It was a package of small size, about fifteen inches long, and was covered by newspaper. In fact it contained fireworks, but there was nothing in its appearance to give notice of its contents. The fireworks when they fell exploded. The shock of the explosion threw down some scales at the other end of the platform many feet away. The scales struck the plaintiff, causing injuries for which she sues.

The conduct of the defendant's guard, if a wrong in relation to the holder of the package, was not a wrong in its relation to the plaintiff standing far away. Relative to her, it was not negligence at all. Nothing in the situation gave notice that the falling package had in it something dangerous. The railroad employees were just trying to help someone late for a train, someone who concededly didn't look the slightest bit suspicious or dangerous. That conduct could hardly be criticized except by hindsight. On the contrary, in today's lawsuit-conscious world, it probably is much easier to imagine the employees thinking that the guy with the parcel would sue them if they didn't get him safely on the train, and even in the kinder, gentler world of 1928, that kind of reasoning is very plausible.

It doesn't take much imagination to see the judges involved in this case going through the same kinds of thought processes, and the two opinions in this case more than most are unusually candid expressions of how the justices (of what was then the most prestigious state appellate court) wrestled with this problem. The moral: significant developments in the law are most likely to emerge when existing doctrines seem out of step with our intuitive sense of justice and fairness.

Palsgraf is an example of such a development. However significant it is, no case causes students more grief than *Palsgraf*, partly because Justice Cardozo's opinion proceeds more like a geometry proof at first, and also because his approach was entirely unrelated to that taken by Justice Andrews in the dissenting opinion written in the case. Cardozo ruled that the railroad did not breach any duty to the plaintiff because its employees could not have foreseen the possibility of injury to her.

Before we analyze the substance of this case excerpt, let us ask a preliminary question: Without resorting to any deep legal analysis, are you comfortable imposing some kind of liability on the railroad for this rather bizarre set of circumstances?

Having just invoked a concept of reasonable care, does it make reasonable sense to impose liability? Even in this day of metal detectors and bomb-sniffing dogs, many of you probably answered that it would be unfair or unjust, that is (and with due apologies to those many philosophers who have devoted deep thought to the concept), out of step with our fundamental shared sense of how we all want or think of danger. Except for a few exceptions, we will discuss in the next chapter, the actor is liable for the ultimate result of his or her conduct (the consequences which actually ensue therefrom) even if those particular consequences could not themselves have been foreseen.

Justice Andrews, on the other hand, thought that the problem presented in the case could be solved by applying something called "proximate cause," which we will discuss in the next chapter. And, in fact, as we shall soon see, it can.

But the essence of this excerpt from Justice Cardozo, the single principle that underlies it is this: the duty of reasonable care includes only those risks that can reasonably be foreseen from the actor's perspective.

Reasonable care does not include a duty to foresee every possible risk attendant upon one's conduct. Instead, there is a **"zone of danger"** attendant upon all conduct. This zone may be larger or smaller depending upon a number of factors, including the intrinsic risks of the conduct in which our actor is engaged and the likelihood of injury to others. It is this zone into which the actor must peer, and for which he or she is responsible. Without a foreseeable risk, the actor is not liable.

In modern terms, the extent of the *Palsgraf* zone of danger depends upon weighing

- the risk intrinsic in the actor's conduct (compare the risks in playing tennis, say, with those in blasting)
- the foreseeability of harm to another
- the likelihood of injury to someone in the zone of danger against the social utility in the conduct
- the burden of guarding against the injury
- the consequences of placing the burden on defendant to avoid the harm.

Foreseeability

Foreseeability is the most important of these factors; or, putting the matter a different way, the greater the danger that is known or reasonably to be anticipated, the greater the degree of care required.

> *Foreseeability.* The quality of being anticipatable.

Once the zone of danger is known, it no longer matters whether the actual method by which the injury occurs was itself foreseeable. Inside the zone of danger, the duty is to guard against injury, not forms of injuring.

The seminal case on point is *In re Polemis and Furness, Withy & Co.*, which is usually called the *Polemis* case.[7] There, a dockhand involved in repairing a ship dropped a large plank into the open hold of the vessel. When the plank hit the bottom of the open hold, it created a spark that ignited built-up fuel vapors. The ship burned to a crisp. The English court that heard the case found that it was foreseeable that harmful consequences would flow from dropping the plank, and so the repair company was liable even if no one could have foreseen the existence of the fumes.

We are told that one who drives at reckless speed through a crowded city street is guilty of a negligent act and therefore a wrongful one, irrespective of the consequences. If the same act were committed on a speedway or a racecourse, it would lose its wrongful quality. The risk reasonably to be perceived defines the duty to be obeyed.

Inside the zone of danger, the area of foreseeable risk, the actor's obligation is to avoid all harm from his or her conduct, not merely those consequences that he or she can foresee.

Admittedly, this is rather deep, but we can distill it down to a manageable level. The idea of foreseeable risk following from conduct can be thought of as an obligation to keep a lookout and to protect those within the range of the lookout from any harm that may flow from your conduct. If you are engaged in something that is intrinsically very risky — for example, running a bungee cord jumping center — or the magnitude of the injury that could result from your actions, however innocuous the actions are, is very high, the zone of danger — the extent to which you must keep a lookout and the scrutiny you must use — is larger, your duty to take the precautions a reasonable person would take is correspondingly higher.

So, as a section summary, consider the duty of reasonable care — the essential benchmark against which a person's obligations to another are measured in tort — as one of a zone of danger. The zone's reach is as far as a reasonable person in your shoes would perceive to be the risks attendant upon your conduct, bearing in mind its intrinsic riskiness, the foreseeability of harm to another, the likelihood of injury to someone in the zone of danger against the social utility in the conduct, the burden of guarding against the injury, the ability of others to protect themselves, and the consequences of placing the burden on defendant to avoid the harm.

Inside the zone of danger, your obligation is to take steps to avoid all unreasonable harm to those who share the zone with you, even if the nature of the harm or the method by which it comes about are completely unanticipated by you. As we will see shortly, some other factors influence this general and far-reaching test, but it remains the benchmark from which all of our later analysis will proceed.

Now let us see who fits into the "reasonable person" pigeonhole.

How General is the Standard?

Both Herbert and Holmes hint that there may be some limits on the reasonable person/reasonable care concept, and each of them implicitly or explicitly points to that limit as somehow being dependent in whole or part upon who it is that we expect to be reasonable. The author, and indeed most courts, often address this question in terms of children, those with some form of mental disability, and those with physical disabilities as candidates for exemption from the basic standard of reasonableness. Somewhat surprisingly, there are fewer exemptions from the standard of reasonable care than one might at first believe, as an exploration of these three alternatives demonstrates.

It is convenient to start our examination of how far the duty of reasonable care goes by examining the companion issues of our obligation to exercise care toward children and their obligation to exercise care toward us.

It should come as no surprise that reasonable people exercise a higher degree of care toward children. To see the principle in application, let us consider the following discussion of an all too common problem:

Garafola v. Rosecliff Realty Co.
17 24 N.J. Super. 28, 93 A.2d 608
Superior Court of New Jersey Appellate Division
1952

Eastwood, J.:

More care must be exercised toward children than toward persons of mature years. Children of tender years and youthful persons generally are entitled to care proportioned to their inability to foresee and avoid the perils that they may encounter, as well as to the superior knowledge of persons who come into contact with them. The duty to avoid doing them an injury increases with their inability to protect themselves, and with their childish indiscretions, instincts and impulses.

We are of the opinion that defendant might well have anticipated that children of early years are likely to become highly emotional and considerably overactive while they are enjoying the thrills and excitement of an amusement park and that they would move about and become physically active, without the foresight and perception of possible danger that would be expected from an adult or mature person. In light of this situation and considering the reasonable apprehension of the unpredictable proclivities of children of tender years, we perceive that the [jury] should consider these circumstances in resolving the question of the defendant's proper use of care to protect patrons from possible danger [in the ride].

In other words, since kids can't, don't, or won't use reasonable care themselves, as just about every parent would tell every judge, adults must do so for them.

Returning briefly to our "reasonable sense" idea, does it make sense in these circumstances to turn reasonable or ordinary care into something more? The answer for most of us would certainly be affirmative, at least up to the point that the child was truly able to look after himself or herself. The idea of a higher standard of care where children are concerned strongly agrees with our general understanding that children should be nurtured and protected, and that it is everyone's duty to do so.

But even without such a strong foundation in public policy, we can reach the same conclusion simply by looking back at the nuts and bolts of the reasonable person standard.

Recall from our initial discussion of "reasonable care" that two of the factors that go into determining what is reasonable are

- the likelihood of harm to others
- the ability of the others who may be within the zone of danger to protect things.

In other words, the reasonable person knows that kids do the darndest things. Clearly, without regard to any overriding societal policies, younger children often are more likely than adults to be hurt by the same action and less likely to know to protect themselves. Hence, there exists a strong internal basis for imposing a higher degree of care in these circumstances.

Why go to the trouble of explaining this heightened degree of care solely by reference to the internal workings of our definition, when the public's belief in protecting kids is reason enough and undoubtedly the true basis for the rule? The answers are simple. This kind of analysis tests the flexibility of our rule; it tells us how capable it is of accommodating and accounting for differing situations. The more flexible, the better.

Second, this exercise in analyzing the importance of factors that are part of a test helps demonstrate how the process works. In many different situations, courts apply similar kinds of tests, all involving the weighing of various factors, and lawyers representing the parties who may be affected by the weighing attempt to "put their thumb on the scales" by having the court weigh more heavily those factors that work in favor of their client's position. You should not be surprised at the attorney who argues in favor of a balance of factors that is anathema to you personally or to a client your team represents.

But to go back to our weighing of the factors that go into the standard or reasonable care, we see that reasonable care can mean a higher degree of care than one would exercise if the only people to enter the zone of danger are adults. The question then arises: What if we look at this problem with a child's eyes?

To understand the basis for the rule concerning the level of care that must be exercised by children, we introduce a new character, the American Law Institute (ALI) and its contribution to legal development:

the *Restatement of American Law*. The ALI is a body of prominent judges, practitioners and legal scholars who meet from time to time in an effort to restate — set forth in summary fashion — essential principles in various fields of law. Often these principles cause little uproar, but sometimes they can extend or change principles of law as they presently exist, and occasionally, as we soon shall see, a *Restatement* principle becomes the basis for a revolution in a field.

What does the *Restatement* say about the duties owed by a child to others?

> *Restatement* (2d), Torts § 283 A. Children
>
> If the actor is a child, the standard of conduct to which he must conform to avoid being negligent is that of a reasonable person of like age, intelligence, and experience under the circumstances.

Wait a minute! This is more or less the same algorithm we used for defining the care owed by adults. Or is it? Let's compare the *Restatement*'s view of the care owed by adults:

> Unless the actor is a child, the standard of conduct to which he must conform to avoid being negligent is that of a reasonable person under like circumstances.

As you can see, the key difference is in the addition of the words, "like age, intelligence, and experience...." This sets the comparative norm with a child's peers rather than with people with more age and experience.

Each *Restatement* section includes a comment that explains why or how the ALI reached the position it takes. The comment for children helps us understand the basis for the principle:

The special standard to be applied in the case of children
arises out of the public interest in their welfare and
protection, together with the fact that there is a wide
basis of community experience upon which it is
possible, as a practical matter, to determine what is to be
expected of them. A child of tender years is not required
to conform to the standard of behavior which it is
reasonable to expect of an adult. His conduct is to be
judged by the standard of behavior to be expected of
like age, intelligence, and experience. A child may be so
young as to be manifestly and utterly incapable of
exercising any of those qualities of attention, perception,
knowledge, experience, intelligence and judgment
which are necessary to enable him to perceive a risk and
to realize its unreasonable character. On the other hand,
it is obvious that a minor who has not yet attained his
majority may not be quite as capable as an adult of
exercising such qualities.

The prevailing view is that in tort cases no such arbitrary limits can be
fixed. Undoubtedly there is a minimum age, probably somewhere in the
vicinity of four years, below which negligence can never be found; but
with the great variation in the capacities of children and the situations
that may arise, it cannot be fixed definitely for all cases.

The fact that the child is mentally retarded, or that he or she is unusually
bright for his or her years, is to be taken into account; but once such
account is taken, the child is still required to exercise the judgment of a
reasonable person of that intelligence. Likewise to be taken into account
are the circumstances under which the child has lived, and his or her
experience in encountering particular hazards, or the education the child
has received concerning them. If a child is of sufficient age, intelligence,
and experience to understand the risks of a given situation, he or she is
required to exercise such prudence in protecting him or herself, and such
caution for the safety of others, as is common to children similarly
qualified.

An exception to the rule "may arise when the child engages in an activity which is normally undertaken only by adults, and for which adult qualifications are required. [In such situations, the child] may be held to the standard of adult skill, knowledge and competence, and no allowance may be made for his immaturity."

When is the child no longer a child for purposes of this section? The ALI comment explicitly sets forth one situation in which a child is not treated as such for purposes of establishing a tort obligation: When the child, no matter how old he or she is, engages in activities normally done only by adults — driving and flying are two examples commonly used — an adult standard of care applies.

Similarly, the standard of care applied to children generally begins to fall away in favor of the adult standard regardless of activity, somewhere between 14 and 16 in most states. Certainly, by the age of 16 everyone is obligated to hew to the same standard of care as "adults."

But the long excerpt quoted above is important for another reason: It enables us not only to see the differences between the obligations owed by adults and children, but to recall several important aspects of the idea of reasonable care.

First and very significantly, the standard of care owed by a child essentially is an individual one that is dependent upon many specific factors. Compare this idea with that applied to adults, in which the only standard permitted is a non-specific one, in which evidence of individual traits is irrelevant, and even prohibited.

Second, putting the matter a little more generally, the test applied to children essentially is subjective. It depends almost entirely upon the individual whose conduct is being evaluated. With adults, however, the test is almost entirely objective and in no way dependent upon any person's traits. This distinction between the subjective and objective will be vital in a number of areas we will consider, particularly when we discuss questions of an individual's intent or lack of it.

Third, the idea that subjective elements can be grafted onto a fundamentally objective standard has considerable appeal, because it appears to be a way to "fine tune" the roughness out of what could be a harsh standard when applied to those adults least able to cope with the world, the mentally and physically disabled.

In practice, it doesn't work out that way as the following excerpts show.

> *Restatement* § 283 B. Mental Deficiency.
>
> > Unless the actor is a child, his insanity or other mental deficiency does not relieve the actor from liability for conduct of a reasonable man under like circumstances.
>
> *Restatement* § 283 C. Physical Disability.
>
> > If the actor is ill or otherwise physically disabled, the standard of conduct to which he must conform to avoid being negligent is that of a reasonable man under like disability.

The principle announced in section 283 B certainly comes as a slap in the face after the subjective factors considered in section 283 A, which immediately precedes it. Why such a harsh rule? There are three reasons.

First, whatever the organic cause of a mental deficiency, for our analysis it is the effect upon the actor that matters. In many cases, those effects cannot be distinguished from other forms of behavior, temperament, balance, and intellect that do not arise from a diagnosable cause. The difficulty that exists in drawing lines between what can or cannot be excused on the basis of an abnormal or pathological process suggests that a line cannot, and therefore should not, be drawn.

Second, experience with insanity and incompetence defenses in criminal law suggests rather strongly that the whole process is awkward, unsatisfactory, or even unreliable as a vehicle to avoid obligations. It often is easy to feign insanity,[8] but even if the insanity is real, it still must be asked, "How much of what is enough to escape responsibility?"

And, having asked this, we must also ask whether the standard of insanity should apply or even has any bearing on a civil case, where the standard is objective rather than subjective, and the focus of relief is on redressing injury rather than punishing wrongdoing. After all, in most tort cases, the "why" behind the act is not generally material to the outcome.

Third, given the fact that redress in civil matters generally is limited to payment of monetary damages, requiring those with mental deficiencies to be responsible for their wrongdoing gives incentive to those who must care for them to protect others. Admittedly, in today's world, when the number of those with mental deficiencies living outside of any form of care is so high, this factor has somewhat less relevance than it once had. However, it remains a reason for the general rule that those with mental deficiencies are held to the same standard as those of the general populace.

These three basic principles have long been enough to prevent any change in the basic principle that mental deficiency should not be taken into account in assessing responsibility for tortious conduct. It is a harsh standard on its face, but in application rarely if ever has there been an outcry to change it, usually one of the factors to be considered in deciding if a standard generally works well enough to endure.

Why, then, the apparently different standard for those with physical difficulties? Why are they judged against those with like disabilities when those with mental deficiencies are not? It certainly sounds as though persons with mental deficiencies are judged against a tougher standard. But is this really so?

A *gedanken* experiment[9] suggests otherwise. Consider John Doe, who is blind. Should he be responsible for the injuries he causes if he drives a car? What if he is a quadriplegic?

In the first situation, our "comparison with a reasonable person with the same condition" standard requires us to make Doe liable for any injuries he inflicts while behind the wheel. This is because the reasonable person would have been aware of the limitations imposed by his or her blindness and, based upon that awareness, not gotten behind the wheel to begin with.

By contrast, depending somewhat upon the level and severity of their injury, some quadriplegics can drive and, if so, they are subject to the same restrictions as anyone else behind the wheel and subject to the additional consideration that a "reasonable quadriplegic" would act with additional caution in driving in congested or dangerous conditions where his or her condition would not permit the quadriplegic to respond.

Giving some thought to the standard of care applied to those with physical disabilities thus reveals that it is not any less stringent than the standard of care applied to nondisabled individuals or those with mental deficiencies. In fact, it may be more stringent in the sense that reasonable care requires the physically challenged to understand any limitations imposed by their condition and to proceed with regard to those limitations as they would affect a reasonable person in the same position. The disabled person who works hard and overcomes a physical limitation may face the likelihood of being held legally to a standard that a less capable individual must meet.

Thus, as we can see, the reasonable person standard in effect is universal as to adults, whether or not they are physically or mentally challenged. That universality is a pervading factor in much, if not all, of what we will study during the rest of this book.

Smarter People, Higher Care?

As we have read through the materials that develop the reasonable care/reasonable person standard, it is apparent that our "reasonable person" is pretty average. We have not, in other words, assumed that he or she has any particular amount of special skill or expertise in any particular area or field. You may rightly be asking at this point whether people with such skills and expertise have a higher or different obligation. Back to the cases to find out!

King v. Williams
276 S.C. 478, 279 S.E.2d 618
Supreme Court of South Carolina
1981

Littlejohn, J.:

Defendant Eston E. Williams, Jr., a general practitioner of medicine at Loris, South Carolina, appeals the jury verdict ... against him for his negligent diagnosis and treatment of plaintiff Joe D. King....

In February 1974, King suffered various scrapes, bruises and injuries after losing control of his vehicle and hitting several trees. The following day he entered Loris Community Hospital where he was examined and treated by Dr. Williams.

Among other injuries, King suffered a painful and swollen left foot. Dr. Williams ordered x-rays of only the ankle region and personally observed and manipulated the foot. Based upon his reading of the x-rays, as well as the report of the radiologist, Dr. Williams diagnosed and treated the injury as a severe ankle sprain. He expected the pain and swelling to subside in about one month. King was released in early March and allowed to walk on the foot using a walking cast.

When the cast was removed in March, the foot remained swollen and blue. Dr. Williams considered this condition to be normal and continued the same treatment. Over the next nine months the foot did not heal; instead, King suffered ongoing agony, discomfort, and inconvenience from the extreme pain in his foot. Additional x-rays of the ankle region were ordered and read by Dr. Williams during this interval, but his evaluation and treatment remained unchanged. Continued pain medication was prescribed in addition to use of an Ace bandage and an arch support.

In January 1975, at the insistence of King and his wife, Dr. Williams referred King to orthopedic specialists in Myrtle Beach and Columbia. The specialists x-rayed the entire foot, including areas other than the ankle. Each diagnosed a fracture dislocation of the foot, and corrective surgery was subsequently performed in June 1975. King suffered a 30% disability.

By our previous decisions, a physician has been held to a degree of skill and learning which is ordinarily possessed and exercised by members of his profession in good standing in the same general neighborhood or in similar localities.... The rationale underlying this "locality" rule has been that the education, training, equipment, facilities, libraries, contacts, and opportunities for learning vary among regions, as, for example, between a country doctor and a city doctor.... However, this logic has gradually deteriorated with the advance of required higher education, wide dissemination of medical information, and increased access to updated medical facilities....

Having reconsidered and examined the viability of the "locality" rule in South Carolina today, we hereby discard this rule and adopt a standard of care not bound by any geographical restrictions. More specifically, we agree [that] the standard [should be] as follows: The "locality rule" has no present-day vitality except that it may be considered as one of the elements to determine the degree of care and skill which is to be expected of the average practitioner of the class to which he belongs.

The degree of care that must be observed is, of course, that of an average, competent practitioner acting in the same or similar circumstances. In other words, local practice within geographic proximity is one, but not the only, factor to be considered. No longer is it proper to limit the definition of the standard or care which a medical doctor must meet solely to the practice or custom of a particular locality, a similar locality, or a geographic area. Other factors meriting consideration include the type of injury involved ... and the medical facilities available....

King v. Williams teaches us a number of important lessons concerning the standard of care applied to professionals.

The first is that a "reasonable professional" is an average practitioner — that is, one with an average amount of skill and knowledge — in the "class" to which the defendant belongs.

The rule applies equally to all professions: doctors, lawyers, accountants, engineers, and so on. As the profession becomes more specialized — cardiovascular surgeon, say — the "average amount of skill and knowledge" goes up to the median for that specialty, rather than for general practitioners. Make the specialty narrower — cardiovascular transplant surgeon, this time — and the median goes up again. But the level is always at the center of the bell curve for the profession or specialty, just as it is at the center of the bell curve of "all of us" for the nonspecialist.

The second lesson to be gained from this excerpt is buried in the idea of a "locality rule." It is tempting and in fact partially correct to think that the locality rule arose from the disparity in facilities and equipment that long existed between healthcare facilities in large cities and those in the country. But in fact the "locality rule" developed less for that reason than because of the fact that medical knowledge and information was not so much in books as in the skilled specialists and practitioners who for many years generally worked in major cities. That this is so can be inferred from the passage in the *King* opinion in which the Court suggested that the defendant physician ultimately was able to refer the plaintiff to orthopedic specialists in Myrtle Beach and Columbia.

Would the result have been the same if those specialists had not been available? Perhaps not, but the fact that the question could be asked in the first place was the real justification for the existence of such a rule.

Finally, as we shall soon see, cases like *King v. Williams* teach us how jurors learn about what the standard of reasonable care should be. For this, we need to travel to the next chapter.

But before we do, let us sum up briefly this most important of concepts. The idea of **reasonable care** — or its human exemplar, the reasonable person — is an objective standard for determining the nature and extent of obligations that we owe toward each other and that all of us are expected to fulfill. The level of obligation generally is that of the median or center of a hypothetical bell curve, usually representing the care that would be exercised by most people in the same circumstances, and it runs to the limit of the intangible but otherwise very real "zone of danger," the area in which the reasonable person would see his or her activities as posing risk to others.

For certain people, however, the standard is higher, either explicitly, if we are considered a professional or expert in a particular field, or implicitly, as when we suffer from physical disability, in which case application of the "same or similar circumstances" aspect of the principle puts those who overcome a disability at somewhat greater risk than those who have not done as well.

The only time that subjective criteria — criteria based solely upon the individual defendant rather than the hypothetical bell curve of people — enter into our thinking about reasonable care is when children are involved, and then the exception is somewhat limited.

That we can summarize such a basic concept in so few words is a testament to its enduring quality and dynamic simplicity. Juries every day in courts all over America work with it competently and effectively to reach answers that accord both with the facts and our notions of fairness. Not bad for a bunch of lawyers, huh?

Key Words and Phrases

blameworthy conduct
foreseeability
negligence
omission
ordinary prudence
reasonable care

reasonable person
"zone of danger"

Review Questions

1. Society generally accepts that adults, being (supposedly) more mature, have a duty to protect children. How does this concept square with assaults, in schools and other venues, committed by teenagers and ever younger children?

2. Find out at what age an individual is treated as an "adult" in your state. Does it vary, depending on the activity (for example, purchasing liquor, voting, or committing a crime)?

3. Visit and browse the web page of the American Law Institute at www.ali.org. Because the ALI is a source of *Restatements* and model codes in all aspects of law, you should be familiar with this organization.

---

[1] In England, this idea sprang from cases such as *Vaughan v. Menlove*, 3 Bing. N.C. 468, 132 Eng. Rep. 490 (1837) (Tindal, C.J.).

[2] Holmes, *The Common Law*, at 85 (Howe ed. 1963).

[3] 60 Mass. 292 (1850).

[4] Holmes, *supra* note 2, at 84–85 [emphasis added].

[5] A.P. Herbert, *Misleading Cases in the Common Law*, 12–16 (1930).

[6] Holmes, *supra* note 6, at 85.

[7] *In re Polemis and Furness, Withy & Co.*, 3 K.B. 560 (1921)

[8] *See, e.g., Anatomy of a Murder*, probably the best courtroom drama of all time, in which the insanity defense figures quite prominently. In addition to being intelligently acted, this movie, based on a book by a judge who later became

Chief Justice of the Michigan Supreme Court, is the most realistic portrayal of courtroom banter the author knows. Nice ending, too.

[9] Done in our head. German for "thought experiment," it signifies an analysis of a hypothetical situation and its results.

Chapter Four

REALITY CHECK: ESTABLISHING THE STANDARD OF CARE IN THE COURTROOM

In the last chapter, we discussed very formally and rather academically the standard of reasonable care and where it comes from. But all of that discussion took place in something of a vacuum, because it ignored the essential first step in all standards which have evolved from court cases: the testimony and evidence — the record — put on by real legal professionals in a real courtroom.

Chief Justice Shaw and the dog bite, Chief Judge Cardozo and the package of fireworks, even Justice Littlejohn and poor Mr. King ... all of the principles we have discussed came about because of **evidence** and **argument** prepared and presented in a trial court by lawyers, paralegals, and the other professionals who served as someone's advocates.

So, with all due respect to teachers of evidence (who think of the following as their preserve), let us use this as an opportunity to glimpse the process by which these legal standards come to life.

A Competitive Process

That process is a competitive one. Each party involved in a trial has the right to argue for application by the court of any and all legal principles, including the standard of care to be applied, that it feels that the court should adopt. Each party has the right to put on evidence and testimony to support that argument, subject only to evidentiary rules and the principles of legal ethics.

So long as it does not distort the truth improperly or otherwise violate the principles of ethics, each party to litigation is expected to take the position it feels is most persuasive, plausible, and advantageous for its position.

What keeps this process from becoming a fiasco? Obviously, the rules of evidence limit the kinds of testimony and exhibits that can be introduced. The canons of ethics and court rules applicable to all legal professionals limit the methods that they can use to advocate for a client.

But even more than that, one explicit and two implicit rules operate as checks on overzealous advocates. The first, sometimes humorously known as the **Gander Rule**, reads as follows: "What's sauce for the goose is sauce for the gander." In other words, just as you get to put on the arguments and evidence you want, so also do your opponents. The more extreme you are in advocating a position, the more likely the court is to permit your opponent to be just as extreme. Every proffer of extreme or inflammatory testimony carries with it the possibility that the other side will be able to do something even more extreme.

The other two are related rules of credulity, and they are simply these. You can argue for whatever you want, but the more extreme it is, the less likely it is to be accepted. The same principle applies equally to evidence presented during trial. The more extreme the evidence, generally speaking, the less likely the jury will believe it. In litigation, it is particularly true that what goes around comes around. Using inflammatory tactics can be counterproductive because they invite others in the case to do the same thing. Putting both more formally, there is an inverse relationship between extraordinarily zealous advocacy and persuasion. Thus, mastery of the facts and prudent argument are more likely to persuade than dizzying flights of rhetoric.

What Evidence *Can* Be Used?

However, with this said, the question on the floor is what kinds of evidence or principles can be used to establish a standard of care. Generally, there are four such sources:

1. testimony of laypersons
2. testimony by experts
3. evidence of objective standards, statutes or regulations
4. inference.

Each one has an established place in the law of torts.

Testimony by Laypersons

Having talked so long about the reasonable person, it is logical to suppose that testimony by ordinary individuals is an important part of proving the standard of reasonable care. As our next excerpt shows, this is indeed the case.

Blackburn v. Murphy
737 S.W.2d 529
Supreme Court of Tennessee, at Nashville
1987

Drowota, Justice:

This action arose from an automobile accident in Nashville. Plaintiff Natalie A. Blackburn brought this suit to recover damages from Defendants Charles H. Murphy and Rachel D. Murphy due to the alleged negligence of Rachel Murphy. Defendants asserted the defense of unavoidable accident due to the weather conditions prevailing on the morning of the accident.

During the night and early morning of February 28, 1984, a light snow fell in Nashville, leaving the streets and highways in the area hazardous. Plaintiff was a passenger in a car driven by her husband, Kennard Blackburn. As they were driving to work along Interstate 40 West between 6:00 and 6:30 a.m., Mr. Blackburn was traversing an interstate overpass, following a car driven by a witness in this case, Yvonne Parks, when he saw a truck fishtail ahead of himself and Mrs. Parks. At about the same time, he and Mrs. Parks moved from the left lane in which they were traveling into the right lane to avoid the truck. As they changed lanes, they collided lightly and then pulled over into the emergency parking lane on the far right of the interstate. Little property damage and no personal injuries resulted from this collision; however, while Mr. Blackburn and Mrs. Parks were examining their vehicles for damage, a car driven by Mrs. Murphy came around the curved overpass, lost traction, and slid into the rear of Mr. Blackburn's car, causing extensive damage to Mr. Blackburn's car and injuring Mrs. Blackburn, who had remained in the Blackburn automobile after the first accident. Mrs. Blackburn was taken to a local hospital for emergency treatment of a neck injury....

Mrs. Parks was called to testify for Plaintiff, stating that she had been traveling to work on this morning when Mr. Blackburn bumped into the rear of her car. They had pulled over into the emergency lane to check for damage. While standing on the side of the road, Mrs. Murphy's automobile struck Mr. Blackburn's car. She could not make any estimate of Mrs. Murphy's speed.

On cross-examination, she stated that the roads were very slick and driving was hazardous, noting that the overpasses were especially dangerous and that this particular overpass not only curved but sloped downhill. She testified that she and Mr. Blackburn had collided because they slid on ice on the overpass. She witnessed a number of accidents while waiting at the scene of the accident, estimating that perhaps 20 cars had been involved in several accidents during the period she remained at the scene. The entire area was very slick.

She stated that she and Mr. Blackburn had both been traveling slowly when they bumped and that all the cars she saw seemed to be exercising caution. When asked again about Mrs. Murphy's speed, she stated that she did not remember how fast she [Mrs. Murphy] was going and remarked that the "main thing that stands out in my mind is the impact itself."

Continuing on cross, after Mrs. Parks reiterated that road conditions were slippery, the following exchange then occurred:

* * * *

Q: Okay, now the question I believe was, did you tell me as far as you can recall this was an accident that couldn't be avoided?
A: Okay, yes, sir, it could not have—it was a slick day. Everyone was driving with caution and it was just, you know, one of those things. There were accidents all over town that day.
Q: Even though people were driving with caution they were still having accidents?
A: Yes, sir.

* * * *

We start with the general proposition [that] the ordinary witness must confine his testimony to a narration of facts based on firsthand knowledge and avoid stating mere personal opinions.... The obvious purpose served by the general rule is to preserve the primary fact-finding role of the jury, since [i]t is the function of the witness to state evidentiary facts and the function of the jury to draw such conclusions as the facts warrant.

* * * *

Nevertheless, exceptions to this general rule precluding admission of lay opinion testimony do exist. Non-expert opinion testimony can be admissible when such testimony describes observed facts in the only way in which they can be clearly described. [Citation omitted.] The admission of lay testimony is thus limited to those circumstances [w]here facts perceived by the senses are numerous, and it is difficult to describe them adequately to the jury, and the conclusion or inference to be drawn from such facts is simple and within the range of common experience, and the witness can relate what he has seen more accurately and more easily by stating his conclusion than by attempting to detail the [evidentiary] facts, [then] the conclusion or inference of the witness is admissible.

Upon proper foundation, where necessary, lay opinion is commonly admitted on whether a person is intoxicated ... or regarding recognition or identification of a sound.... Distances and speed are regularly estimated by lay witnesses; even a person's physical condition may be a subject of lay opinion testimony on occasion; the value of property may be given by a lay witness.... These examples are not intended to constitute an exhaustive catalogue, but merely indicate the nature of the opinion testimony that a lay witness may be qualified to give.

In this case, while Mrs. Parks could clearly state whether the roads on which she drove were hazardous or icy, she should not have been permitted to state her opinion as to whether the accident could or could not ultimately have

It should now be obvious that the standard of care at issue in *Blackburn* was whether a reasonable person would have been going as fast as the defendant in the conditions that existed in the "snowstorm,"[1] with plaintiff asserting that a reasonable person would have driven more slowly and defendant asserting that there was nothing anyone could have done to avoid the accident. But that obscures an important point. Why use the victim herself to answer this question?

We cannot truly know the answer to this question, but the defense lawyer was probably concerned that someone else — an expert witness or a police officer that investigated the accident — would have said that defendant Murphy should not have been out in the first place. And this obviously would not be the kind of testimony that would help a defense based upon the idea that the accident was unavoidable.

Clearly, the accident was avoidable simply by staying off the road. So, if one of the victims would admit that the accident might be unavoidable, the defense lawyer would bolster his own case straight from the plaintiff's mouth, as it were, and probably avoid a nasty round of cross-examination.

As the excerpt demonstrates, a lay witness cannot testify to anything but personal observations and facts. By extension, a **lay witness** — an ordinary observer — cannot testify as to what constitutes reasonable care or whether given conduct meets it.[2] But lay witnesses can, and do, provide the factual basis for establishing a standard of care.

As noted by the Tennessee Supreme Court, there are many subjects on which a lay witness can draw conclusions, including speed, intoxication, distance, value, and dozens of others. In addition, even if a trial judge would not permit a lay witness to state such opinions on the witness stand, you can see from the excerpt how tantalizingly close to such conclusions the actual testimony was. Good advocacy and some careful thought by the trial team were almost enough to get the defense team where it wanted to be.

Testimony by Experts

Suppose that this kind of advocacy is not enough. Suppose that the trial team needs someone to say that a professional of average skill and knowledge in the defendant's field would not have done it that way. How does that kind of testimony get to the jury?

King v. Williams, the case concerning the level of reasonable care applied to professionals that we studied in the last chapter, explains how. Let us return to South Carolina, remembering as we go that King sued Dr. Williams for negligent diagnosis and treatment of the fracture and dislocation in King's foot.

King v. Williams (Part Two)
276 S.C. 478, 279 S.E.2d 618
Supreme Court of South Carolina
1981

Littlejohn, J.:

At trial, Dr. Harry Rein of Orlando, Florida, testified on King's behalf, over objections, to the following:

a) That the injury to King's foot was a common one treated similarly by all physicians throughout the country;

b) That he was generally familiar with the standard of medical care in Loris, South Carolina; and

c) That Dr. Williams failed to meet the standard of care in Loris or similar localities in his diagnosis and treatment of King's foot (e.g., failure to order proper x-rays or diagnose the injury; failure to consult other physicians; failure to earlier refer the patient to a specialist).

* * * *

Even without Dr. Rein's testimony, the jury reasonably could have inferred that King's injury was proximately caused by negligence of Dr. Williams. King suffered a foot injury. Dr. Williams x-rayed the ankle region only and diagnosed a "severe sprain." While the initial examination and diagnosis was arguably not negligent ... the subsequent events clearly infer a failure to use proper skills.

Dr. Williams expected general recovery of the foot in three weeks to one month; yet despite persistent pain and swelling, he failed to x-ray areas of the foot other than the ankle for almost eight months. Furthermore, he failed to consult a specialist until almost one year later in spite of abnormal developments, (e.g., failure to timely heal, fallen arch and demineralization)

> While King did see a specialist in July 1975 (about five months after the injury), Dr. Williams failed to consult the specialist either before or after the appointment. Dr. Williams admitted that King followed the prescribed medication. The law is well-established that expert testimony is not required where the common knowledge or experience of laymen is capable of inferring lack of proper care.... We think the jury was justified under these circumstances in finding actionable negligence by Dr. Williams even absent the expert testimony.

Poor Dr. Williams thus answers the basic question left for us. To establish the standard of care, legal professionals ordinarily use expert witnesses, people who by training or experience in a field have special knowledge that is likely to be of use to a jury in discharging its function as the trier of fact.

Expert witnesses have training or experience in a field that can help the jury to understand scientific, technical, or other specialized issues. Expert witnesses are allowed to give opinion testimony.

Qualifying Your Expert

Before a person may testify as an expert, he or she must be shown by questioning to possess adequate experience, education, or training to offer opinion testimony. The process by which this is done is known as **qualification**.

And notice how it was done. First, plaintiff's counsel undoubtedly qualified Dr. Rein. That is, the attorney asked questions, and Dr. Rein's answers showed that he (Rein) had enough training and experience to have the special knowledge necessary to help the jury determine what a practitioner in Dr. Williams' position would have done.

Next, the attorney would have established that Dr. Rein was familiar with the standard of care at issue. Usually this is done by asking a straightforward series of questions that probably went something like this, changing the names to protect the innocent.[3]

Q: Now, Dr. Shlabotnik, are you familiar with the standard or level of care that should be afforded by general practitioners like Dr. Williams in communities like Loris?

A: I am.

Q: And before I ask you to describe for the jury what that standard or level of care is, would you tell the jury how you came to be familiar with it?

A: [Dr. Shlabotnik explains what training and experiences he has that would make him familiar with how the care should be given. Often this answer will be interlaced with a discourse on why Dr. Shlabotnik is a fantastic doctor.]

Q: Now, Dr. Shlabotnik, have you had an opportunity to read Dr. Williams' medical records concerning his treatment of Mr. King?

A: I have.

Q: And based upon your review and experience, can you tell the jury whether or not there are any differences in the way physicians in different parts of the country treat an injury like Mr. King's?

A: It would be the same everywhere.

Q: And again, based upon your review of the medical records, and on your training and expertise and your familiarity with the kinds of care that should be given, do you have an opinion as to whether or not Dr. Williams failed to provide Mr. King with the kind of medical care that a reasonable practitioner would have given for Mr. King's condition?

A: I do.

Q: And what is that opinion?

[At this point, there is a strenuous objection from opposing counsel, almost always overruled summarily.]

A: Dr. Williams failed to order proper x-rays or diagnose the
    injury. He failed to consult other physicians, and he failed to
    refer the patient earlier to a specialist.

A review of most trial transcripts reveals similar exchanges in many
cases involving everything from automobile accidents to professional
malpractice to defective product cases. Experts are an essential element
of most causes of action.

What gives them this essential role? Note again the court's statement in
King v. Williams: "The law is well-established that expert testimony is
not required where the common knowledge or experience of laymen is
capable of inferring lack of proper care...."

The problem is that most, if not all, laymen lack much (if any) expertise
in the ins and outs of medical care, product design, professional care or
conduct, and all manner of other subjects dealt with in the courtroom.
The expertise can only come from those who have such knowledge and
skills, and that is what experts provide in the courtroom.

This is not to say that the role and use of expert testimony in a trial is
free from controversy,[4] but in most situations it is the expert's job to
explain what the standards of care are.

Expertise or standards are not necessarily limited to witnesses, however, as the next excerpt demonstrates:

Mele v. Sherman Hospital[5]
838 F.2d 923
United States Court of Appeals for the Seventh Circuit
1988

Manion, Circuit Judge:

Plaintiff Sheila Mele (Mele), desiring to have her tubes tied (a "tubal ligation"), entered Sherman Hospital (the Hospital) in Elgin, Illinois, for a laparoscopy and tubal ligation to be performed by Dr. Joe Han....

The Hospital did not employ Dr. Han. Rather, as an independent physician with Hospital staff privileges, Dr. Han could admit his patient into the Hospital and treat the patient there when his patient required those facilities.

The Hospital's bylaws provide that "a surgical operation will be performed only on consent of the patient ... except in emergencies." After admission Mele signed a form captioned "authorization for medical and surgical treatment." This form had been prepared by the Hospital and bore the Hospital's name on top. The form left blank spaces for the treating physician to fill in the patient's name, the physician's own name, and the treatment the patient has authorized. The form's remainder featured prepared provisions.

One preprinted provision authorized the physician to employ additional procedures if unforeseen conditions should arise during surgery....

* * * *

By signing the consent form, Mele authorized Dr. Han to perform a "laparoscopic tubal coagulation." A nurse filled in that procedure as directed by Dr. Han. The consent form did not mention a laparotomy. Mele testified that Dr. Han did not tell her about the surgery's risks. Dr. Han testified that he informed Mele of some risks, but did not tell her about the possibility of nicking a membrane in her abdomen because he believed the chance of that complication arising was slight.

During the operation, Dr. Han nicked a membrane inside Mele's abdomen.... He consequently performed a laparotomy to discover the bleeding's source.... As a result of the laparotomy, Mele has a scar on her abdomen.

* * * *

Mele did not establish that the standard of care the Hospital had to meet included warning a patient of possible bad results from surgery to be performed by an independent treating physician. At most, she established that the standard of care included requiring such a physician to warn his patients of the risks of surgery.

It is established that a hospital's duty to its patients requires it to conform to the standard of reasonable conduct in light of the apparent risk. Th[is] standard of care ... is capable of proof through a wide variety of evidence including expert testimony, hospital bylaws, statutes accreditation standards, customs and community practice.... [T]he Hospital's bylaw—which allows surgery only with a patient's informed consent—does not obligate the Hospital to guarantee that a patient has tendered informed consent....

* * * *

Mele's expert witness, Dr. Hasson, testified that the filled-in form Mele signed was incomplete because it did not disclose the possibility of a laparotomy.... But Mele's expert candidly acknowledged that he did not believe that it was the Hospital's responsibility to place upon the form that Mele might need a laparotomy. Instead, he testified that it is the doctor's responsibility to inform a patient of surgical risks.... The only standard of care derivable from Mele's evidence is that of putting in place a system to facilitate a doctor's consent....

There may seem much to digest in this excerpt, but notice two main points. Initially, we see that bylaws, formal standards or procedural manuals, regulations, and even custom and practice in a community can be used to establish the standard of care. The field is a fertile one. Many hospitals, for example, maintain detailed internal procedure manuals governing all sorts of daily operations, and they subscribe to standards of practice imposed by accreditation agencies or governmental bodies. It is very common in tort litigation for plaintiffs to seek internal procedure manuals, rule books, and other similar documents or materials in an effort to show that the employees of a given organization or the members of a particular profession failed to abide by the guidelines given in such documents.

The second point to be learned from this excerpt is that procedural manuals are not necessarily the strongest evidence of a standard of care. There are several reasons for this. The first is simply that procedures developed for one institution or group of people may not translate well as guides to the obligations of others or serve as definitive statements of what someone should do. This is the problem that the plaintiff in *Mele* could not overcome. The second problem is that standards often become outdated or even obsolete, sometimes to the point that they are entirely ignored or even irrelevant to any issue that may be important to a case. A rule governing use of a 1950s vintage fluoroscope has little if any relevance to operating the latest in nuclear magnetic resonance or positron-electron tomography systems.

Finally, it should be recalled that organizations sophisticated enough to draft rule books or procedure manuals are also sophisticated enough to realize that plaintiffs will attempt to take advantage of them, and thus the documents are usually drafted with enough forethought to make them as self-serving as possible.

A Damaging Expert Witness

But before we consider this issue of regulation — even of statutory law — as a basis for a standard of care, let us examine briefly the final significant lesson from *Mele*, which is that expert witnesses can be every bit as harmful to your position as they can be helpful.

The expert Mele used ultimately was a large factor in the undoing of her case, as can be seen from the Court's comments about some of the questions:

Cross-examination of Mele's expert produced the following typical exchange:

Q: You're not saying that Sherman Hospital should have put
     something on the form that the physician didn't put on the
     order, are you.
A: No, I can't say that. (*See* 838 F.2d at 925.)

One can almost see the plaintiff's lawyer wilting as Mele's own expert
gave answers that torpedoed important parts of the case.

And that is the final lesson of *Mele*, one that all manner of legal
professionals have to learn over and over again. Experts can be a little
like nitroglycerine; very useful but occasionally prone to go off in
inopportune ways!

Proper preparation of expert witnesses — indeed, of all witnesses — is
essential to effective testimony. More generally, it is a great lesson of
the trial game — one that could be seen being ignored over and over
again in the O. J. Simpson criminal trial — that it is vital not only to
prepare one's witnesses, experts included, but also to get them on and
off the stand expeditiously. Even for the best witnesses, there is a direct
relationship between the time spent on the stand and the likelihood of
saying something regrettable.

The care and feeding of experts is an enduring subject of debate, lore
and even urban legend among trial types, and something more properly
addressed in courses on evidence and trial practice. These excerpts,
however, give you some idea of how important this area is to the
substantive law of torts.

Evidence of Objective Standards, Statutes, or Regulations

Statutes often have an important role in establishing a standard of care.
The question that follows is whether or not they do play such a role in
real life. Again we turn to the case law to find out.

Palmer v. Shearson Lehman Hutton, Inc.[6]
622 So.2d 1085
District Court of Appeal of Florida,
First District
1993

Zehmer, Chief Judge:

* * * *

These cases primarily arise out of relationships created and regulated under ... the Florida Securities Act. This Act regulates the sale of securities in Florida and requires that dealers and associated persons[7] be registered with the [Florida] Department [of Banking and Finance] before selling or offering to sell securities to any person in this state.... Registrations of associated persons[7] are specific with respect to the securities dealer identified at the time the registration is approved. Thus, each time an associated person is terminated from employment with a dealer, whether voluntarily or involuntarily, the dealers must notify the Department of that person's termination and the reason therefor; and to become associated with another dealer, the terminated associated person must reregister with the Department.

* * * *

From 1978 until January 1984, David Kury was registered as an associated person of E. F. Hutton & Co., Inc.... In early 1983, Kury's supervisor, Fred Brown, discovered that Kury had taken money from several of his customers in exchange for personal and corporate promissory notes.... Brown testified in the administrative disciplinary proceeding against Kury that he was aware that Kury's actions violated SEC regulations as well as Hutton's internal rules and that in January 1984, he asked for and obtained Kury's resignation. Subsequently, Hutton filed a Uniform Termination Notice For Securities Industry Registration (a "Form U-5") ... stating that Kury had voluntarily resigned. On this form, Hutton falsely reported that it had no reason to believe that Kury had violated any state or federal law or regulation, or that Kury had engaged in any conduct inconsistent with just and equitable principles of trade.

* * * *

In 1986 ... Luther and Marlene Young visited Kury at his [new employer] Associated [Planners Securities Corporation] and employed him to provide them with financial planning services. In early 1987, Kury induced Luther and Marlene Young ... to purchase a $50,000 corporate promissory note issued by Kury Financial.... In July 1987... he induced Young to purchase a $30,000 promissory note from Kury Financial.... In December 1987, Kury induced Palmer to pay $20,000 for a promissory note from Kury Financial.

In May 1988, the Department commenced an investigation of Kury's activities and as a consequence filed an administrative complaint against Kury and Kury Financial [alleging] that he had engaged in the sale of unregistered securities.... In March 1989 [Young and others] filed [lawsuits] against Hutton and other securities dealers. Count V of each complaint alleged Hutton's negligence in covering up Kury's fraud and falsely advising the Department regarding his termination....

* * * *

The law is settled that a statute creates a duty of care on one whose behavior is the subject of the statute to a person who is in the class designed to be protected by the statute, and that such duty will support a finding of liability for negligence when the injury suffered by a person in the protected class is that which the statute was designed to prevent.... Although the violation of a statute establishing a duty to take precautions to protect a particular class of persons from a particular injury or type of injury constitutes negligence *per se* ... the fact of negligence *per se* resulting from a statutory violation does not necessarily mean that there is actionable negligence.... It must also be shown that the plaintiff falls within the class of persons that the statute was designed to protect, that the plaintiff suffered an injury of the type the statute was designed to prevent, and that the violation of the statute was the proximate cause of this injury....

The broad legislative purpose underlying the enactment of ... the Florida Securities Act [...] was to protect the investing public from fraudulent and deceptive practices by persons selling securities in the securities market.... The reporting provisions ... and the prohibition on filing false reports with the Department ... are designed to enable the Department to timely obtain truthful information about the conduct of persons registered to sell securities

---

so that it can discipline or otherwise prevent registered persons from practicing fraud on members of the investing public.

[The Palmers, the Youngs and other investors] are within the class of persons [these statutes were] designed to protect because they are investors in securities and dealt with Kury as a registered broker. Likewise, the investors suffered the kind of injury the statutes were designed to prevent because they lost moneys invested as a consequence of the fraudulent acts of the registered dealer, Kury.

* * * *

To summarize, we hold that the facts shown in these cases by [Plaintiffs'] allegations in the complaints and responses to discovery requests asserting Hutton's violation of the statutory reporting requirements are legally sufficient to show the existence of a legal duty owed by Hutton to [the Plaintiffs]....

Negligence *Per Se*

Here we have another "new" concept — that of **negligence** *per se* — in which statutory obligations designed to protect the public form the basis of a duty in tort. "New" is in quotes because such an idea should come as no surprise to you, since reasonable person (an individual of average intelligence taking reasonable care) obeys the law.

The concept of negligence *per se* really is about that simple. The elements of negligence *per se* are

- the existence of a statute or similar official enactment designed to protect the public or some class of persons
- the plaintiff is within the class of people the statute is designed to protect.

The duties imposed through negligence *per se* are cumulative to those that arise through the concept of reasonable care. Thus, they are an additional way of demonstrating the existence of an obligation. This cumulation of obligation is commonly seen in automobile collision cases, where it is routine to see a pleading in which the plaintiff alleges that the defendant breached his or her duty of reasonable care by, for instance, going too fast or making an improper turn and then alleging that the defendant breached the separate statutory prohibitions of these things contained in the applicable traffic laws.

Are the "reasonable person" and negligence *per se* obligations necessarily redundant? Not at all. We can easily imagine situations in which it would not be unreasonable in the abstract to be driving faster than the posted speed limit — on a well-designed freeway in the desert with no traffic nearby — so that the only obligation not to exceed the speed limit comes from the statutorily-imposed speed limit itself. Even the *Young* case we just read held that the brokerage house had no duty to report that it had terminated Kury except for the one created by statute:

> Under the common law, a person has no duty to control the tortious or criminal conduct of another or to warn those placed in danger by such conduct unless there is a special relationship between the defendant and the person whose behavior needs to be controlled or the person who is a foreseeable victim of such misconduct.... Kury was not in the employ and control of Hutton at the time the alleged injuries occurred, and Hutton had not employed him for several years.... Hutton owed [the Plaintiffs] no duty under the common law, apart from any relevant regulatory requirements, with respect to the alleged negligent conduct. (*See* 622 So.2d at 1089.)

Thus, negligence *per se* exists as an overlapping but independent body of obligations, one that often complements the obligations imposed by the more general standard of the reasonable person. As long as legislatures enact new statutes and agencies create new regulations, negligence *per se* will remain a lively field of tort law.

Res Ipsa Loquitur

Earlier in this chapter, we called the last of our four sources for obligation "inference," but the traditional legal phrase for it is *res ipsa loquitur*, Latin for "the thing speaks for itself."

> *Res ipsa loquitur.* The principle that, in certain circumstances, the fact that an accident occurred raises an inference of negligence sufficient to establish a *prima facie* case.

Res ipsa, as the doctrine sometimes is known, is one of inference with roots in medical malpractice, where the victim too often was anesthetized and incapable of observing what happened while it happened. By way of example, consider the following.

Connors v. University Associates in Obstetrics and Gynecology, Inc.[8]
4 F.3d 123
United States Court of Appeals for the Second Circuit
1993

Altimari, Circuit Judge:

* * * *

On October 28, 1986, Mary Jane Connors had surgery performed, including a hysteroscopy and a laparoscopy, in order to assist her in her efforts to become pregnant.... Within a few days after surgery, Connors began to experience severe pain in her left leg and hip. This pain continues today and has been accompanied by a permanent loss of function of the leg....

At trial, Connors attempted to show that the physicians performing the surgery had negligently employed an O'Connor-O'Sullivan self-retaining retractor during the operation. A retractor is a device that is inserted into an incision and keeps the operative area open while the surgeon is working. Connors alleged that the negligent use of the retractor had entrapped her lateral femoral cutaneous nerve ("LFCN"), damaging the nerve and causing her injury. Experts for both parties agreed that the standard of care in the use of the retractor dictated that ... the doctor ensure that the retractor blades are not impinging on various structures, and that the doctor check the blades during surgery to ensure that the retractor is not pressing on nerves or muscles.

Experts at trial disagreed, however, over whether Connors' injury could have occurred even if this standard of care had been followed. Connors' experts opined that the injury could not have occurred if not for the negligent use of the retractor, and reasoned that Dr. Brunstead and the other physicians [who performed the surgery] had violated the standard of care in employing the retractor. Dr. Brunstead testified for the defense, stating that he could not recall if he used a self-retaining retractor in the operation but that he was sure that he would have followed proper procedures if he had.

Other defense experts opined that Connors' injury was due to the fact that her LFCN was abnormally positioned, an anatomical rarity that the performing physicians could not have anticipated. These experts also testified that nerve injuries in operations of this type were sometimes unavoidable complications not attributable to negligence.

* * * *

At the close of the ... trial, over University Associates' objection, [the court] issued the following instruction to the jury:

> In ordinary cases, the mere fact that an accident or injury happened does not furnish evidence that it was caused by any person's negligence. And the plaintiff must prove some negligent act or omission on the part of the defendant. This is the method of finding negligence that I have just described to you.
>
> Nevertheless, I instruct you in this case that you may find the defendant, University Associates, negligent if you find that the plaintiff has proved each of the following elements by a preponderance of the evidence; first, that an injury to the plaintiff was proximately caused by the self-retaining retractor used during her surgery; that at the time of the accident or injury, the self-retaining retractor was in the exclusive control or management of Dr. John Brunstead and/or his surgical assistants, so that the defendant had superior means for determining the cause of the accident and injury; and third, that in the normal course of events this type of injury would not have occurred without the negligence of the person having control and management of the self-retaining retractor.

I say that you may so find. You are not compelled to so find. You should consider all the facts and circumstances in evidence and also the defendant's explanation. You are reminded that the plaintiff has the burden of proving the defendant's negligence by a preponderance of the evidence.

[R]es ipsa loquitur is a form of circumstantial evidence that allows a jury to infer from the circumstances of an injury that the defendant has been negligent.... The term "*res ipsa loquitur*," literally translated, is Latin for "the thing speaks for itself," and derives from the landmark English case *Byrne v. Boodle* ... allowing the inference of negligence where a barrel of flour rolled out of a warehouse window [ ]. The doctrine has traditionally been invoked in cases where the jury has a basis of past experience which reasonably permits the conclusion that such events do not ordinarily occur unless someone has been negligent....

There are four elements of *res ipsa loquitur*: (1) a legal duty of the defendant to exercise a certain degree of care; (2) control by the defendant; (3) causation; and (4) the requirement that the event which brought on the plaintiff's harm is such that it would not ordinarily occur except for the want of requisite care on the part of the defendant as the person responsible for the injuring agency....

University Associates contend[s] that *res ipsa* should not apply to medical malpractice cases in which expert testimony is presented. The basis for this contention is that *res ipsa* is a doctrine traditionally grounded on the theory that jurors share a common experience that allows them to make certain inferences of negligence. If expert testimony is needed to support the inference, then the inference does not come from common experience but from uncommon experience (*i.e.*, specialized medical knowledge).

University Associates has raised an issue that has divided jurisdictions across the country. Unless a medical malpractice case is factually simple (i.e., leaving a sponge in the patient), jurors' common experience will not provide them with the requisite insight to determine whether certain injuries can only be the result of negligence.

This is clearly the type of case in which expert testimony was appropriate and necessary. To find otherwise would place Connors in a "Catch-22," presenting her with the choice of either introducing expert testimony or foregoing a *res ipsa* instruction. By making do with only one or the other, however, Connors' ability to present her case would have been severely impaired.

If the *res ipsa* instruction were to be given without the expert testimony, the jury would be given the opportunity to find the defendants negligent without proof, but the jury would lack the acumen to be able to determine whether the injury was truly the type that could not occur but for the defendant's negligence.

Alternatively, Connors could introduce the expert testimony but do without the *res ipsa* charge.... This would give the jurors the ability to evaluate the injury, but would not instruct them that they can make the leap to inferring negligence from the fact of injury. Expert testimony in this case was not able to prove conclusively that negligence caused Connors' injury. Rather, Connors' experts opined that there was nothing unusual about Connors' anatomy ... and that the injury could only have occurred if the doctors had negligently used the retractor. This does not, by itself, support finding of negligence. A *res ipsa* instruction was needed to allow the jury to make the inference. The *res ipsa loquitur* instruction in this case was important guidance to the jurors, informing them that, if they credited the testimony of Connors' experts, they could infer that the physicians were negligent simply because the injury occurred.

A *res ipsa loquitur* instruction is given in order to allow a plaintiff with no ability to show actual negligence the opportunity to prove negligence through inference. It is especially necessary in medical malpractice cases, since the plaintiff is in no position to testify about what happened to her in surgery.

* * * *

The elements of *res ipsa loquitur* are

- a legal duty of the defendant to exercise a certain degree of care
- control by the defendant
- causation

- the requirement that the event that brought on the plaintiff's harm is such that it would not ordinarily occur except for the want of requisite care on the part of the defendant as the person responsible for the injuring agency.

Can *res ipsa loquitur* be used in cases other than medical malpractice involving the unconscious? The answer, of course, is yes, and the doctrine has been used in everything up to and including one notable case involving an allegedly defective hand grenade.[9]

Regardless of the setting, however, the doctrine depends upon two essential steps for the inference to be drawn.

First, the thing, product, or action that caused the injury must have been under the exclusive control and management of the defendant.

Second, the character and circumstances surrounding the accident must be such that it can reasonably be believed that the accident would not have occurred in the absence of negligence.

Both steps are necessary to keep extraneous circumstances from intervening to cause a problem or injury; hence, both are necessary to support application of the doctrine. Courts tend to be rather strict in requiring someone who wishes to meet the *res ipsa* challenge to come forward with evidence that satisfies these criteria.

These, then, are the main sources for the standard of care that our friend, the reasonable person, must meet:

- common experience
- the expertise of qualified witnesses, especially in cases involving technical or scientific issues
- negligence *per se*
- *res ipsa loquitur*.

They are a fertile and seemingly limitless field in which the law of torts can work.

Key Words and Phrases

argument
bylaws
custom and practice
evidence
expert testimony
expert witness inference
inference
lay testimony
lay witness
negligence *per se*
procedure manuals
qualification of an expert witness
res ipsa loquitur
standards

Review Questions

1.   Think about *res ipsa loquitur* as a device for establishing
        negligence. List several situations in which the doctrine might
        apply. Having done so, can you see whether there is some factor
        about the plaintiff's situation in each case that is conceptually
        the same?

2.   We have talked as though the standards for reasonable care
        apply to defendants. Do they also apply to plaintiffs? Explain
        your reasoning. Give examples of situations that are particularly
        appropriate for application of these standards to plaintiffs.

3.   Analyze the following situation. Smith claims to have been
        injured when he dove into an aboveground pool. Your
        supervisor has asked you to develop information that would bear
        upon what standards of care might apply to the pool's
        manufacturer (*i.e.*, what must the manufacturer have done to use
        reasonable care in the design and sale of the pool). Provide your
        supervisor with specific kinds of resources that can be used

(*e.g.*, standards set by the Consumer Products Safety Commission) to understand whether the manufacturer did use such care.

4.   For a doctor's take on the subject of medical experts, see "First Kill All the Experts" by Dr. Al Davies, found (as of publication) in the 'Lectric Law Library at www.lectlaw.com /filesh/ medscn1.htm.

---

[1] Here we put the word "snowstorm" in quotations to still the snickering of readers from places such as Buffalo, Duluth, or Great Falls, for whom this would be heavy dew.

[2] The reasons for this rule are largely historical, but they rest in large measure on the theory that the quality of opinion or conclusion drawn by a non-expert witness presumably is no better than the conclusion that a juror could draw simply by listening to observation or factual recitation. If laypersons were permitted to give such opinions, the theory goes, every witness would do so, and a trial would become nothing more than a giant "op ed" page with little time spent on the facts and much time spent on the irrelevant. Obviously, this rule was developed by people who foresaw the O. J. Simpson case, in which it was largely ignored.

[3] Warning: the next several questions usually differ from court to court, because of differences in local practice, applicable rules of evidence, and the preference of the person asking the question. This exchange is, however, rather typical.

[4] *See, e.g., Daubert v. Merrell Dow Pharm., Inc.,* 509 U.S. 590 (1993).

[5] Some internal citations and quotations omitted.

[6] Internal footnotes, quotations, and some citations omitted.

[7] "Associated persons" here means stockbrokers employed by a registered brokerage house

[8] Internal quotations omitted.

[9] *McGonigal v. Gearhart Indus., Inc.,* 788 F.2d 321 (5th Cir. 1986).

Chapter Five

NO CAUSE FOR ALARM: THE CONCEPT OF CAUSATION IN THE LAW OF TORTS

In our preceding discussion, we explored the general basis for the law of torts, and found our way to the reasonable person, the individual who personifies the idea of reasonable care. However, simply having a standard of care and knowing what it is doesn't get us very far.

Have you cheated a bit on a red light lately? Driven home late at night a little too fast after one too many? Failed to use safety glasses or a safety belt? Of course, we have. Everyone — the author, your instructor, even you — frequently does things that a jury might find to be a failure to use reasonable care. We do these things without the slightest adverse consequence and certainly without being hauled into a courtroom. The reason should be obvious, of course. There is no link between these lapses and injury or harm to anyone or anything else.

There are two rather large issues in that last sentence, one of **linkage**, which we discuss in this chapter, and another of **injury** or **harm,** which we will discuss more fully later in this book because of its relevance in other contexts. For right now, learning what constitutes a sufficient link between breach of an obligation and injury to another will be quite enough.

Linkage

Legal professionals refer to the necessity for a link between breach and injury as **causation.**

Causation. The act or process of causing or producing an effect; also, the relationship between cause and effect.

Perhaps the best way to begin to get an idea of the concept is to return to the *Palsgraf* case we discussed in Chapter Three.

You remember the facts — the commuter with the package of fireworks being helped onto the departing train ... the falling package ... the explosion ... the falling scale ... Mrs. Palsgraf's being hurt — an exceedingly odd set of circumstances altogether.

When we discussed this case before, we noted that Chief Justice Cardozo found that the railroad could not be liable for the acts of its employees because they (the employees) could not have foreseen the explosive consequences of their actions in helping the passenger. We also noted that Justice Cardozo did not speak for a unanimous Court of Appeals. Three Justices, led by Justice Andrews, dissented, and their opinion is as famous as the majority opinion.[1]

Palsgraf v. Long Island Railroad Co. [Part II]
248 N.Y. 339, 162 N.E. 101
1929

ANDREWS, J., dissenting:

* * * *

The right to recover damages rests on additional considerations. The plaintiff's rights must be injured, and this injury must be caused by negligence. We build a dam but are negligent as to its foundations. Breaking, it injures property down stream. We are not liable if all of this happened because of some reason other than the insecure foundation. But, when injuries do result from our unlawful act, we are liable for the consequences. It does not matter that they are unusual, unexpected, unforeseen, and unforeseeable. But there is one limitation. The damages must be so connected with the negligence that the latter may be said to be the proximate cause of the former.

These two words have never been given an inclusive definition. What is a cause in a legal sense, still more a proximate cause, depends in each case upon many considerations, as does the existence of negligence itself. Any philosophical doctrine of causation does not help us. A boy throws a stone into a pond. The ripples spread. The water level rises. The history of that pond is altered to all eternity. It will be altered by other causes also. Yet it will be forever the resultant of all causes combined. Each one will have an influence.... Each is proximate in the sense it is essential. But that is not what we mean by the word....

* * * *

What we do mean by the word "proximate" is that, because of convenience, of public policy, of a rough sense of justice, the law arbitrarily declines to trace a series of events beyond a certain point....

* * * *

The proximate cause, involved as it may be with other causes, must be, at the least, something without which the event would not happen. The court must ask itself whether there was a natural and continuous sequence between cause and effect. Was the one a substantial factor in producing the other? Was there a direct connection between them without too many intervening causes? Is the effect of cause on result not too attenuated? Is the cause likely, in the usual judgment of mankind, to produce the result? Or, by exercise of prudent foresight, could the result be foreseen? Is the result too remote from the cause, and here we consider remoteness in time and space? ... Clearly we must so consider, for the greater the distance either in time or space, the more surely do other causes intervene to affect the result. When a lantern is overturned, the firing of a shed is a fairly direct consequence. Many things contribute to the spread of the conflagration—the force of the wind, the direction and width of the streets, the character of the intervening structures, other factors. We draw an uncertain and wavering line, but draw it we must as best we can.

One again it is a question of fair judgment, always keeping in mind the fact that we endeavor to make a rule in each case that will be practical and in general keeping with the understanding of mankind....

Well, that all sounds rather metaphysical, now doesn't it? And to a certain degree, it is. But in historical context, both of the *Palsgraf* opinions were efforts to address the same problem: given the fact that obligations imposed by tort are general in nature, is it proper to limit the extent of those duties in some fashion? If so, what method should be used?

Think of the problem in terms of the facts of *Palsgraf* itself, a highly improbable series of events culminating in injury. Is it fair to the parties — is it credible as a premise for a system of obligations — that any connection between an injury and a breach of obligation should make the injury compensable? The need for some limitation on liability ought to be apparent, for the obvious reason that, without it, no one could ever do anything without the fear that he or she could be liable for it later in entirely unimagined ways. As Justice Andrews conceded in his opinion, "A line has to be drawn somewhere."

A Difference in Method

What differed in the two *Palsgraf* opinions was the way the two groups of judges proposed to solve the problem. Cardozo advocated a **zone of danger** as a limitation on a tortfeasor's duty, while Andrews suggested **proximate cause** as a limitation on the linkage between breach of obligation and injury.

Why the trip by Justice Andrews into metaphysics, to rippling ponds and flowing streams? The glib answer is that lawyers aren't very good at dealing with deep questions of philosophy, but the better response is that the amount of linkage we are willing to permit, like the extent of the obligation we are willing to impose, varies from situation to situation.

Assuming that the "zone of danger" is infinite for a moment, and thus that potential obligation is equal, it is perfectly reasonable to accept on policy grounds alone fewer limitations upon liability, because as the potential effects of an activity spread farther geographically or last longer in time. He who pours hundreds of tons of toxic waste into a creek or river has less to complain about on policy grounds if someone far downstream suffers an odd injury than does the person whose backyard compost heap washes away in a rainstorm. Thus, there is a need for some amount of line drawing; otherwise, the actionable consequences of tortious behavior could well be unlimited.

The Proximate or Legal Cause Standard

> ***Proximate or legal cause.*** A cause that is legally sufficient to result in liability and that directly produces an event and without which the event would not have occurred. .

If you have doubts about the propriety of line-drawing or the need to do it in the real world, the next excerpt may change your mind. This issue — the need for application of the policy side of the proximate cause standard — attracted the attention of some of the best judges of the United States Court of Appeals for the Second Circuit in a series of opinions that arose out of a highly unusual series of events in Buffalo, New York.

Better than almost any other decision, the last of the major opinions in the cases shows how the policy side of proximate cause works.

Petition of Kinsman Transit Co., et al.[2]
388 F.2d 821
United States Court of Appeals for the Second Circuit
1968

IRVING R. KAUFMAN, Circuit Judge:

The difficult question presented by this appeal is whether certain expenses incurred by claimant[s] Cargill, Inc. (Cargill) and Cargo Carriers, Inc. (Cargo Carriers), as a result of an unusual concatenation of events on the Buffalo River during the night of January 21, 1959, are recoverable as a matter of law.

The misadventures leading to the catastrophe on the river that fateful evening were set forth when this litigation was previously before this court....[3] For our purposes it is sufficient to state that as a result of the negligence of the Kinsman Transit Company and the Continental Grain Company, the *S.S. MacGilvray Shiras* broke loose from her moorings and careened stern first down the narrow, S-shaped river channel. She struck the *S.S. Michael Tewksbury*, which in turn broke loose from her moorings and drifted down stream—followed by the *Shiras*—until she crashed into the Michigan Avenue Bridge. The bridge collapsed and its wreckage, together with the *Tewksbury* and the *Shiras*, formed a dam which caused extensive flooding and an ice jam reaching almost three miles upstream. As a result of this disaster, transportation on the rivers was disrupted until approximately March 13, 1959—a period of about two months....

At the time of the accident, Cargill had some 336,000 bushels of wheat stored aboard the *S.S. Donald B. Gillies* berthed in Buffalo harbor below the Michigan Avenue Bridge. (It is apparently not an uncommon practice for companies to "winter storage" wheat in this manner.) Cargill, it appears, was under contract to deliver 124,000 bushels of the *Gillies'* wheat during the period from January through March 1959. Because of the accident, the vessel could not be moved to Cargill's elevators located above the collapsed bridge so that it could be unloaded. In order to comply with its contractual obligations, Cargill was required to secure replacement wheat in the Midwest. The [trial court] allowed Cargill $30,321.38 for its extra transportation costs and $8,232 for increased "storage costs."

Cargo Carriers' claim is somewhat different. When the calamity occurred it was in the process of unloading a cargo of corn from the *S.S. Merton E. Farr* at elevators located above the Michigan Avenue Bridge. Apparently, the *Farr* was struck by one of the two free-drifting ships. Its cargo was undamaged, but it broke loose from the dock at which it was moored. The by-product of this was that an ice jam formed between the *Farr* and the dock and normal unloading became impossible; the city fireboat and the harbor tugs which ordinarily would have broken up the ice jam were below the bridge wreckage and thus could not be of any assistance. The consequence of this was that Cargo Carriers, which was under contract to transfer 10,322 bushels of the *Farr's* corn, was required to continue the unloading with the aid of specially rented equipment. The [trial court] awarded it $1,590.40 for these increased expenses.

* * * *

[W]e conclude that recovery was properly denied on the facts of this case because the injuries to Cargill and Cargo Carriers were too "remote" or "indirect" a consequence of defendants' negligence.

Numerous principles have been suggested to determine the point at which a defendant should no longer be held legally responsible for damage caused "in fact" by his negligence. Such limiting principles must exist in any system of jurisprudence for cause and effect succeed each other with the same certainty that night follows day, and the consequences of the simplest act may be traced over an ever-widening canvass with the passage of time. In Anglo-American law, as Edgerton has noted, "except only the defendant's intention to produce a given result, no other consideration so affects our feeling that it is or is not just to hold him for the result as its foreseeability...."

When the case was last here we held ... that it was a foreseeable consequence of the negligence of the City of Buffalo and Kinsman Transit Company[4] was that the river would be dammed. It would seem to follow from this that transportation on the river would be disrupted and that some would incur expenses because of the need to find alternative routes of transportation or substitutes for goods delayed by the disaster. It may be that the specific manner was not foreseeable in which the damage to Cargill and Cargo Carriers would be incurred but such strict foreseeability — which in practice would rarely exist except in hindsight — has not been required....

On the previous appeal we stated aptly: "Somewhere a point will be reached when courts will agree that the link has become too tenuous—that what is claimed to be consequence is only fortuity...." We believe that this point has been reached with the Cargill and Cargo Carriers' claims. Neither the *Gillies* nor the *Farr* suffered any direct or immediate damage for which recovery is sought. The instant claims occurred only because the downed bridge made it impossible to move traffic along the river. Under all of the circumstances of this case, we hold that the connection between the defendants' negligence and the claimants' damages is too remote to permit recovery. The law does not spread its protection so far.

Kinsman is as clear an example as American case law permits of the policy arm of the proximate cause concept in action. As Judge Kaufman noted in a footnote in the decision,[5] it is entirely foreseeable that the collapse of the bridge and the interruption of river traffic would impede those who relied upon the Buffalo River as a thoroughfare for their cargoes. Equally clearly, the collapse and interruption of damages was a factor without which the claimed damages would not have occurred, so it would meet Judge Andrews' cause-in-fact/substantial factor test.

If you *still* have doubts, consider the offhand comment in the opinion about what the result would have been if either Cargill or Cargo Carriers had claimed that their barges had sustained damage in the disaster. It appears that the court might well have allowed such a recovery.

What makes the difference — and this is a concept to which we soon will return — is the fact that it took much more than just the negligence of Kinsman and the City of Buffalo to result in "damage" to Cargill or Cargo Carriers. For there to be harm, it also took the fortuitous positioning of the tugboats and the fireboats on the wrong side of the dam.

Since those events hardly could be called negligent, it became very difficult to impose liability. Indeed, if, as the opinion seems to indicate, there would not have been any damages if the tugboats had been on the correct side of the river, it is difficult to see how the negligence can be called a substantial factor in, and therefore a proximate cause, of the injuries.

None of this is to say that the policy side of the proximate cause concept comes into play very often. The fact of the matter is that it rarely, if ever, plays a major role in most cases. It takes the kind of amazing coincidences that cases like *Kinsman* provide for there to be a test of this limitation. But its existence is a perennial check on the extent to which the breach of an obligation can give rise to a claim in tort.

Having just had described to us as unlikely a series of events as can be imagined and been told so casually that these events all were within the zone of danger, it is entirely possible to suppose that the cause-in-fact arm of proximate cause is a dead issue, and that any combination of events producing direct damage without too much intervention from outside sources is enough. See if you feel the same way after the next excerpt.

Boyd v. Fuel Distributors, Inc.
795 S.W.2d 266
Texas Court of Appeals, Austin
1990

Aboussie, J.:

* * * *

[O]n February 23, 1988, 18-year-old Robert Kruse, along with 18-year-old Neal Boyd, drove to a "Pay-less" convenience store operated by [defendant Fuel Distributors, Inc.]. Kruse and Boyd entered the store. and Kruse purchased a 12-pack of beer. The store clerk, Yvonne Peeler, did not ask Kruse for proof of his age. Kruse and Boyd returned to Boyd's apartment, where they spent the next hour drinking the beer and playing board games. Kruse drank six beers.... Kruse and Boyd decided to purchase more beer. While Boyd remained at the apartment, Kruse and his girlfriend, Kristi Roberts, drove to the Pay-less store. Roberts remained in the car while Kruse entered the store alone and purchased a six-pack of beer from Peeler. When Kruse and Roberts returned to the apartment, Boyd and Kruse resumed their drinking and visiting for the next hour and a half. Kruse and Boyd consumed no alcohol other than what Kruse had purchased at the Pay-less store.

Roberts received a call from a former boyfriend during this period which upset Kruse. Kruse and Boyd then decided to go for a drive. Kruse does not remember who made the decision, but one of the friends at the apartment, Tiffany West, stated in an affidavit that Kruse insisted on going for a drive and that Boyd agreed to go out of concern for Kruse. Boyd drove his car, and Kruse rode as a passenger. Boyd lost control of his vehicle and collided with an embankment. The car vaulted into a tree, killing Boyd and severely injuring Kruse. Subsequent tests showed that Boyd's blood alcohol level was 0.14, and that Kruse's was 0.17.

[Boyd's family and Kruse] sought recovery on several grounds. The first was for the alleged violation of [Texas Alcoholic Beverage Code] §§ 2.01-2.03. These statutes create a cause of action based upon providing, selling, or serving an alcoholic beverage to one who is obviously intoxicated when the recipient's intoxication is a proximate cause of damages.

* * * *

Proximate cause consists of two elements: the act or omission was a cause-in-fact of the plaintiff's damages and that it was foreseeable to a reasonable person that such act or omission would lead to a result of the general character as the one that obtained.... To constitute a cause-in-fact, the act or omission must be a substantial factor in bringing about injury and without which no harm would have been incurred....

We hold that Kruse's intoxication could not be a cause-in-fact of the automobile accident and resulting damages. Boyd was operating his own vehicle at the time of the accident. Kruse was a passenger. There was no suggestion that anything Kruse did interfered with his operation. Boyd lost control of his car and hit an embankment. This was the cause-in-fact for the accident and the resulting injuries. Kruse's intoxication played no part in bringing about the wreck.

[The plaintiffs] claim that Kruse's intoxication could have been a cause of the accident if, due to his impaired state, Kruse persuaded Boyd to go for a drive despite their intoxicated condition and did not recognize the seriousness or danger of doing so. In other words, [plaintiffs] insist that but for Kruse's intoxication, Boyd would not have been driving. While this may be true, this could not have been a cause-in-fact of the car hitting the embankment because the accident could have occurred if Kruse had nothing to drink that night. An act or omission cannot be a substantial factor in bringing about harm if the harm would have been sustained regardless of the act....

* * * *

[The plaintiffs] also suggest that the accident was reasonably foreseeable because it was foreseeable that in his impaired state Kruse might share the alcohol he obtained with a friend who might then drive and cause an accident. We need not consider the argument. Because [Fuel Distributors] conclusively proved that Kruse's intoxication was not a cause-in-fact, it could not be a proximate cause.

A brief note on the outcome here, which may seem rather harsh given the obvious basis of statutes that make the sale of alcoholic beverages to minors and intoxicated persons a crime. In Texas, as in other states, statutory rather than decisional law controls the extent to which a person may recover damages for injuries caused by the sale of alcoholic beverages. The statute requires the person seeking recovery to show that the "intoxication of the recipient" was the proximate cause of the injuries.[6] This provision results in the kinds of limitation on recovery that we see in the *Boyd* case, limits that might not otherwise exist at common law. Nevertheless, the logic behind the *Boyd* decision reminds us that cause-in-fact is alive and well and is very much a part of the law of torts.

The Concept of More Than One Proximate Cause

In examining the concept of proximate cause, we have confined our discussion thus far to consideration of the linkage between one tortfeasor's alleged breach of obligation and an injury. The questions that follow concern whether similar rules apply when there is more than one cause for an injury, or when more than one person commits a tort. These problems have fueled great controversy over the years and kept law professors in business just about as long! We can see why this is so by looking at the next excerpt.

Callahan v. Cardinal Glennon Hospital
863 S.W.2d 852
Supreme Court of Missouri, *En Banc*
1993

THOMAS, Judge:

Daniel Callahan ("Danny") was born on August 7, 1978. For the first three and one-half months of his life, Danny was basically healthy and normal. On November 4, 1978, Danny received Orimune, a live polio vaccine. This vaccine is an attenuated poliovirus, which means that it is a weakened strain of polio. Until the end of November, Danny remained basically in good health. On November 30, 1978, Danny's mother noticed a red area between Danny's anus and scrotum. The resulting events...eventually led a jury to find that Danny was the victim of medical malpractice, which caused him to be a permanent triplegic. The jury returned a $16 million verdict in Danny's favor.

[Author's synopsis: Danny's red area developed into a boil with a fever. His parents took him to Cardinal Glennon Hospital, where he was examined by a nurse practitioner, Nurse Schwarz, who did not lance the boil or take a culture of what kind of bacteria might be causing it. Dr. Venglarcik, a resident physician employed by St. Louis University [SLU] on the hospital staff, prescribed oxycillin, which is effective only against certain kinds of bacteria. Danny and his parents went home, with instructions to see their regular pediatrician on Monday, two days later. Danny did not improve over the weekend, so his parents took him to their pediatrician on Monday, December 4, 1978. The pediatrician did not drain the abscess or take a culture.

By December 5, Danny's parents noticed that his legs appeared to be "floppy," but when they called the hospital, it told them that children with fevers were less active and that Danny did not need to be brought in. Finally, the next day, Danny's legs were still floppy, and his eyes were rolling back in his head. His parents took him back to Cardinal Glennon, where the abscess was drained and shown to contain bacteria that did not respond to oxycillin. The physicians also found that Danny's legs and one arm were paralyzed.

The Callahans retained experts who opined that the failure to treat the abscess properly caused Danny's paralysis because the bacteria suppressed his immune system so as to render him susceptible to the poliovirus in the vaccine. They sued Cardinal Glennon, St. Louis University [SLU], the employer of the resident physician, the manufacturer of the vaccine, and their pediatrician. All but SLU settled before or during trial. On appeal, SLU argued that the trial judge had applied the wrong standard of causation in the case.]

Plaintiff contends that because this injury resulted from multiple tortfeasors and more than one cause, the substantial factor test should be applied rather than the "but for" test.... The "but for" causation test provides that "the defendant's conduct is a cause" of the event if the event would not have occurred "but for" that conduct.... Put simply, "but for" causation tests for causation in fact. Mere logic requires causation in fact.... The substantial factor test has become popular because in the complex litigation of today, courts are often forced to deal with claims that the conduct of more than one tortfeasor caused the harm. When considering the multiple causes it is misleading to talk about "the" cause, and changing the terminology to "a" cause is too insignificant an alteration to communicate to the jury the idea of contributing causes. The upshot is that lawyers and judges feel more comfortable using "substantial factor" language with multiple causes because it is consistent with and better communicates the idea of more than one cause....

* * * *

One reason for the confusion as to when a "but for" test is required is because the *Restatement (Second) of Torts* uses "substantial factor" in a different way than [other authorities.] Section 430 of the *Restatement (Second)* requires "legal cause" for liability. Section 431 provides that legal cause is present if the defendant's conduct is a substantial factor in bringing about the harm. Section 432 provides that the conduct is not a substantial factor unless it meets the "but for" test, which is always required except for the very narrow exception where there are two independent torts, either of which by itself would have caused the injury.

* * * *

Some lawyers and judges have come to look upon the "but for" test as a particularly onerous and difficult test for causation. Nothing could be further from the truth. "But for" is an absolute minimum for causation because it is merely causation in fact. Any attempt to find liability absent actual causation is an attempt to connect the defendant with an injury or event that the defendant had nothing to do with. Mere logic and common sense dictates that there be some causal relationship between the defendant's conduct and the injury or event for which damages are sought.

Two causes that combine can be tested easily by a "but for" causation test. How would such a test for causation be applied to the negligent conduct of SLU in the present case? If Dr. Venglarcik was informed by Nurse Schwarz of Danny's presence and condition at the hospital but failed to see Danny, or even if Dr. Venglarcik saw Danny but failed to incise and drain the abscess, then the jury could conclude that "but for" the doctor's negligent conduct, Danny would not have contracted paralytic polio. In this instance, Dr. Venglarcik's negligent conduct would meet the "but for" causation test and would be a contributing cause to Danny's paralytic polio.

* * * *

If Cardinal Glennon was still a party to this case, how would the "but for" causation test be applied to Nurse Schwarz's negligent conduct? If Nurse Schwarz had failed to inform Dr. Venglarcik of Danny's presence and condition at the hospital, and the doctor had no other source of information, then a jury could have concluded that "but for" the nurse's failure to inform the doctors, Danny would not have developed paralytic polio. As such, her conduct meets the "but for" test and, in that respect, it is causal. This is the classic example of applying the "but for" test to two contributing causes.

On the other hand, if the doctor had another source of information as to Danny's presence and condition at the hospital, such as the medical records, then the doctor's negligence would have been independently sufficient to cause the injury to Danny. In this circumstance, Nurse Schwarz's conduct would not have met the "but for" causation test because, if the doctor already knew about Danny's condition, then Nurse Schwarz's failure to tell the doctor something he already knew would not be causal....

The court's discussion in *Callahan* may seem confusing, but with a little review and analysis, it becomes easier to understand.

Start with the idea that one or more persons may breach an obligation that they owe to another. If only one person is involved, our task is simple. We ask if the injury would have occurred "but for" the breach of obligation by the single defendant. Putting the matter a little differently, we ask whether the injury would have occurred as it did without the defendant's tortious conduct.

If the answer is no — and if there are no policy factors involved — the defendant's breach of obligation was the cause-in-fact of the plaintiff's injury. If two or more people are involved, the issue is more complex and the possibilities wider. The possibilities are as follows. Each person's breach of obligation could independently be the cause of an injury. As the court described it in *Callahan*,[7]

> The law school example of this ... type of case is where two independent tortfeasors set fires on opposite sides of [a] mountain, the fires burn toward the cabin at the top, and either is sufficient to destroy the cabin. Under these circumstances, the "but for" test fails accurately to describe causation in fact because the absence of either fire will not save the cabin. Applying the "but for" causation test to fire number one results in the conclusion that the cabin would have burned even if fire number one had not occurred because fire number two would have burned the cabin. For the same reason, applying the "but for" causation test to fire number two leads to the conclusion that the cabin would have burned even if fire number two had not occurred because fire number one would have burned the cabin. Nevertheless, it is obvious that both fires are causes-in-fact.

This situation, sometimes called the two-fires case, demonstrates the rule that applies when two or more independent causal breaches of obligation are responsible for an injury.

The next possibility is the one more often seen and the one represented in *Callahan*: a situation in which two or more breaches of obligation, none of which is sufficient without the other to cause an injury, combine to cause and injury. A bit of editorial magic to our last excerpt, and we have it:

> The law school example of this ... type of case is where two independent tortfeasors set fires on opposite sides of [a] mountain, the fires burn toward the cabin at the top, and [neither] is sufficient to destroy the cabin. [The fires combine, and the resulting larger fire destroys the cabin.]

In addition to showing that law teachers have an unhealthy fascination with fires,[8] this situation, also sometimes described as the two-fires problem, shows how the concept of "but for" causation works with multiple dependent causal agencies. Here neither fire is enough by itself to cause harm to the cabin, yet "but for" its existence and merger with the other fire, there would be no damage, because without those events the larger fire could not come into existence.

The same kind of situation existed in *Callahan*, as the Missouri Supreme Court explained in its opinion. Even using the somewhat different "substantial factor" language, we can see that the physician's breach of obligation and the nurse's breach of obligation each was a substantial factor in bringing about Danny Callahan's injury.

Substantial Factor

The confusion between "but for" and "substantial factor" probably springs from the use of the word "substantial," which implies that the causal connection must have some sufficient size in order to "count" as a factor in the resulting injury. In reality, however, this is not the case. Even if there are a hundred or even a thousand other causal factors operating, any single one of them is "substantial" if the injury could not have occurred without it. In this way, we can reconcile "but for" and "substantial factor," the terms most often used in describing this matter.

Each person whose breach of obligation results in injury is theoretically responsible for all of the damages sustained by the plaintiff, because "but for" the breach there would not be an injury. When confronted with this kind of proposition the earnest and serious law student often says, "But that's not fair! How can someone whose breach of obligation wouldn't be a proximate cause of injury without the actions of dozens of others be responsible for all of the plaintiff's damages?"

Here there can be two limitations upon liability. One is the policy arm of the proximate cause concept, which can serve to limit liability, as we have seen. The other lies in the way damages are awarded, a concept we will return to in a later chapter. Modern methods of distributing responsibility have largely erased our friend's concern.

On occasion, independent lines of causation (each involving dependent events) can combine to cause injury. Here, we apply both rules. Each independent line of events is a proximate cause of the injury, as in the two-independent-fires problem discussed earlier. Inside each line, each dependent "sub-event" counts as a causal agent if that line of events would not have occurred without it. Again, the rules complement each other and apply to take account of any situation.

All of these notions are sometimes called "**concurrent causation**," and the concept often turns up in a variety of odd situations.

Concurrent causation. The principle that an event is brought about by one of two or more causes that alone could not have brought about the event.

As a coda to our discussion of the point, consider the events in our next excerpts.

State Farm Mutual Automobile Insurance Co. v. Partridge
10 Cal.3d 94, 514 P.2d 123, 109 Cal. Rptr. 811
Supreme Court of California, *En Banc*
1973

Tobriner, J.:

* * * *

We begin our analysis with a brief review of the facts of the case, which are not in dispute. The circumstances resulting in the accident at issue reveal an instance of what can only be described as blatant recklessness. Wayne Partridge, the named insured of the two insurance policies issued by State Farm, was a hunting enthusiast who owned a .357 Magnum pistol. Prior to the date of the accident, Partridge fired the trigger mechanism of his pistol to lighten the trigger pull so that the gun would have "hair trigger action"; the trial court specifically found this modification of the gun to be negligent act, creating an exceptionally dangerous weapon.

On the evening of July 26, 1969, Partridge and two friends, Vanida Neilson and Ray Albertson, were driving in the country in Partridge's four-wheel drive Ford Bronco. With Vanida sitting between them in the front seat, Partridge and Albertson hunted jackrabbits by shooting out of the windows of the moving vehicle; Partridge was using his modified .357 Magnum. On the occasion in question here, Partridge spotted a running jackrabbit crossing the road, and in order to keep the rabbit within the car's headlights, Partridge drove his car off of the paved road onto the adjacent rough terrain. The vehicle hit a bump, the pistol discharged and a bullet entered Vanida's left arm and penetrated down to her spinal cord, resulting in paralysis. At the time of the accident, Partridge was either holding the gun in his lap or resting it on top of the steering wheel pointed at Vanida.

If any case represents concurrent causation in a nutshell, this surely is it. Without the "hair trigger," the bump in the terrain has no effect on the unfortunate Vanida, and without the bump, the "hair trigger" merely is a hazard. Each is dependent on the other to result in the injury; thus, each is a concurrent cause of the harm.

But what about the following situation? Is it concurrent causation?

Duncanville Diagnostic Center, Inc. v.
Atlantic Lloyd's Insurance Co.
875 S.W.2d 788
Texas Court of Appeals, Eastland
1994

McCloud, C.J.:

On October 19, 1989, Erica Portlock was treated at Duncanville Diagnostic Center. She died at home later the same day. In two different lawsuits, Erica's parents sued the Center, its president Kenneth W. Perry, and Cheryl Heckard and Linda Cole, who were radiological technicians employed by the Center....

* * * *

Raymond and Mary Portlock alleged a number of acts and omissions constituting negligence on the part of the Center, its president, and the two technicians: (1) the administration to Erica of an overdose of chloral hydrate, a sedative; (2) the failure to obtain a proper medical diagnosis of the overdose when Erica remained unconscious both when the tests were completed and when Mr. Portlock called the Center later that day; (3) the failure to adequately hire, train, and supervise the Center's employees; and (4) the failure to institute adequate policies and procedures.

On October 19, 1989, the Portlocks took Erica, their four-and-a-half year old daughter, to the [Duncanville Diagnostic] Center for routine radiological examinations of her urinary tract, bladder and kidneys. Cheryl Heckard and Linda Cole, two radiological technicians employed by the Center, prepared a dosage of chloral hydrate. Heckard and Cole did not properly measure the dosage and administered too much of the sedative to Erica. Erica became unconscious. The tests were performed, and the Portlocks were told to take Erica home in her unconscious state. Later that day, Mr. Portlock called the Center because he was concerned that Erica was still unconscious. Instead of conveying this information to a physician at the Center, the receptionist put Mr. Portlock on hold and spoke with a technician. The receptionist then told Mr. Portlock not to worry and that it would be normal for Erica to sleep well into the evening or the next morning. After more time had passed without Erica's awakening, Mr. Portlock again called the Center, but no one answered the phone. Erica never awoke, and she died later that day. The medical examiner attributed Erica's death to acute chloral hydrate intoxication.

* * * *

The [Portlocks' lawsuits] alleged two operative causes of Erica's death: that the radiological technologists administered to Erica a massive overdose of chloral hydrate and that the Center's employees failed to obtain a proper medical diagnosis of the fact that Erica had been given an overdose of chloral hydrate when she remained unconscious....

* * * *

The doctrine of concurrent causation does not apply to this case. There would have been no injury in this case and no basis for the Portlocks' lawsuits without the negligent rendering of professional medical treatment. Stated more specifically, Erica's death could not have resulted from the negligent hiring, training and supervision or from the negligent failure to institute adequate policies and procedures without the negligent rendering of professional medical services. The negligent acts and omissions were not independent and mutually exclusive; rather they were related and interdependent....

What is the difference between *Partridge* and *Duncanville Diagnostic*? Why is the former a case of concurrent causation and the latter not?

The answer lies in the mutual dependency of the causal agents. In *Duncanville Diagnostic*, the negligent supervision and hiring could not cause any harm without the administration of chloral hydrate, but even the most stringent hiring and supervision might not have been enough to prevent the improper overdose from occurring. Thus, there was no mutual dependence of causal factors, and without that dependence, no concurrent cause could exist.

Whether alone or concurrent, causal elements are part of every tort action. Their role in negligence cases is to serve as a limit upon liability.

Key Words and Phrases

"but for"
causation
concurrent causation
linkage
proximate cause
substantial factor
zone of danger

Review Questions

1.   Visit http://courts.state.ny.us/Sterk.htm, where Stewart Sterk calls *Palsgraf* "perhaps the most famous torts opinion written during the 20th century." Do you agree with Justice Cardozo's limiting duty to an established zone of danger, or do you agree with Justice Andrews' argument that a situation must be traced to its proximate cause? Read all of *Palsgraf*. (Yes, you'll have to look it up in a book!)

2.   Drawing upon your local newspaper or a legal newspaper as a resource, find a factual situation in which it was alleged that "but for" an event, the damaging event would not have occurred. Share the news item or court case with your colleagues in class.

3.   Using the same resources, find a factual situation in which it was alleged that the damaging event was a foreseeable consequence. Share the news item or court case with your colleagues.

---

[1] A note here about concurring and dissenting opinions: Most appellate courts hear cases through panels of judges, usually three or more. In many cases, all the judges agree about what the court should do. In these cases, a single judge usually writes a single opinion for the unanimous court. When, however, the judges disagree, either as to the approach that should be taken in deciding the case or in the proper outcome, they can write separate opinions expressing the extent of their agreement (concurring opinions) or disagreement (dissenting opinions).

These concurring and dissenting opinions serve an important function in our jurisprudence, because they are a vehicle by which judges can put forward ideas that may ultimately persuade other members of the court or the bar.

They also can serve as cries of conscience that, if well written, can persuade by the power of their feeling. Depending on the author, these separate opinions can also give clues as to the internal thinking of collegial courts.

[2] Internal footnotes and citations omitted.

[3] Author's note: That opinion, *Petition of Kinsman Transit Co.*, 338 F.2d 708 (2d Cir. 1964), was written by Judge Henry J. Friendly, one of the most formidable minds on a court full of them. If you find this subject interesting, his opinion, which dealt with the zone of danger side of the *Palsgraf* equation, is well worth the time.

[4] The City's negligence was in failing to raise the Michigan Avenue drawbridge. If it had done so, the barges would not have collided with it and made the dam. Kinsman was negligent in failing to secure the vessels properly.

[5] 388 F.2d 821, 824, n.8.

[6] Texas Alcohol Beverage Code Annotated, §2.02(B)(2).

[7] 863 S.W.2d at 861.

[8] Do not assume from these hypothetical situations that all law teachers are unduly fascinated with fire. Only some of them are.

Chapter Six

"DEE-FENSE, DEE-FENSE":
DEFENSES TO CLAIMS
OF NEGLIGENCE

Except for damages, which we will discuss in Chapter Eight, in the preceding chapters we have looked at the elements of negligence that must be proven by a plaintiff to establish the defendant's liability: the existence of a duty or obligation, its breach, and causation.

Negligence, however, is not a one-way street. The defendant has an opportunity to show that the plaintiff is not entitled to recover. In this chapter, we discuss how defendants can defend themselves against claims of negligence.

Affirmative Defenses

This can be done in two ways. First, a defendant can defeat a plaintiff's claim of negligence if the plaintiff fails to meet its burden of proof on any of the elements we have discussed, or (as we will see) if the plaintiff fails to prove that it has suffered any injury.

The second is by prevailing on an affirmative defense — that is, by putting on evidence that establishes a legally-recognized reason that the plaintiff can not recover even if the defendant would otherwise be liable.

In this chapter, we will discuss the main affirmative defenses to negligence, which are

- contributory negligence
- comparative negligence
- assumption of the risk

- intervening cause
- last clear chance.

Since each of these defenses and the idea of showing that the plaintiff should not recover, all are bound up with the idea of "burden of proof," our discussion begins with a brief review of this important concept.

Everyone has some idea of what a **burden of proof** is.[1] The need for proof **beyond a reasonable doubt** is well known to anyone who reads crime or lawyer paperbacks or who watched the O.J. Simpson criminal trial on television.

Burden of Proof. A party's duty to
prove a disputed assertion at trial.

There also is a burden of proof in civil cases, but it is considerably lower than in criminal matters. Generally speaking, to prevail in a civil case, the plaintiff need only prove its *prima facie* case by a **preponderance of the evidence**.

What is a preponderance of the evidence? The law professor's cliché response is to say, "Imagine that we are weighing the evidence offered by each side to support its case. If the weight of the evidence on the plaintiff's side of the scales is enough to outbalance the weight of the defendant's evidence, the plaintiff has carried its burden of proof and wins."

Preponderance of evidence. In a civil case, the plaintiff needs
to prove its *prima facie* case by a preponderance of evidence.

For once, the cliché response is about as right as a "real world" answer. A preponderance of the evidence really is just enough credible evidence to outweigh the evidence that the defendant puts on. It doesn't matter if the evidence comes in one large, weighty chunk or as hundreds or even thousands of small pieces. The plaintiff prevails so long as the total weight of this evidence is even the slightest amount greater than what the defendant puts on.

Nevertheless, there is one rather significant point hidden in this: The person with the burden of proof has to put on evidence to win. The person who does not have the burden of proof has no obligation to put on evidence. Why? Think about the idea of weighing again. When the trial begins — before either side puts on evidence — the proverbial scales of justice are equally balanced ... and empty. As long as they stay that way, the defendant wins. Therefore, the plaintiff has to put on some evidence before it can prevail.

Negating Evidence

Why the clichés? The old-fashioned idea of weighing the evidence in the scales of justice suggests that defendant can win not only by putting on evidence that outweighs what the plaintiff puts on. The defendant can prevail also by showing that the plaintiff's evidence has "no weight." In other words, a defendant can prevail if it shows that the plaintiff's evidence is not credible or sufficiently related to the elements that must be proven to justify its consideration by the jury or trier of fact.

This does not mean that a defendant prevails merely by cross-examining the substance out of a plaintiff's case. Although this can happen, and just about every defense lawyer fantasizes about doing it, the result usually comes about because the defendant puts on evidence that negates or offsets points made by plaintiff. The witness with a different view of the accident, the internal memorandum that contradicts a story, the telltale mark that shows that a document is not authentic, an expert who refutes testimony by plaintiff's experts — each of these and many others are "negating evidence," and all of them can be important in the defense of a negligence case. Finding and developing this "negating evidence" is a key part of trial work for all members of the litigation team.[2]

Nevertheless, this chapter is about affirmative defenses, which, as we have noted, defeat a claim of negligence even if the defendant would otherwise be liable. We call the defenses affirmative because the party who asserts them in a case has the burden of proving them. Again applying the old "scales of justice" approach, we see that the defendant asserting an affirmative defense must put on more evidence to support the defense than plaintiff does to undercut it. Ties on the weight of evidence in affirmative defenses go to the plaintiff, just as ties on the plaintiff's case go to the defendant.

An Illustration in Drama: Act the First

But saying all of this does not explain what the affirmative defenses to a tort action truly are. For this purpose, we need a demonstration or two, and a couple of volunteers from the audience. Let me therefore introduce our cast members for this little play, which is called:

Defenses to Negligence with Virginia and Sarah[3]

Dramatis Personae

Dazed and Confused Parent, *a dazed and confused parent*[4]
Sarah, *a young adult*
Virginia, *sister of* Sarah *and another young adult*

Act I—Contributory Negligence

Before the curtain rises, a loud scream and cry of "Watch it!" is heard. Enter DCP *to find* Sarah *in cheerleading clothing and* Virginia *in a gymnastics outfit.* Sarah *has a split lip.* Virginia *looks pitiful.*

DCP [*bravely and forcefully*]: What's going on here? Sarah, why is your lip bleeding? Virginia, what happened?

VIRGINIA: I just was doing a back walkover and.... [*She begins sobbing.*] I wasn't doing anything!

SARAH: I was just standing here doing a cheer ... you know, "Ka-*boom* Dy-nuh-mite, Ka-*boom* Dy-nuh-mite," and all of a sudden, she just kicked me in the mouth with her foot.

DCP: I'm sure she didn't mean to kick you in the mouth. [*He turns suddenly.*] Virginia, why were you doing gymnastics in the house? Didn't I tell you not to do gymnastics in the house?

VIRGNIA [*shuffling her feet*]: Weeeeeellll ... yes.

SARAH [*sensing her advantage*]: You told her a bunch of times not to do it. Send her to her room. Ground her for a century. You'd never let me get away with it. You never let me do anything. What a loser!

DCP [*still bravely and forcefully*]: Sarah, didn't I tell you not to do any cheers in the family room?

SARAH: As if ...

DCP [*when she doesn't finish*]: As if what?

SARAH: Well ... yes.

DCP [*feeling he is almost there*]: O.K., Virginia, you apologize to your sister. In addition, Sarah, you apologize to your sister. [*He pauses, looking at them both intently.*] Now.

SARAH [*hurt*]: But she should be the only one who has to do anything.... I didn't do anything. You just don't understand.

Curtain

Contributory Negligence

During the intermission, let's take a moment to savor Act I of our little play by examining the doctrine of contributory negligence as described in the next excerpt.

McIntyre v. Balentine[5]
833 S.W.2d 52
Supreme Court of Tennessee
1992

Drowota, Justice:

* * *

In the early morning darkness of November 2, 1986, Plaintiff Harry Douglas McIntyre and Defendant Clifford Balentine were involved in a motor vehicle accident resulting in severe injuries to Plaintiff. The accident occurred near Smith's Truck Stop in Savannah, Tennessee. As Defendant Balentine was traveling south on Highway 69, Plaintiff entered the highway (also traveling south) from the truck stop parking lot. Shortly after Plaintiff entered the highway, his pickup truck was struck by Defendant's Peterbilt tractor. At trial, the parties disputed the exact chronology of events immediately preceding the accident.

Both men had consumed alcohol the evening of the accident. After the accident, Plaintiff's blood alcohol level was measured at 0.17 percent by weight. Testimony suggested that Defendant was traveling more than the posted speed limit. Plaintiff brought a negligence action against Defendant Balentine and Defendant East-West Motor Freight, Inc. Defendants answered that Plaintiff was contributorially negligent, in part due to operating his vehicle while intoxicated. After trial, the jury returned a verdict stating: "We, the jury, find the plaintiff and the defendant equally at fault in this accident; therefore, we rule in favor of the defendant."

The common law contributory negligence doctrine has traditionally been traced to Lord Ellenborough's opinion in *Butterfield v. Forrester*, 11 East 60, 103 Eng.Rep. 926 (1809). There, plaintiff, "riding as fast as his horse would go," was injured after running into an obstruction defendant had placed in the road. Stating as the rule that "[o]ne person being in fault will not dispense with another's using ordinary care," plaintiff was denied recovery on the basis that he did not use ordinary care to avoid the obstruction....

The contributory negligence bar was soon brought to America as part of the common law, see *Smith v. Smith*, 19 Mass. 621, 624 (1824), and proceeded to spread throughout the states.... This strict bar may have been a direct outgrowth of the common law system of issue pleading; issue pleading posed questions to be answered "yes" or "no," leaving common law courts, the theory goes, no choice but to award all or nothing.... A number of other rationalizations have been advanced in the attempt to justify the harshness of the "all-or-nothing" bar. Among these: the plaintiff should be penalized for his misconduct; the plaintiff should be deterred from injuring himself; and the plaintiff's negligence supersedes the defendant's so as to render defendant's negligence no longer proximate....

[T]he rule as initially stated was that "if a party, by his own gross negligence, brings an injury upon himself, or contributes to such injury, he cannot recover;" for, in such cases, the party "must be regarded as the author of his own misfortune...." In subsequent decisions, we have continued to follow the general rule that a plaintiff's contributory negligence completely bars recovery....

Equally entrenched in ... jurisprudence are exceptions to the general all-or-nothing rule: contributory negligence does not absolutely bar recovery where defendant's conduct was intentional ... where defendant's conduct was "grossly" negligent ... where defendant had the "last clear chance" with which, through the exercise of ordinary care, to avoid plaintiff's injury ... or where plaintiff's negligence may be classified as "remote."

In Act I of our little play, Sarah could not get the relief she wanted — having Virginia grounded for a century — because both had violated the rules of the house. Sarah's own breach of an obligation had contributed to the problem in which she was involved and operated to deprive her of a right to recovery.

Likewise, plaintiff McIntyre could not recover damages from defendant Balentine because each had in some way been negligent. Generalizing, under this contributory negligence rule, the plaintiff's own negligence, no matter how slight, operates to preclude any recovery, no matter how negligent the defendant has been.

OK, you may be asking, how can this possibly be fair? How can we deny any recovery to a plaintiff, even if his or her negligence played only the slightest role in causing the accident or injury?

Historically, the rule seemingly arose in cases where the plaintiff's own conduct had been a very significant reason for the accident or injury; the rule operated as an early and primitive check on lawsuit abuse because it provided a real check on the indifferent and reckless. Even in terms of proximate cause, it is possible to argue that if a plaintiff's own negligent conduct was sufficient to be a "but for" cause in fact of the injury, the accident would not have happened without it, and therefore the plaintiff should not be allowed to recover.

Still the rule on paper was absolute, and judges soon began to try to limit its expansiveness.

Based upon the author's own experience trying cases under the **contributory negligence rule** and the **comparative negligence doctrine** we soon will discuss, juries also tried to limit the harshness of the contributory negligence doctrine. In practice, real jurors usually were reluctant to turn away an injured person entirely. So, instead of entirely rejecting a claim, the jury often awarded a significantly lower amount of damages, especially where the plaintiff was only slightly responsible for having caused the accident. In real courtrooms, contributory negligence only operated to prevent recovery by plaintiffs whose negligence was a major reason that the accident took place.[6]

As time went on, everyone recognized that contributory negligence was being honored mostly in the breach, and earnest efforts began in legislatures and courts to change the rule, as we can see by returning to Act II of our little play.

An Illustration in Drama: Act the Second

ACT II—Comparative Negligence

As the scene opens, we hear a series of screams from a darkened stage. The lights come up upon Sarah *and* Virginia *struggling over a pair of retro bellbottom '60s mod pants, such as would be worn on* Friends.

SARAH: But they're my pants! Mom bought them for me!

VIRGINIA: But you said I could wear them to school today.

SARAH: I did not. I said you could wear 'em if I didn't want to, and I want to. Give them to me.

VIRGINIA: No! *I'm* going to wear them.

SARAH: *I* am!

[*Enter* DCP, *still dazed and confused.*]

DCP [*still bravely, but less forcefully*]: O.K., what's going on here?

SARAH: She has my new pants, and I want to wear them to school. I don't think you should ever let her wear them again.

VIRGINIA: Sarah said I could wear 'em.

SARAH: *Did* not!

VIRGINIA: *Did* too!

DCP: Both of you stop right now. Sarah, when we bought the pants, didn't we agree that you'd share them with your sister?

SARAH: Weeeeeellll ... yes.

DCP: And Virginia, didn't we agree that the person who picked out the pants could wear them first?

VIRGINIA: Weeeeeellll ... yes.

DCP: Here's what we'll do. Sarah, you wear the pants to school tomorrow, but because you wouldn't share, Virginia will get to wear them for a week. Then, Sarah, you'll get to wear them again because Virginia wouldn't let you wear them to school, and then we'll see if you two can share. Now, each of you apologize to each other and then go to your rooms till I tell you that you can come out ... which may be next year! GO!

SARAH [*disgusted*]: Awwwwwwww....

VIRGINIA [*smirking*]: Fine....

Blackout

Now, as Sarah and Virginia have just learned, the immediately apparent difference between comparative negligence and contributory negligence is that in comparative negligence, rather than a simple yes-no, there is a balancing of relief when all parties have breached an obligation. The relative fault of the parties is cumulated and then, in essence, prorated in order to fashion relief.

For a more formal analysis of the concept, let us return to our excerpt, which also discusses the subject:

McIntyre v. Balentine (Part II)[7]
833 S.W.2d 52
Supreme Court of Tennessee
1992

Drowota, Justice[8]

[C]omparative fault has long been the federal rule in cases involving injured employees of interstate railroad carriers, see Federal Employers' Liability Act ... and injured seamen....

Similarly, by the early 1900s, many states, including Tennessee, had statutes providing for the apportionment of damages in railroad injury cases.... While Tennessee's railroad statute did not expressly sanction damage apportionment, it was soon given that judicial construction. In 1856, the statute was passed in an effort to prevent railroad accidents; it imposed certain obligations and liabilities on railroads "for all damages accruing or resulting from a failure to perform said dut[ies]...." Apparently this strict liability was deemed necessary because "the consequences of carelessness and want of due skill [in the operation of railroads at speeds previously unknown] ... are so frightful and appalling that the most strict and rigid rules of accountability must be applied.... "

Between 1920 and 1969, a few states began utilizing the principles of comparative fault in all tort litigation. Then, between 1969 and 1984, comparative fault replaced contributory negligence in 37 additional states. In 1991, South Carolina became the 45th state to adopt comparative fault....

* * * *

Two basic forms of comparative fault are utilized by 45 of our sister jurisdictions, these variants being commonly referred to as either "pure" or "modified." In the "pure" form, a plaintiff's damages are reduced in proportion to the percentage negligence attributed to him; for example, a plaintiff responsible for 90 percent of the negligence that caused his injuries nevertheless may recover 10 percent of his damages. In the "modified" form, plaintiffs recover as in pure jurisdictions, but only if the plaintiff's negligence either (1) does not exceed ("50 percent" jurisdictions) or (2) is less than ("49 percent" jurisdictions) the defendant's negligence.

Although we conclude that the all-or-nothing rule of contributory negligence must be replaced, we nevertheless decline to abandon totally our fault-based tort system. We do not agree that a party should necessarily be able to recover in tort even though he may be 80, 90, or 95 percent at fault. We therefore reject the pure form of comparative fault.
We recognize that modified comparative fault systems have been criticized as merely shifting the arbitrary contributory negligence bar to a new

ground.... However, we feel the "49 percent rule" ameliorates the harshness of the common law rule while remaining compatible with a fault-based tort system.... We therefore hold that so long as a plaintiff's negligence remains less than the defendant's negligence the plaintiff may recover; in such a case, plaintiff's damages are to be reduced in proportion to the percentage of the total negligence attributable to the plaintiff ... in cases of multiple tortfeasors, plaintiff will be entitled to recover so long as plaintiff's fault is less than the combined fault of all tortfeasors.

Systems Used by States

As of the date of publication, the states line up as follows in terms of the comparative negligence systems they use.

Thirteen states use pure comparative fault: Alaska, Arizona, California, Florida, Kentucky, Louisiana, Mississippi, Missouri, Michigan, New Mexico, New York, Rhode Island, and Washington.

Twenty-one states use the "50 percent" modified form: Connecticut, Delaware, Hawaii, Illinois, Indiana, Iowa, Massachusetts, Minnesota, Montana, Nevada, New Hampshire, New Jersey, Ohio, Oklahoma, Oregon, Pennsylvania, South Carolina, Texas, Vermont, Wisconsin, and Wyoming.

Nine states use the "49 percent" form: Arkansas, Colorado, Georgia, Idaho, Kansas, Maine, North Dakota, Utah, and West Virginia.

Two states, Nebraska and South Dakota, use a slight-gross system of comparative fault.

It sometimes can be difficult to see how a system of comparative fault operates in a real courtroom, but looking at a series of jury instructions can demonstrate more clearly how a real jury confronts these questions.

Texas Civil Pattern Jury Charges
1996

PJC 4.1—Broad Form—Joint Submission of Negligence
and Proximate Cause[9]

QUESTION ___

Did the negligence, if any, of the persons named below
proximately cause the [occurrence] [injury] [occurrence
or injury] in question?

Answer "Yes" or "No" for each of the following:

    a. Don Davis   _____
    b. Paul Payne   _____
    c. Sam Settlor   _____
    d. Responsible Ray   _____
    e. Connie Contributor   _____

* * * *

PJC 4.3—Proportionate Responsibility

If you have answered "Yes" to Question ___ [4.1 or
other applicable liability question] for more than one of
the persons named below, then answer the following
question. Otherwise, do not answer the following
question.

QUESTION ___

What percentage of the negligence that caused the
[occurrence] [injury] [occurrence or injury] do you find
to be attributable to each of those found by you, in you
answer to Question ___ [4.1 or other applicable liability
question], to have been negligent?

The percentages you find must total 100 percent. The
percentages must be expressed in whole numbers. The
negligence attributable to a person named below is not
necessarily measured by the number of acts or
omissions found. The percentage attributable to a person
need not be the same percentage attributed to that
person in answering another question.

a.	Don Davis	_____	%
b.	Paul Payne	_____	%
c.	Sam Settlor	_____	%
d.	Responsible Ray	_____	%
	Total	___100___	%

Percentage of Fault

As you can see, the idea that each person involved in an accident or
event is responsible for a percentage of fault — up to a maximum of 100
percent, of course — solves a problem left over from our discussion of
proximate cause and cause in fact. A person whose negligence played a
small part in causing an accident or injury no longer has to bear more
than a fair share of the responsibility. The jury simply imposes a
percentage of fault corresponding to the actor's role in bringing about
the accident, and this prevents any actor from being unfairly singled out
for a disproportionate share of responsibility.

Comparative negligence is almost universally recognized as the better
way to apportion responsibility for injury or damage arising from
negligent conduct. It is simple, comprehensive, and relatively easy for
juries to apply. As we will see in a later chapter, the doctrine is not
without limitations, but they are problems that are much easier to deal
with than those that arose in carving out artificial exceptions to the
contributory negligence doctrine.

Before we come to those limitations, however, we need to return to the primary defenses to claims of negligence and that means it's back to Sarah, Virginia and their Dazed and Confused Parent:

An Illustration in Drama: Act the Third

ACT III—Sarah Assumes the Risk

As the lights come up, we find Sarah, Virginia *and* DCP *at the dinner table eating stew.* Sarah *is holding a bottle of Tabasco sauce over her stew. She is ready to pour.*

DCP [*neither brave nor forceful, just tired*]: Sarah, be very careful! The Tabasco is very hot. You'll burn your mouth.

SARAH: As if.... I'm only using a little.

[*She pours a substantial amount into her stew, stirs it around and spoons some into her mouth.*]

SARAH: Waaaaaaaaaaaaaaaaaaaaaaaaaaaaah! Mah mouf izon fahr![10]

VIRGINIA: Hahahahahahahahahahahahaha. That'll teach you.

Blackout

It might be assumed that the doctrine of comparative fault had swept all before it, and that it had replaced older defenses to negligence. While this generally is true, two defenses, assumption of the risk and last clear chance, have clung to life even in a purely comparative world.

Assumption of Risk

Our heroine Sarah has just given us a vivid demonstration of what assumption of the risk is all about. The next excerpt explains the doctrine and how it interacts with ideas of comparative negligence.

Howell v. Clyde
533 Pa. 151, 620 A.2d 1107
Supreme Court of Pennsylvania
1992

Flaherty, J.:

* * * *

Daniel Howell was attending a party at his neighbors' house and was injured when a fireworks cannon owned by the host-neighbors exploded. Howell then sued the neighbors, Theodore and Pamela Clyde, for damages associated with his injuries. ... The evidence established that there was conversation at the party concerning a fireworks cannon fabricated by Clyde's grandfather. The guests, including Howell, visually inspected the cannon and expressed an interest in firing it. Howell went to his residence next door to retrieve black powder for use in the cannon, and upon returning with two cans of black powder, Howell held a flashlight while Clyde filled the bore of the cannon half full of black powder. Howell stood back approximately 40 feet while Clyde ignited the cannon, which exploded, injuring Howell.

* * * *

The present case may also be analyzed from different perspectives.

If the case is viewed from the perspective of a duty analysis, the evidence presented at trial establishes that Howell voluntarily encountered a known risk, thereby obviating any duty that might otherwise have been owed him by Clyde. Under this analysis, the case is controlled by the assumption of risk principle that one who voluntarily undertakes a known risk thereby releases the defendant from any duty of care.

A second analysis is that Howell was negligent in participating in the cannon episode and that his negligence must be compared with Clyde's.

Such a comparison is for the jury, and if Clyde is found to be negligent, Howell will recover at least some proportion of his damages so long as his negligence does not exceed Clyde's.

A third analysis is that this is a type 4 assumption of risk case. Type 4 assumption of risk, as defined by the *Restatement*, is that in which:

> the plaintiffs' conduct in voluntarily encountering a known risk is itself unreasonable, and amounts to contributory negligence. There is thus negligence on the part of both plaintiff and defendant; and the plaintiff is barred from recovery, not only by his implied consent to accept the risk, but also by the policy of the law which refuses to allow him to impose upon the defendant a loss for which his own negligence was in part responsible.

Thus, under a type 4 analysis, a plaintiff who negligently assumes a risk is barred from recovery because he was, in part, at fault.

Fourth, the case may be analyzed as a type 2 or 3 assumption of risk case. Those types of assumption of risk are described as follows by the *Restatement*:

> 2. A second, and closely related, meaning is that the plaintiff has entered voluntarily into some relation with the defendant that he knows to involve the risk, and so is regarded as tacitly or impliedly agreeing to relieve the defendant of responsibility, and to take his own chances. Thus a spectator entering a baseball park may be regarded as consenting that the players may proceed with the game without taking precautions to protect him from being hit by the ball. Again the legal result is that the defendant is relieved of his duty to the plaintiff. As to such implied assumption of risk, *see* § 496C.

> 3. In a third type of situation, the plaintiff, aware of a risk created by the negligence of the defendant, proceeds or continues voluntarily to encounter it. For example, an independent contractor who finds that he has been furnished by his employer with a machine that is in dangerous condition, and that the employer, after notice, has failed to repair it or to substitute another, may continue to work with the machine. He may not be negligent in doing so, since his decision may be an entirely reasonable one, because the risk is relatively slight in comparison with the utility of his own conduct; and he may even act with unusual caution because he

is aware of the danger. The same policy of the common law that denies recovery to one who expressly consents to accept a risk will, however, prevent his recovery in such a case.

Either type 2 or 3 assumption of risk might apply to the present case. In type 2, Howell may be said to have voluntarily entered into "some relation" with Clyde that he knows to involve risk (i.e., the joint enterprise of firing the cannon); and in type 3, Howell may be said to have voluntarily proceeded to encounter a risk created by Clyde's cannon, seeing the risk of injury as slight, and proceeding cautiously, nonetheless, because of the risk.

Assumption of risk types 2 and 3, then, deal with situations not treated by comparative negligence. In comparative negligence, each of the parties must have been negligent: there must be negligence on both sides to compare. In assumption of risk types 2 and 3, the plaintiff may or may not have been negligent in encountering the risk. He is barred from recovery not because of his negligence, but because of the policy that a person may not recover for injuries which he himself has chosen to risk.

If types 2 and 3 assumption of risk were to be abolished, this idea would be lost. But the policy against recovery for "self-inflicted" injuries remains as viable today as it ever was. Because it is desirable to preserve the public policy behind assumption of risk types 2 and 3, but to the extent possible, remove the difficulties of application of the doctrine and the conflicts that exist with our comparative negligence statute, to the extent that an assumption of risk analysis is appropriate in any given case, it shall be applied by the court as a part of the duty analysis, and not as part of the case to be determined by the jury. This approach preserves the public policy behind the doctrine while at the same time alleviating the difficulty of instructing a jury on voluntariness, knowledge, and scope of the risk.

Assumption of the risk thus differs from concepts of fault or negligence, because it arises even in situations where no one is being negligent. It certainly can be — and indeed it has been — argued that there should be better screens to protect patrons at baseball games and other sports events, but even if we accept that this is true, the doctrine would still apply to participants in the game itself. Injuries are possible even with proper warm-ups and equipment on the best-maintained fields, and this is why the doctrine of assumption of risk refuses to go away entirely.

Some activities involve inherent amounts of risk, and so long as the injury is within that inherent risk, there cannot and should not be liability. Why do we not simply invoke the doctrine of unavoidable accident in such cases? The reason, of course, is that the accident is avoidable if one simply avoids playing the game or taking part in the event. Thus, the unavoidable accident doctrine does not apply.

Assumption of the risk lives on the margins of tort law, important in certain areas and as a conceptual limitation on the extent to which comparisons of fault can apply.

Everything we have discussed so far in this chapter has rested upon the relatively simple idea that the parties who are involved in an accident go about their business oblivious to the fact that the others also were breaching obligations. That can be a big assumption, however, as Sarah and Virginia are about to demonstrate.

An Illustration in Drama: Act the Fourth

ACT IV—Can Virginia Avoid an Accident?

The lights come up on a situation best described as deja vu. Sarah *is standing in the middle of the floor dressed in her cheerleading outfit holding a bloody lip. Once again,* DCP *enters to sounds of recrimination and whimpering.*

DCP: What's going on here? Sarah, why is your lip bleeding? Virginia, what happened?

VIRGINIA: I just was doing a back walkover and.... I wasn't doing anything.

SARAH: I was just standing here doing a cheer ... you know, "Ka-*boom* Dy-nuh-mite, Ka-*boom* Dy-nuh-mite," and all of a sudden she kicked me in the mouth. Only this time I think she saw me and did it anyway.

DCP: I'm sure she didn't mean to kick you in the mouth. [*He turns suddenly.*] Virginia, why were you doing gymnastics in the house? Didn't I tell you not to do gymnastics in the house?

VIRGINIA [*shuffling feet*]: Weeeeeellll ... yes.

SARAH: You told her a bunch of times not to do it. Send her to her room! Ground her for a century! You'd never let me get away with it. You never let me do anything. What a loser!

DCP: Sarah, didn't I tell you not to do any cheers in the family room?

SARAH: Well ... yes.

DCP: And Sarah, since you say that Virginia could see you, you must have been able to see her coming too. Right?

SARAH: Yes.

DCP: WHAT?

SARAH: Well ... yes.

DCP: O.K. Virginia, you apologize to your sister right now. But, Sarah, if you see her coming and you don't get out of the way ... well, I guess you really can't complain, now can you?

SARAH: I sure can. She gets her way all the time. It's ... like ... so unfair. What a loser!

DCP: To your rooms ... now!

Blackout

For those who insist upon less family-oriented approaches to legal problems, here's how the Missouri Supreme Court solved this problem and reconciled the issues with which Sarah and Virginia have so recently grappled against the idea of comparative fault.

Gustafson v. Benda[11]
661 S.W.2d 11
Supreme Court of Missouri, *En Banc*
1983

Welliver, J.:

* * * *

The case involves a collision between plaintiff-respondent's motorcycle and defendant-appellant's automobile. The motorcycle was in the act of passing the automobile as the parties approached a "T" intersection. The accident occurred when appellant turned toward the left. The sole issue involved and certified for our reexamination is the definition of "the point of imminent peril" or "the point of immediate danger." If that point is as we have previously defined it ... it is at the point at which appellant's automobile physically began to turn left, and, upon the facts of the case, respondent cannot recover....

The common law doctrine of last clear chance comprises three basic situations: (1) a plaintiff in a position of actual peril and a defendant who knows of that peril; (2) a plaintiff in a position of actual peril and a defendant who in the exercise of the requisite degree of care should know of that peril; and (3) a plaintiff who because of his inattentiveness or obliviousness is in a position of peril and a defendant who knows of the plaintiff's position and knows or has reason to know of his obliviousness.... Missouri's "humanitarian" doctrine allows recovery in a fourth situation, in which a plaintiff is in a position of peril because of his inattentiveness or obliviousness and a defendant is negligent only in his similar inattentiveness or obliviousness to plaintiff's peril....

For many years, authorities addressing the last clear chance doctrine have recognized and [a] number of commentators have observed that last clear chance is one step, and a rather significant one, toward a system of

---

comparative negligence. As pointed out by Fleming James, the first cases of contributory negligence dealt with situations where the plaintiff's negligence was later in point of time than the defendant's. The directness of the relationship between the act and the injury was emphasized rather than the negligent quality of the act. As the idea of negligence gained recognition, there was a shift to the culpability of the conduct involved.

Whatever the difficulties implicit in the application of the doctrine of last clear chance, it did represent an attempt to shift the loss to the party who was more to blame. It was thus ethically and morally preferable to the prior rule that the slightest degree of negligence would bar the plaintiff's recovery. If all the intricacies of proximate cause, sequential negligence, and last opportunity are brushed aside and the problem viewed simply and realistically, it will be seen that the last clear chance cases represent nothing more or less than a comparison of fault.

As Dean Prosser[12] has so aptly pointed out, however, the trouble with last clear chance is that it shifts the entire loss to the defendant. "It is still no more reasonable to charge the defendant with the plaintiff's share of the consequences of his fault than to charge the plaintiff with the defendant's; and it is no better policy to relieve the negligent plaintiff of all responsibility for his injury than it is to relieve the negligent defendant. The whole floundering, haphazard, makeshift device operates in favor of some plaintiffs by inflicting obvious injustice upon some defendants; but it leaves untouched the greater number of contributory negligence cases in which the necessary time interval or element of discovery does not appear and the last clear chance cannot apply." The obvious solution was a system of comparative negligence, the adoption of which can be traced to a century of experience with last clear chance....

Despite the apparent demise of "last clear chance" as an independent doctrine, the concepts it contains remain an important factor in the law of negligence. Knowledge of another person's danger and the ability to act in such a way as to prevent harm to that person are obviously factors that should go into analysis of the scope of a duty and the zone of danger; for example, we can easily see how the result in *Palsgraf* might have changed if the passenger's package had said, "DANGER!!! Explosives," instead of being wrapped in plain newspaper.

Similarly, the idea of knowledge may have an impact on "but for" causation analysis. If I know that someone else is in peril and can adjust my conduct so as to prevent that person from becoming involved in an accident, it is quite possible to argue that the other person's negligence is not a "substantial factor" or a "but for" cause of the injury. Why? Because once I know that another person is in danger and can influence the situation one way or the other, the mutual interdependence of which we spoke.

This is not to say that a person who sees that another is in peril has any duty to go to the rescue, because the law does not require it. But it does create certain kinds of responsibility to avoid accidents, and that responsibility has survived even the transition to a system of comparative negligence.

All of the defenses we have discussed in this chapter share a common characteristic: They involve only the plaintiff and possible defendants. There is, however, one important, remaining defense to claims of negligence that rests upon the actions of third parties. Our next excerpt discusses it.

Coyne v. Taber Partners I
53 F. 3d 45
United States Court of Appeals for the First Circuit
1995

Selya, Circuit Judge:

* * * *

On July 8, 1992, a local union representing taxi drivers and tour operators, frustrated by competition from hotel-operated taxis and other amateurs, declared a strike that virtually paralyzed transportation services at San Juan's municipal airport. Despite a beefed-up police presence, strikers congregated at various points, including Baldorioty de Castro Avenue (the main thoroughfare leading to and from the airport). The labor unrest was open and notorious; reports of a strike appeared, *inter alia*, in the July 9 edition of a major newspaper, the San Juan *Star*.

Carol Coyne, a resident of Massachusetts, blissfully unaware of the strike, flew into the airport on July 9. Because she had reserved accommodations at the Ambassador Plaza, Taber dispatched a driver, Angel Marrero, to transport her from the airport to the hotel. While waiting for Taber's emissary to arrive, plaintiff witnessed several confrontations between strikers and motorists.

Following the same practice he had thrice utilized that day, Marrero crossed the picket line driving a red Ford rented by the hotel. When he reached the terminal, he refused to alight from the vehicle and plaintiff noticed that he seemed frightened. Once he had collected the plaintiff, other prospective guests, and their luggage, Marrero headed for the hotel. After the Ford reached Baldorioty de Castro Avenue, a man stepped in front of it and blocked its path. Other persons began hurling objects at the car. One such projectile shattered a window and injured the plaintiff. Marrero eventually managed to extricate the vehicle from this precarious situation and immediately sought medical attention for plaintiff.

Some time elapsed. Then plaintiff, striking a blow of her own, sued Taber in Puerto Rico's federal district court.... [T]he [district] court found plaintiff's claim wanting ... because ... the harm of which plaintiff complained "was not foreseeable or causally related to any acts or omissions" attributable to Taber.

* * * *

Even if a jury could find that Taber violated a duty owed to plaintiff, a breach of duty is not actionable absent a causal relationship between the breach and the ensuing harm. ... For this causal relation to exist the damage must have been foreseeable and avoidable had the omitted action been timely taken....

This does not mean that foreseeability is always a jury question. To establish the foreseeable character of an event, the evidence must be such that the risk complained of is among the universe of risks recognizable by reasonably prudent persons acting with due diligence in the same or similar circumstances.... Because a defendant will not be relieved of liability by an intervening cause which could reasonably have been foreseen, nor by one which is a normal incident of the risk created ... criminal acts of third parties can sometimes fall within the ambit of foreseeability....

Intervening Cause

And with this dilemma, the First Circuit gives us its Sherlock-Holmes-dog-that-didn't-bark-in-the-night version of **intervening cause.**

> *Intervening cause.* An event occurring before an initial event, but after an end result, which changes the course of events that would have resulted in an actionable injury.

The presence of an intervening cause breaks the causal chain and relieves the defendant of liability for what otherwise might be an actionable breach of obligation.

Probably the most common intervening cause asserted as a defense to liability is the criminal act of a third party, which, of course, is what happened in *Coyne. The Common Law* would have recognized such conduct as an absolute defense in all but two situations, that of a common carrier, such as a stage coach or railroad, and that of an innkeeper, which the defendant in *Coyne* happened to be. From medieval times forward, innkeepers had special duties to protect the persons and goods of their guests. The duties imposed on common carriers were an outgrowth of this special relationship and a recognition that a stage coach or railroad car was, in essence, simply a moving inn.

But as time went on — and perhaps because crime increased — courts came to believe that reasonable innkeepers, common carriers, and — ultimately — everyone else would recognize that a certain amount of crime was possible or even inevitable. And (you guessed it) the moment crime became foreseeable, it became just another factor to be taken into consideration in establishing both the zone of danger and the cause-in-fact element of proximate cause.

Intervening cause still exists as a viable defense to negligence liability, but only as a matter of fact rather than as a matter of law. All of the circumstances surrounding the allegedly intervening cause must be taken into account. If the event constitutes a genuine "gotcha," that is, it constitutes something a reasonable person in the shoes of the defendant would not have foreseen, it remains an intervening cause and a defense to liability.

Key Words and Phrases

assumption of the risk
beyond a reasonable doubt
burden of proof
comparative negligence
contributory negligence
contributory negligence rule
intervening cause
last clear chance
negating evidence
preponderance of the evidence

Review Questions

1.   On page 134, you have found a list of the states' comparative negligence systems as of publication. First, see if your state's has changed from the method listed thereon. Next, evaluate that system. Is it as fair to your state's citizens as the other systems? Discuss with your colleagues.

2.   From a form book or the Internet, obtain and review a copy of the standard civil jury charges in your state. If you are using the Internet, a good source is www.findlaw.com, entering "jury instructions" for your search term.

3.   Should Virginia be grounded for a century? Will DCP survive long enough to enforce the grounding? Discuss with your own sibling.

---

[1] And if they didn't before, the O.J. trial probably gave them an idea!

[2] The defense strategy in the O.J. Simpson criminal trial was a continuing object lesson in "negating evidence." Virtually every step taken by the defense —

from showing the violations of crime lab procedure to the impeachment of Mark Furman with his prior statements — was done with the objective of negating the weight of the prosecution's case. A similar process often occurs in civil litigation, but rarely with the intensity that was evident in the Simpson criminal trial.

[3] The author originally had intended to name these characters "Piss" and "Vinegar" but has refrained from doing so because he promised Sarah and Virginia that he would never do that again. Ever. Really.

[4] Tonight the part of A Dazed and Confused Parent will be played by the author.

[5] Internal citations and quotations omitted.

[6] Although the author's feeling in this regard rests upon a fairly unscientific reading of jury verdict reports and anecdotal evidence, the change from contributory to comparative negligence in Missouri did not have any substantial impact on either the number of verdicts for plaintiffs or the amount of damages being awarded. This was a strong suggestion that juries ameliorated the potentially harmful effects of the rule through their deliberations.

[7] Internal citations and quotations omitted.

[8] For those who are counting, this is the second excerpt I have used from Justice Drowota. No relation. Honest.

[9] Author's note: The names used in these jury instructions are taken from an illustrated pattern.

[10] Tabasco talk for "My mouth is on fire!"

[11] Internal citations omitted. Some footnotes edited into text for clarity.

[12] A note about Dean William Prosser. Universally regarded as America's most influential scholar on the subject of torts, William Prosser served as a law professor and ultimately as Dean of the Vanderbilt University School of Law. His textbook on torts, entitled *The Law of Torts*, has been through five editions and has been known as "Prosser on Torts" to generations of law students.

Chapter Seven

THE SPECIAL DUTIES
OF LANDOWNERS

The common law was fascinated with real property. In early times, this fascination most often took the form of deciding what interests or "estates" in real property could be owned or passed. But defining the estates inevitably meant that common law courts would be called upon to figure out what rights and obligations went with each estate. After all, the person who owned or lived on a piece of real property would want to know what he or she could or could not do with it. And having said that, the next step was to determine obligations that landowners and holders had toward other people who came onto their property. These efforts resulted in a specialized — and somewhat complicated — system of obligations whose connection with tort law has always been a little uneasy.

Nevertheless, most states apply this system of obligations in cases involving what we now call "premises liability," that is, cases where someone coming onto another's property suffers an injury. Our next excerpts show how this system operates.

Basso v. Miller[1]
40 N.Y.2d 233, 352 N.E.2d 868, 386 N.Y.S.2d 564
Court of Appeals of New York
1976

Breitel, Chief Judge, concurring:

* * * *

Under traditional common law analysis, in actions based on negligence, a possessor's duty to one on his property is measured by the status of that person, namely, by the circumstances under which he came or remained on

---

the property. The injured person is classified as trespasser, licensee or invitee, that is, how did he come there or what was he doing there — burglar, social quest, or one on the possessor's business, or the like.

Generally, a trespasser is one who enters upon or remains on property without privilege or the consent of the owner. A possessor has a duty to refrain only from inflicting willful, wanton or intentional injuries upon a trespasser. Maintenance of an artificially created, inherently dangerous but deceptively innocent instrumentality or condition, commonly referred to as a "trap," is equated to a willful, wanton or deceptive act.

A licensee is one who is permitted to enter upon or remain on property with the possessor's consent, express or implied. The duty of care owed to a licensee is sometimes said to be much the same as that owed to a trespasser, that is, to refrain from inflicting willful, wanton or intentional injury, or maintaining a "trap...."Other cases have, however, imposed a broader duty that includes the obligation to refrain from committing acts of "affirmative negligence" and to exercise reasonable care to disclose dangerous defects known to the possessor and unlikely to be discovered by the licensee.... This seemingly broader duty is in effect an expansion of the concepts of "wanton" or "willful" conduct or a "trap."

An "invitee" is subdivided into two categories, a public invitee and a business visitor. A public invitee is one who, as a member of the public, is invited to enter or remain on property that is held open to the public. A business visitor is one who is invited to remain on property for a purpose directly or indirectly connected with business dealings with the possessor of the property.

The duty owed to an invitee is to use due care to keep the property in a reasonably safe condition so that invitees will not unnecessarily be exposed to danger. This includes an obligation to warn an invitee of any hidden danger if the possessor is unable to maintain the property in a reasonably safe condition.

* * * *

[These] three categories make out as a general pattern, a rough sliding scale, by which, as the legal status of the visitor improves, the possessor of the land owes him more of an obligation of protection. The sliding scale thus reflects the foreseeability of injuries to others, the obligation of the injured person to foresee the precautions likely to be taken for his benefit, and the varying economic burdens justifiably placed on the possessor to protect those on his property against harm.

What a set of pigeonholes! In this context, liability depends both on the pigeonhole into which the person entering on the land fits *and* on the kind of danger involved. How does this system work in the real world? The next case excerpt should give you some idea.

Bishop v. First National Bank of Florida, Inc.[2]
609 So.2d 722
District Court of Appeals of Florida, Fifth District
1992

Gridley, W.C., Associate Judge:

* * * *

Michael Bishop was injured when he swung from a rope swing located on the landowners' property, dived into the Weeki Watchee River and struck his head on the bottom of the river or on an unknown submerged object.

According to the record on appeal, Bishop and two companions rented a boat from a location unassociated with the landowners and proceeded up the Weeki Watchee River to an area where they saw ten to fifteen people playing in the water, having mud fights and swinging from a ledge on a rope attached to a tree limb. The tree is located on the landowners' property. Bishop watched six or seven people swing on the rope into the water. He determined that the water in the landing area was over his head, and he noticed that no one had any trouble in entering the water in the landing area. He then took a turn swinging and entered the water at approximately the same place as the others. He entered the water in a dive-jump position, and when he resurfaced, he had a laceration on his head and numbness in his legs.

The landowners own 260 acres of undeveloped land surrounding the bank of the river where the accident occurred. The land is bounded by a chainlink fence and the river. Although "No Trespassing" signs are normally posted in this area, there were none posted on the date of the accident. The landowners were aware that rope swings are continually put up by persons traveling on the river, and the landowners routinely looked for such rope swings and removed them.

Bishop submits that his status on the premises should be elevated to that of an invitee. Specifically, he claims that he was either a "public invitee," who was impliedly invited on the premises, or a "licensee by invitation...." We disagree.

The two variations of invitee status, namely, "public invitee" and "licensee by invitation" ... were developed for different reasons that should be recognized in order to apply this technical area of the law in a logical and practical manner.

The "public invitee" category ... was introduced to broaden the invitee category to cover persons who were invited onto the premises, without any business purpose connection, as a member of the public for a purpose for which the land is held open to the public.... [T]he invitation test bases the "invitation" on the fact that the occupier, by his arrangement of the premises or other conduct, has led the entrant to believe that the premises were intended to be used by visitors for the purpose that the entrant was pursuing and that such use was not only acquiesced in by the owner or possessor, but that it was in accordance with the intention and design with which the way or place was adopted or prepared. Further, when premises are thrown open to the public, assurances of reasonable care or safety are ordinarily given.

In [1973, the Florida Supreme Court] expanded the ... invitation test by allowing social guests to be raised to the same status as business visitors or public invitees. The court called these social guests "licensees by invitation" and said that the invitation may be either an express invitation or a reasonably implied invitation. In so ruling, the court continued to recognize the category of "uninvited licensees," which it defined as "persons who choose to come upon the premises solely for their own convenience without invitation either expressed or reasonably implied under the circumstances."

So ... the categories of invitee and licensee were redefined. The status of invitee was expanded to include business visitors and public invitees as well as licensees by invitation. What remains of the licensee category is the uninvited licensee and its twin, the discovered trespasser. The category of trespasser was not affected.[3]

Under the circumstances of this case ... Bishop was not invited onto the premises as a social guest. Accordingly, Bishop does not qualify as a "licensee by invitation" [which] is founded upon a social guest relationship that requires some sort of effort by the landowner or agent to initiate a relationship with the entrant. Here there was no [such] initiative made by the landowner....

It would appear that the more accurate subcategory for the consideration of Bishop's status would be as a "public invitee" who was impliedly invited on the land. Bishop claims that he was impliedly invited on the property because the property was held open to the public for recreational purposes, because there were no posted signs or fences or any other indications that the property was not public property, and because the particular area was

All of this sounds a whole lot like the TV ad in which the low-rent mechanics assure the car's owner that "We'll make it fit," as they try to jam the battery into a car in which it just won't fit. The three basic pigeonholes of **invitee, licensee,** and **trespasser,** are subdivided into an ever expanding array of "subpigeonholes" depending on the purpose of the visit, express or implied invitation, and the occupier's knowledge of what's happening.

Despite this rather obvious problem, the great majority of states continue to use these classifications in much the same way as occurred here.

By the late 1950s, for example, English law abandoned the pigeonholes by statute. Some states have attempted to address the problems with the trespasser-licensee-invitee trichotomy by moving in other directions, as a return to the case of *Basso v. Miller* shows.

Basso v. Miller[4] (Part II)
40 N.Y.2d 233, 352 N.E.2d 868, 386 N.Y.S.2d 564
Court of Appeals of New York
1976

Cooke, Judge:

* * * *

Ice Caves Mountain, Inc., operates a large scenic park as a tourist attraction
on property leased from the village of Ellenville. During the summer
months the premises are open to the public from approximately 8 a.m. until
a half hour before dark on the payment of an admission fee.

In the late afternoon of that September day, Jeffrey Shawcross, a patron,
walked off the main trail up a hillside and fell into a 40-foot crevice where
he remained until rescued about four and a half hours later. Another
customer, 17-year-old Frederick Coutant, after hearing of the accident, went
down into the hamlet of Cragsmoor and told "a couple of people" about it,
among them the plaintiff and defendant Miller. These two, riding on
Miller's motorcycle, proceeded up to Ice Caves Mountain. Miller drove.
Plaintiff sat behind as a passenger on the single seat, with his arms wrapped
around Miller's midriff and his feet on the exhaust pipes. It was still
daylight when the two arrived at the entrance. Plaintiff testified that Miller
stopped the motorcycle, got off, went into the house where tickets were
sold, spoke to the girl on duty, returned and the two, plaintiff and Miller,
proceeded by motorcycle through the raised barrier along the mountain
drive to the parking lot. After waiting about 45 minutes, plaintiff testified
that he received instructions pursuant to which he carried first aid
equipment and rope down the fissure into which Shawcross had fallen. On a
second trip, plaintiff testified he carried a stretcher and additional
equipment, assisted a nurse and eventually helped carry Shawcross, on the
stretcher, to the ambulance. Once the rescue was completed, plaintiff and
Miller returned to the motorcycle, resumed the riding position as previously
described and, following the road traveled on earlier, left the parking area at
what plaintiff estimated to be a speed of 20–30 miles per hour. It was now
9:30 or 10:00 p.m. As the motorcycle approached a curve, plaintiff testified
that it hit a series of holes, went out of control, slipped from one side to the
other and threw both driver and passenger out onto rocks. Plaintiff testified

that he had been a summer resident of Cragsmoor for the past 16 years, had been to Ice Caves Mountain several times, that he had a 1972 season's pass but had only been there once before that summer.

While several issues are raised, the one of paramount importance relates to the duty of care owed by the owner or occupier of land to one upon his property. In New York, for long, it has been the status of the plaintiff which has been determinative of the duty and often ascribing the status has been a difficult task. In the instant case, for example, much of the testimony in the nearly 1,000-page record was elicited in order to enable the jury to classify the plaintiff as a trespasser, licensee or invitee. As a further complication, not only did the jury have to weigh and evaluate the differing testimony as to status at any particular time, but also had to determine whether the status of the plaintiff shifted as the afternoon turned to evening.... [I]t remains a curiosity of the law that the duty owed to plaintiff on exit may have been many times greater than that owed him on his entrance, though he and the premises all the while remained the same.

Rather than to demand continued attempts to fit a plaintiff into one of three rigid categories, the court pauses instead to reflect, to reconsider the necessity for such classification and to state today that the distinctions no longer need to be made. Taking a broad view, we note that ... the distinctions between licensees and invitees have been abolished by statute in England.... [T]he United States Supreme Court ... leveled direct criticism at this aspect of tort law.

* * * *

Application of the single rule in the instant case amplifies its good sense, for the duty of keeping the roads of Ice Cave Mountain in repair should not vary with the status of the person who uses them, but, rather, with the foreseeability of their use and the possibility of injury resulting therefrom. While the likelihood of plaintiff's presence had been an implicit consideration in the determination of status and the duty commensurate therewith, it now becomes a primary independent factor in determining foreseeability and the duty of the owner or occupier will vary with the likelihood of plaintiff's presence at the particular time and place of the injury. While status is no longer determinative, considerations of who plaintiff is and what his purpose is upon the land are factors which, if known, may be included in arriving at what would be reasonable care under the circumstances.

Now this is quite a debate, isn't it? On the one hand, those who argue for a single standard assert that it will provide a uniform duty based upon a full consideration of all relevant factors without having to try to fit people and situations into inconvenient pigeonholes. It certainly makes life easier, at least when the time comes to prepare jury instructions.

It also makes a great deal of sense to say that a landowner's duty to keep property free from hazards should not depend upon who is on the land, and that the landowner's obligation does not depend upon why the persons are there.

Yet, is it very different to have a single standard of care when all of the evidence that would have been admitted under the old trespasser-licensee-invitee rules would still be admissible? Isn't the jury doing the very same thing that it did under the old standard, except with less specific instructions?

And, even if the trichotomy was evolving on a case-by-case basis, isn't that what common law is supposed to do? And is it so bad to make the plaintiff's reason for being on land an express factor in deciding when the plaintiff can recover? Would you want the obligation to exercise the same degree of care toward trespassers as toward people you asked to come onto your property?

In fact, based upon this rather unscientific analysis of the cases, changing from a trespasser-licensee-invitee standard to a single foreseeability rule probably has not made very much difference in how cases are tried or even in how they come out. It may be that "undiscovered trespassers" do a bit better under a single standard, but there simply seems not to have been any real change in who wins or who loses depending on what instructions are used.

The point is that the difference between the two methods of testing for premise liability seems to be one of convenience rather than substance. Whichever standard is used in the state where you work, however, you should be aware of all of the factors that go into an analysis of a landowner's liability to persons coming onto its property. It seems clear that they always will be relevant, regardless of the legal standard being applied.

In the Case of Children

Does the trespasser-licensee-invitee standard apply to children? The answer is ... well, maybe not ... as our next excerpt demonstrates.

Haddad v. First National Stores, Inc.
109 R.I. 59, 280 A.2d 93
Supreme Court of Rhode Island
1971

Kelleher, Justice:

* * * *

First National has a place of business located on Broad Street in Central Falls. It consists of a supermarket and a large parking lot which abuts the sidewalk. There are no barriers, fences or other restrictions which prevent access to the parking lot by any pedestrian who might be walking along the sidewalk.

June 4, 1967, was a Sunday. The supermarket was not open for business. Tamara [Haddad], who was then five years old, and several young friends, walked onto the parking lot. There was a number of the supermarket's shopping carts standing in the lot. Tamara climbed into one of the carts. When she did, one of her companions pushed the cart around the parking area. One of the cart's wheels struck a rock. The cart tipped over throwing Tamara to the ground. She sustained a fractured left arm which necessitated hospitalization and surgery.

The trial justice, in granting First National's motion for summary judgment, emphasized that he was bound by the Rhode Island law, which holds that an owner or possessor of land owes no duty to a trespasser or licensee, even one of tender years, except to abstain from willfully subjecting him to injury.

The plaintiffs urge us to ... adopt the standard set out in *Restatement (Second) Torts* § 339.... That section requires a landowner to use reasonable care in making artificial conditions on his land reasonably safe for foreseeably trespassing children. As such, the *Restatement* view represents a modification and the modern view of the so-called "attractive nuisance" doctrine. The rule, as set forth in § 339, has been adopted by the majority of the courts in this country.

In early times there was no age deferential shown a trespasser. Whether he was six or sixty, he was owed no duty of reasonable care by the landlord.... [T]he initial indication that special consideration might be accorded the young trespasser came in [an 1841 English case.] There the court allowed recovery for personal injuries where the child was injured as he fell off an unattended horse and cart. The court in permitting the child to sue said that although he was a trespasser, he had been "tempted" to come onto the wagon. One of the first instances in the United States where it was demonstrated that there would be a different rule for the young trespasser came in [1875. In that case,] a child was injured by an unlocked, unguarded turntable. Such a device was described as an "allurement" which caused the child to be drawn to hidden danger. The possessor's act of maintaining such a device was deemed to be an invitation, and the child was the invitee to whom a duty of care was owed. This case and several others making a similar ruling gave rise to what became known as the "attractive nuisance" doctrine. With the passage of time, the element of allurement has been discarded by most courts. Today, the basis for the landowner's liability in cases involving trespassing children is his duty to take reasonable measures against a child's foreseeable conduct, a breach of that duty and resulting injury.... This is the view expressed in the *Restatement*. It might be described as the trespassing child doctrine.... Rhode Island is one of but seven states which has rejected the rule or any qualification thereof.

* * * *

Although it is unreasonable to require a landowner to provide for the safety of an unwanted intruder when that intruder is a child, such a fact justifies a closer look at the respective rights of the landowner and those of the young trespasser. A young child cannot, because of his immaturity and lack of judgment, be deemed able to perceive all the dangers he might encounter as he trespasses on the land of others. There must and should be an accommodation between the landowner's unrestricted right to the use of his land and society's interest in the protection of the life and limb of its young. When these respective social-economic interests are placed on the scale, the public's concern for a youth's safety far outweighs the owner's desire to use his land as he sees fit.... The *Restatement* rule is a reasonable compromise between conflicting interests....

In adopting the *Restatement* rule, we emphasize that the possessor of land is not the insurer of the safety of the young trespasser. When, however, he knows or should know that children are likely to trespass upon a part of the property on which he maintains an artificial condition which is likely to be dangerous to them, he may be liable for the harm resulting to them.... The *Restatement* affords relief to the young trespasser if he shows (a) the possessor knows or has reason to know that young children are likely to trespass where the condition exists; (b) the condition is one which he knows or has reason to know and which he realizes or should realize involves an unreasonable risk of death or serious injury to such children; (c) the child because of his youth does not discover the condition or realize the risk involved in intermeddling with it or coming within the area made dangerous by it; (d) the utility to the possessor of maintaining the condition is slight as compared to the risk to children; and (e) the possessor fails to exercise reasonable care to eliminate the danger or otherwise protect the children. It is plaintiffs' burden to satisfy all five requirements of the rule.

The landowner's duties toward the child trespasser thus look a very great deal like the single standard of reasonable care used in states like New York; the idea that a different standard applies under the old rules to adults and children certainly gives added impetus to those who argue for a single rule to replace the older trespasser-licensee-invitee trichotomy. We also should recall that the landowner's duties toward a child look very much like those that adults have toward minors in general, more proof of the extent to which the law of torts, like society in general, gives special consideration to children.

Nuisance

In our last section, we discussed situations in which the person injured sustains his or her injury by *coming onto* another's property. A moment's reflection ought to remind us that what we do on our property can have effects outside its borders. Here we discuss some of those problems.

Historically, this area developed in phases. The first phase — nuisance — can trace an honorable ancestry to at least the 13th century.[5] Since that time, however, the concept of nuisance has come to include actions that improperly or unduly interfere with another's use of enjoyment of his or her land. Sometimes these actions involve actions entirely on the land of defendant, but today they more often involve the escape of something — light, noise, fumes, pollutants — from one person's land onto another's.

Nuisance. An offensive condition that interferes
with a person's use or enjoyment of property.

Thus, we will study the concept of nuisance not only in this chapter but also in our section concerning environmental issues; nuisance has a pivotal role in this area.

Vickridge First and Second Addition Homeowners Ass'n, Inc.
v. Catholic Diocese of Wichita
212 Kan. 348, 510 P.2d 1296
Supreme Court of Kansas
1973

Kaul, Justice:

The [Diocese] owns and operates a coeducational parochial high school on the property in question known as Kanpaun-Mount Carmel High School. For many years prior to the events giving rise to this litigation, [the Diocese] operated two separate high schools in east Wichita. One of these was known as Kanpaun, a boys' school, and the other Mount Carmel, a girls' school, was originally located on the tract in question. Within a few years after

Mount Carmel had been in operation, the area surrounding the campus was developed as a residential area and some of the homes were purchased by [the plaintiffs in this case].

In 1969, [the Diocese] commenced consideration of a plan to merge Mount Carmel and Kanpaun, and the result was a decision in 1970 to combine the two schools on the Mount Carmel campus. After study and investigation by committees, together with professional consultants, plans were developed concerning facilities to be constructed in order to serve the function of the combined schools. The original plan to move the Kanpaun High School athletic stadium to the Mount Carmel site was abandoned. Architects employed by [the Diocese] prepared a site plan including locations and grading....

On April 11, 1972, [plaintiffs] filed the petition instituting this litigation.... It was alleged that the construction plans of [the Diocese] clearly show that the creation of a private nuisance to [plaintiffs] would result from the actual construction of the planned facilities for reasons which were alleged in the petition as follows:

(A) That Kanpaun-Mt. Carmel ... has a present student enrollment of approximately 700 and the planned gymnasium facility is capable of seating 1500 ... but yet, the Defendant is providing less [*sic*] than 200 parking spaces ... and is not planning to fence its school.... [T]he clear, necessary and obvious result ... is to burden the entire Vickridge area with a deluge of on-street parking and most assuredly, those persons parking on the streets will [walk] ... across the lawns and between the homes of Vickridge residents.

(B) [B]ecause of the landscape contours of the [high school] and the [Diocese's] construction plans, a serious drainage problem will be created....

(C) * * * [T]he football field, track, and baseball diamond which are to be located within a few feet of the property boundary lines are to be used year round ... to the extent that an almost continuous level of activities will be conducted ... and ... adequate screening cannot be installed to protect the Plaintiffs from the obvious noise, dust and pollution which will be created by the activity.

(D) * * * [T]he effect of [the Diocese's] entire construction project will be ... to seriously devalue the property owned by the Plaintiffs....

* * * *

The question of what constitutes a nuisance has been considered in many decisions of this court. Most recently ... it was held:

> A nuisance is an annoyance, and any use by one which gives offense to or endangers the life or health, violates the laws of decency, unreasonably pollutes the air with foul, noxious odors or smoke, or obstructs the reasonable and comfortable use and enjoyment of the property of another may be said to be a nuisance.

> A private nuisance is a tort related to an unlawful interference with a person's use or enjoyment of his land. The concept of private nuisance does not exist apart from the interest of a landowner....

Nuisances fall into two categories — nuisance *per se* and nuisance *per accidens* or "nuisance in fact." A nuisance *per se* is an act, instrument, or structure which is a nuisance at all times and under any circumstances. A nuisance *per accidens* is an act, instrument, or structure which becomes a nuisance by reason of surrounding circumstances.... Obviously, under the above definition neither a football field nor a baseball diamond or the operation thereof can be said to be a nuisance *per se*.... Since the football field and baseball diamond are not nuisances *per se*, then the critical question ... is whether the proposed construction and uses thereof, under all the surrounding circumstances established by the evidence, substantially interferes with the comfortable enjoyment by [plaintiffs] of the adjacent premises owned by them.

An interesting — and confusing — area. As you can see from the Kansas Supreme Court's analysis, what constitutes a nuisance can be extraordinarily fact-sensitive. All would agree that toxic waste dumps, slaughterhouses, rendering plants and other similar enterprises would be nuisances *per se*. But a baseball diamond, home of America's Pastime, a nuisance? As Casey Stengel would have said, "Who'd of thunk it?"

What makes this area a nuisance — well, such a nuisance — is that it is really a result rather than a tort. As the last excerpt shows, nuisance is really a remedy rather than a tort. Putting the matter somewhat differently, the adjoining landowners in our last excerpt really wanted the diocese not to build the sports fields. To achieve this, they had to persuade a court that the fields would be a nuisance. If the court so found, it then had the power to take steps to correct the problem through awards of damages, abatement (discontinuation) of an existing nuisance, or even by injunction, which could be used to prevent the nuisance from coming into existence in the first place.

But all of this depends on the facts, and if the nuisance only is threatened, the court ordinarily will be extremely unlikely to grant draconian relief.

The final caveat on the field is that the idea of *private* **nuisance**, which, as we have seen, is a private cause of action in tort, is entirely different from *public* **nuisance**, a criminal offense involving behavior or conduct that is offensive to the community as a whole. Private nuisance also is entirely different from an attractive nuisance, the analytical device used to create obligations running from landowners to trespassing minors. Many attractive nuisances are not private nuisances at all.

But no matter how unwieldy the concept is, nuisance is another old concept that lives a rich and full life in the law of torts today. No one working with the field or its relationship to the law of property can afford to be ignorant of this concept.

Ultrahazardous Activities

The other area where tort law imposes limitations upon a landowner's to do as the landowner pleases involves something called **ultrahazardous activities**.

> **Ultrahazardous activity.** An activity that cannot be safely
> performed, even with the exercise of reasonable care.

The idea comes from *Rylands v. Fletcher*, a famous and still
controversial English case handed down in 1868. What is involved in the
field can be understood better by reading our next excerpt.

Miller v. Civil Constructors, Inc.[6]
272 Ill. App. 263, 651 N.E.2d 239,109 Ill. Dec. 311
Appellate Court of Illinois, Second District
1995

Bowman, Justice:

Plaintiff, Gerald Miller ... alleged essentially that defendants were strictly
liable for injuries to plaintiff arising from purportedly "ultrahazardous"
activity for which defendants were legally responsible either because of
their control of the premises or because of the discharge of firearms. In each
instance, plaintiff stated that the defendant, through its officers, agents or
employees knew ... "or in the exercise of reasonable care should have
known" that "discharging firearms is an ultrahazardous, highly dangerous
activity" which was the proximate cause of plaintiff's injuries. The
complaint averred that plaintiff was injured when a stray bullet ricocheted
during the course of firearm practice in a nearby gravel pit and caused him
to fall from a truck....

The issue before us is whether ... the trial court properly dismissed the
counts where plaintiff attempted to state a cause of action premised on a
theory of strict liability by asserting that the discharge of firearms in a
quarry shooting range is an ultrahazardous activity....

* * * *

The doctrine of strict liability, sometimes called absolute liability, has its
genesis in the English rule of *Rylands v. Fletcher* ... wherein strict liability
was imposed on the defendant owners of land for harm resulting from the
abnormal or nonnatural use of defendants' land which arose when water
from defendants' reservoir flooded the adjoining mine of the plaintiff.

Subsequent decisions interpreted this rule to be confined to things or activities which were "extraordinary" or "exceptional" or "abnormal" so that there was some special use bringing with it increased danger to others.... From the decisions of the English courts, the "rule" of *Rylands* which has emerged is that "the defendant will be liable when he damages another by a thing or activity unduly dangerous and inappropriate to the place where it is maintained, in light of the character of that place and its surroundings...."

Most jurisdictions in this country have adopted the rule of *Rylands* to impose strict liability on owners and users for harm resulting from abnormally dangerous conditions and activities.... The best known applications of the *Rylands* rule imposing strict liability on a defendant involve the storing and use of explosives and flammable materials.... Illinois has recognized strict liability when a defendant engages in ultrahazardous or abnormally dangerous activity as determined by the courts, giving particular consideration [among other things] to the appropriateness of the activity to the place where it is maintained, in light of the character of the place and its surroundings....

We are concerned here only with determining as a matter of law whether the use of firearms is an ultrahazardous activity giving rise to strict liability.... Plaintiff concedes that ordinarily the manufacture or the sale of nondefective handguns has been held not to be an ultrahazardous activity....

* * * *

Section 519 of the *Restatement* states the general principle that "[o]ne who carries on an abnormally dangerous activity is subject to liability for harm to the person, land or chattels of another resulting from the activity, although he has exercised the utmost care to prevent the harm." Section 520 of the *Restatement* sets forth several factors which we will consider in determining whether an activity is abnormally dangerous (ultrahazardous):

    (a) existence of a high degree of risk of some harm to the person, land or chattels of others;
    (b) likelihood that the harm that results from it will be great;
    (c) inability to eliminate the risk by the exercise of reasonable care;
    (d) extent to which the activity is not a matter of common usage;

> (e) inappropriateness of the activity to the place where it is
> carried on; and
> (f) extent to which its value to the community is outweighed by
> its dangerous attributes....
>
> While all of these factors are important and should be considered, ordinarily
> the presence of more than one factor, but not all of them, will be necessary
> to declare the activity ultrahazardous as a matter of law so as to hold the
> actor strictly liable. The essential question is whether the risk created is so
> unusual, either because of its magnitude or because of the circumstances
> surrounding it, as to justify the imposition of strict liability even though the
> activity is carried on with all reasonable care. Considerations of public
> policy also enter prominently into the decisions by our courts to impose
> strict liability.... Particular consideration is also given to the appropriateness
> of the activity to the place where it is maintained, in light of the character of
> the place and its surroundings....

Strict liability is a new term for us, and one of considerable
significance.

> ***Strict liability.*** Liability that arises despite
> the absence of negligence or intent to harm.

As you may have guessed from the context, it means liability without
fault. A person is strictly liable when his or her conduct proximately
causes harm to another, even if conducted with more than a reasonable
degree of care.[7] As we shall soon see, it most often arises in the context
of products or goods unreasonably dangerous when put to reasonably
foreseeable uses, but it also is a legacy of *Rylands v. Fletcher.*

Some states, most notably Texas, have refused to adopt the *Rylands*
doctrine in any fashion.[8] Most others limit its application with
considerable rigor to situations such as blasting, which cannot ordinarily
be conducted with complete safety even using the highest possible care.[9]
In some states, transportation or handling of highly toxic substances may

also brush against this doctrine, but less often than blasting cases because most such substances can be controlled and handled safely.

That issue is the key here. If the damages can be avoided by the exercise of proper care, even if the care required is extraordinary, a court is unlikely to invoke the abnormally hazardous doctrine.

Summary

These, then, are the duties that go with occupancy and ownership of land. Though there have been some shifts of emphasis, the basic outlines of responsibility would be familiar to Holmes and even to his legal ancestors. And even the ongoing outcry for a unitary standard of fault cannot mask the fact that what is being argued for may be nothing more than the same old obligations with a "new coat of paint." But whatever side you take in the debate, understanding a landowner's duties is an essential part of understanding the law of torts.

Key Words and Phrases

attractive nuisance doctrine
business visitor
invitee
licensee
licensee by invitation
nuisance
premises liability
private nuisance
public invitee
public nuisance
strict liability
trespasser

Review Questions

1.   Locate a recent nuisance case in your own state. Did plaintiff or
       defendant prevail? Share the facts of the case with your
       colleagues in class.

2.   What is your state's position on the *Rylands* doctrine?
       (Obviously, students in Texas get a free ride on this question!) If
       your state has adopted it, is the application limited, as describes
       on pages 168-169?

3.   A swimming pool or a trampoline in one's backyard are classic
       examples of the "attractive nuisance" or "trespassing child"
       doctrine. Can you think of others?

---

[1] Internal citations and quotations omitted.

[2] Internal citations and quotations omitted.

[3] Author's note: For which we can all be grateful, if the instructor is going to put
this stuff on an exam.

[4] Internal citations and quotations omitted.

[5] *See, e.g.*, McRae, "Development of Nuisance in the Early Common Law,"
1 U.Fla.L.Rev. 27 (1948).

[6] Internal citations omitted.

[7] The other form of liability obliquely referred to in the excerpt, that of an
insurer, omits even the requirement of causation. An insurer — not the same
thing as an insurance company, whose liability rests upon a contract — is
responsibly for any injury occurring "on its watch," even if not caused by any
error, breach of obligations, or other omission of the insurer.

[8] *See Barras v. Monsanto Corp.*, 831 S.W.2d 959 (Tex. App. – Houston [14th
Dist.] 1992, writ denied).

[9] This ought not be surprising, because a blasting charge sufficient to do its
intended work must be big enough that there could be seismic or shock waves

that cause additional damage. The author has represented a number of mining and construction companies doing blasting work, and in most cases, the only issue is the extent of the plaintiff's damages.

Chapter Eight

WHAT'S IT WORTH TO YOU?
COMPENSATORY DAMAGES
IN TORT CASES

In our prior discussions, we have looked at various kinds of torts, more or less assuming that the redress for the wrongs involved followed rather directly. This assumption is thoroughly natural, but it is not quite correct.

History of the Concept of Damages

The legal system has tended to treat damages as a separate and semi-independent branch of analysis. History figures heavily in this separation. The need to settle on appropriate redress for a wrong existed hundreds of years before the idea of negligence had been considered.

Because the common law has roots in many different legal systems, there also was a considerable borrowing of ideas and overlap of concepts, some of which resulted in different awards or remedies.

Legislatures have also played a significant role in shaping the law of damages. Constitutional and statutory provisions often have an impact on what courts and juries can do. In recent times, for example, many states have enacted statutes limiting amounts that may be recovered in a medical malpractice action. At the close of 1999, proposals were presented before Congress and state legislatures to limit recoveries for Y2K-related computer or software losses. Each is an example of a significant limitation on damages that otherwise might be available.

Another factor weighs particularly heavily in issues of damage: factual development of issues at trial. As befits the general proposition that the plaintiff has the burden of proof, the plaintiff generally has the burden of proving the proper amount of damages to be awarded. Areas that seem at first glance to be entirely subjective, such as pain and suffering, can benefit from creative treatment by counsel.

Many areas of damage, such as future medical losses, require careful presentation based upon adequate documentary foundation and expert testimony. This is an area where paralegals and other professionals play a vital part.

Nominal Damages

The first level of damage that can be awarded is **nominal damages**, which means a small award, usually one dollar. Plaintiffs who sue for trespass, assault, battery, and, as we shall see, certain forms of defamation can recover nominal damages simply by proving the other elements of the tort. If they do this, the nominal award is automatic.

So why do it, you ask? In trespass matters, for example, a plaintiff can only recover if it can prove a superior right of ownership over the property in question. Where a dispute has arisen over property rights, a neutral decision on who owns the property may be more important than a sum of money as damage.

Similar desires to achieve vindication may also lead someone to seek nominal damages, although it is the rare plaintiff who does not seek more from a lawsuit. Rare though they are, nominal damages retain their vitality even in today's high-dollar legal world.

Compensatory Damages

At the next level, plaintiffs can seek **compensatory damages** for torts inflicted upon them. As the name implies, compensatory damages exist to compensate — to make a plaintiff whole for an injury inflicted.

At the same time, however, compensatory damages are not intended as a windfall. A plaintiff is not entitled to be better off than he or she was before the tort was committed.

We now take up the question of how to strike this balance in an area given over to specific rules and formulas. We start with two relatively simple cases, the measure of damages for injuries to real property and chattels.

Damages to Real Property

Flora v. Amega Motor Home Sales Inc.
958 S.W.2d 322
Missouri Court of Appeals, Western District
1998

Spinden, P.J.:

* * * *

Flora purchased a double-wide mobile home from Amega in 1994. They agreed that Amega would set the house on a basement foundation constructed by Flora. Flora constructed the basement of unreinforced concrete blocks, contrary to Amega's recommendation that he use steel-reinforced, poured concrete.

After a crew set the house on the foundation, the foundation wall cracked and bowed. Flora's theory of causation was that the crew parked the delivery trailer and set hydraulic jacks for moving the house too close to the basement.

After a small claims court entered a $3,000 judgment for Flora in his negligence action against Amega, Amega obtained a trial *de novo* in circuit court. The circuit court's judgment said, "Court finds from evidence adduced, that defendant is liable for damage occasioned to [Flora's] foundation walls by reason of manner in which mobile home was being placed on [Flora's] foundation." The circuit court awarded Flora $2,695 in damages.

* * * *

In determining the amount of damages, the circuit court accepted the testimony of Flora as to the amount of his repair expenses in fixing the basement. Flora did not present any evidence concerning the value of the property before and after the basement cracked and bowed. The measure of damages in a negligence action for damage to real property is the difference in fair market value before and after the defendant's negligent conduct, or the cost of repair, whichever is less. Further, application of the cost of repairs test is limited to situations where repairs amount to a small percent of the diminution in value.

When a court has no evidence concerning the market value of the damaged property, an award of damages for repairs erroneously applies the law in the absence of any evidence of value. We, therefore, remand the case to the circuit court to determine whether the diminution in value to Flora's property was less than the cost of repairing the basement. If it was, the circuit court shall enter judgment for the lesser amount.

Well, that seems simple enough, and perfectly sensible as well. If a piece of property is worth $1,000, it makes no sense to allow the plaintiff to recover $2,000 to repair it, since that is more than the property was worth in the first place. In this $2,000 repair hypothetical, the plaintiff has benefited $1,000, a violation of the axiom that compensatory damages should do no more than make him whole.

But here is where the formula/technicality issue becomes important, because there are formulas for dealing with losses to crops and trees, as well as real estate. Consider these two short case excerpts as variations on the main real estate theme.

Welter v. Humboldt County
461 N.W.2d 335
Iowa Court of Appeals
1990

Oxberger, J.:

In 1985, Humboldt County had hired Barry and Bruce Raemaker to spray ditches in Humboldt County during the summer of 1985. The plaintiffs, David and Charles Welter, are brothers who farm in Humboldt County and live relatively close to each other.

On June 8, 1985, on a record-setting hot day, Bruce Raemaker sprayed the road ditches next to and across from the David Welter residence with a chemical known as Brayton Brush Killer. The chemical is used to kill weeds and trees growing in the ditches. When Raemaker approached the Welter residence, he shut off the sprayer, since the wind was blowing strongly and Raemaker wanted to avoid any drift of the chemical into the Welter garden. Once past the Welter home, Raemaker resumed spraying.

David and Charles Welter subsequently brought this consolidated action against Humboldt County and the Raemakers on the grounds that the chemical used in spraying the ditches had caused damage to some of the 400 different trees planted on David's property and had tainted the popcorn in Charles' corn crib. David claimed that he had planted the trees two years previously and had planted them for a windbreak and for his own enjoyment. David alleged that nearly twenty trees died or were stunted and that total replacement cost was $3200.

* * * *

Because of the great versatility of trees, it is impossible to state an all-purpose measure of recovery for loss of trees. Iowa courts have through the years devised numerous alternatives to be applied according to the location of the trees and the use to which they were put.... Where trees are put to a special use, such as for windbreaks or shade, the measure is the difference in value of the realty before and after the destruction of the trees.... Where the trees had no special use, the measure is the commercial market value of the trees at the time damages occurred.... Where trees can be replaced, the measure of damages is the cost of replacement. Even if the before and after value of the land is the appropriate measure of damages, the court may consider the intrinsic value of trees to the owner....

Let us change direction slightly and see how the law treats crop damage, again with a short excerpt from Iowa:

Maisel v. Gelhaus
416 N.W.2d 81
Iowa Court of Appeals
1987

Donielson, P.J.:

* * * *

The Gelhauses argue that the trial court erred in awarding Maisel actual damages in the amount of $1,600. The Gelhauses argue that Maisel had admitted that part of the drainage problems existed long before either party owned their land and argued that Maisel admitted during his deposition that he had suffered no loss. At trial, however, Maisel alleged that in 1979 and 1980, he respectively lost the rental value of eight acres due to ponding near the end of the ditch.

The trial court awarded Maisel $1,600, based upon the cash rental value of the land in question. The value was determined by lease agreements, which placed the value of the rented land at $100 per acre. Maisel contends that he had forgotten about the lease provisions at the time of his deposition, but that he promptly introduced them at trial.

Generally, the proper measure of damages for the loss of growing crops is their value in the field at the time of their injury or their value in a matured condition less the reasonable expense of maturing and marketing....
However, the plaintiff, as lessor, did not own the crops that were lost due to flooding. Therefore, the proper damages to be awarded would be the loss of the cash rent value of the land lost....

If we continued this kind of analysis, we would see that there exist well-defined rules for many different kinds of property, all dependent on the particular nature of the property involved, its use, and whether or not it could be replaced. In all of these situations, the rules that exist are a function not only of the general idea of "make-whole-but-don't-overcompensate," but also of long-standing concepts of damage imported from the law of property or contracts.

Even though you probably will not confront them very often, it is important to remember that these special variations on the simple rule governing damage to real property exist.

Damages to Personal Property

On the other hand, you are very likely to confront damage to personal property (sometimes referred to as **chattels**) in your career. This is most likely to take the form of damage to someone's automobile, but it could be other personal property as well. Here there also is a rule, as our next excerpt demonstrates.

Farmers Insurance Co. of Arizona v. R.B.L. Investment Co.
138 Ariz. 562, 675 P.2d 1381
Court of Appeals of Arizona
1983

Hathaway, J.:

Whether the owner of a negligently damaged motor vehicle may be compensated for damages for loss in the fair market value above and beyond the cost of repair, and whether he may be compensated for loss of use of the motor vehicle during the period in which it is being repaired, are questions raised on this appeal....

The trial court held that the compensable damages were limited to the cost of repair. It is from this ruling that the appeal is taken.

We ... believe that the rule is clearly enunciated in the *Restatement (Second) of Torts*, § 928 (1977):

§ 928. Harm to Chattels. When one is entitled to a judgment for harm to chattels not amounting to a total destruction in value, the damages include compensation for

(a) the difference between the value of the chattel before the harm and the value after the harm or, at his election in an appropriate case, the reasonable cost of repair or restoration, with due allowance for any difference

---

between the original value and the value after repairs, and

(b) the loss of use.

Other authority supporting damages for depreciation beyond the cost of repair includes Professor Dobbs, who writes:

> There seems no warrant at all for insisting that the owner content himself with the repair costs if they are less than the depreciation, provided depreciation can be and is adequately proven. However satisfactory the repairs may be in, say, the operation of a car, the owner may quite possibly find that the trade-in value of his car is less when he seeks to purchase a new automobile, or that its cash sale value is less throughout the immediate life of the car. If this sort of depreciation is real, and can be established, there seems no reason at all to deny full compensation by limiting recovery to cost of repairs. (D. Dobbs, *Remedies*, § 5.10, at 380 [1973].)

Jurisdictions that have addressed the issue seem to have generally held that the measure of compensation to the owner of a negligently damaged motor vehicle may include the cost of repair and proven residual diminution in fair market value.... We believe this is the appropriate standard....

Cost of repair plus depreciation seems an easily understood standard, but what about loss during the period that repairs are required? Today the rule is almost universally settled that reasonable expenses for loss of use (for example, for a rental car) should be included.

Somewhat surprisingly, it took an apparently titanic amount of effort to convince most appellate courts that this was appropriate. Again, the issue is in the purported "double dip." Those against recovery for loss of use argued that they already would be included in the diminution of value element of damages.

Putting the issue in somewhat different terms, these individuals argued that the damaged vehicle's value was zero during the period of repairs plus what it still could not do after repairs were completed. Thus, rental car value should properly be included in the diminished value and not separated out. The other side said that juries could differentiate between including rental car costs as a separate line item in a damage award and lumping them in with diminished value costs. Whether this is true or not, it won the day.

If you sense that all of this has something of a convoluted, metaphysical feel about it, you are correct. Many arguments concerning damages are conducted on such esoteric levels. Is an award of damages for pain and suffering different from an award for the loss of enjoyment of life? What is sufficient emotional distress to permit recovery of damages for it? At what point is someone conscious enough to be entitled to an award of conscious pain and suffering? If someone destroys a treasured heirloom of mine, can I recover for the emotional distress I suffer as a result? And how do we value the heirloom? The arguments go on and on ... and will go on and on as long as creative lawyers stand up in courtrooms.

Damages for Bodily Injury

Part of the reason for the continual debate is the inherent difficulty of valuing bodily injuries. The next case excerpt deals with a young man, Frankie Graeff, who sustained injuries when he was struck by a car as he got out of a bus operated by the church he attended. Contrast the standard you are about to study with those you have just left. How do they compare?

Graeff v. Baptist Temple of Springfield
576 S.W.2d 291
Missouri Supreme Court, *En Banc*
1978

Simeone, Special J.:

* * * *

Plaintiff Frank Kenneth Graeff by his next friend and father, Kenneth S. Graeff, filed an action seeking damages for personal injuries in the circuit court of Greene County against the defendant-respondent Baptist Temple of

---

Springfield and defendant-appellant Mr. Emmett M. Davis. The jury returned a verdict in favor of plaintiff, Frank (Frankie) Graeff, against Baptist Temple in the amount of $97,100, and returned a verdict in favor of defendant Emmett M. Davis....

Mrs. Linda Lee Graeff, the mother of Frankie ... [testified that prior] ... to the accident Frankie's leg was normal. He engaged in normal activities, was "very active," and was in the second grade. He enjoyed boxing and swimming.

At the time of the accident, Mrs. Graeff stated, "The next thing I knew, Frank was laying on the ground, screaming." Frankie was underneath Mr. Davis' vehicle at about the center post. "The center post (of the Davis vehicle) was right over the middle of Frank. Frank, from the waist down, was underneath Mr. Davis' car." Mrs. Graeff could see the "bone in his leg sticking out approximately, six inches." Mrs. Graeff pulled him from underneath the car.

Frankie received serious injuries in the collision. The hospital report indicated that he was admitted on April 19, 1975, and dismissed May 10, a total of 21 days. The report indicated that Frankie had received a compound fracture of the left femur.... "Adjacent soft tissues are severely lacerated."

Frankie was operated on by Dr. Newt Wakeman, Jr., an orthopedic surgeon. Dr. Wakeman saw Frankie in the emergency room. "(H)e was a frightened youngster ... the most obvious injury was his left lower limb, where there was a large laceration of approximately one-half the circumference of his lower thigh with a bone protruding from the wound."

He [Dr. Wakeman] determined that an operation was necessary. Surgery was performed, a metallic pin was inserted in the tibia, the wound partially closed over the bone, and about half the wound was left open. Frankie was placed in traction from April 19 to May 10. On April 27, another operation was performed to close the wound. On May 10, Frankie underwent another operation for the removal of the pin, and a body cast was applied. The cast covered all of the left limb, and the right limb to the knee. The upper cast encircled his body "up to approximately the level of his belly button."

After Frankie left the hospital, Dr. Wakeman "saw" him 14 times.... Dr. Wakeman indicated that there would be permanent scarring of the leg and that Frank will have to take precautions with the leg. "Certain occupations might be more hazardous to him than others," and he would have to be selective concerning employment "so as to try to protect the scar tissue there from breaking down and being irritated and being injured." The doctor estimated that he [Frankie] would "have approximately 10% disability, and permanent physical impairment to the lower extremity."

Dr. Ernst Peter Danielsson, a plastic surgeon to whom Frankie had been referred, testified at trial concerning the operations in April 1976, a year after the accident. He examined Frankie and admitted him to the hospital. He [Frankie] was confined from April 11, 1976, to April 30, 1976, 20 days. "(T)here was heavy scarring which extended from the side of his lower thigh down into the back of the knee ... and extending down onto the back and the lateral aspect of the leg...." The doctor recommended surgery.

Two operations were performed, [one on] April 12 for a skin graft, and, because of some drainage, a second operation was performed on April 23, 1976. Frankie was discharged on April 30, but instructions were given by the physician to care for the leg by "soaks." Dr. Danielsson too indicated that there would be permanent scarring; scar tissue "never is normal." The doctor indicated that it is "quite possible" that he [Frankie] may need future surgery.

In the plaintiff's case, the life expectancy tables were introduced showing that a nine-year-old male child had a life expectancy of 64.89 years.

Pause here. Ask yourself what you would suggest as a proper award of damages for plaintiff if your legal team were representing him? What could the defendants' attorney tell the jury? What factors did you consider as you made these evaluations?

With those thoughts in mind, let us skip forward in the *Graeff* opinion:

One of the most difficult decisions facing the jury in a personal injury action is to decide the amount of monetary award, if any, that the plaintiff is entitled to be awarded as compensation for past, present and future pain and suffering.

The measure of damages for pain and suffering in this state is, and has been, what is fair and reasonable. The jury is so instructed by [mandatory form instruction]. There is no fixed measure, table, or standard which the jury can use as an accurate index to establish an award of damages. No method is available to the jury by which it can objectively evaluate such damages, and no witness may express his subjective opinion concerning the matter.

From time immemorial, the judicial measure of damages for pain and suffering has been fair and reasonable compensation ... because there is and can be no established standard, fixed basis of mathematical rule by which such damages may be calculated. In a very real sense, the jury is required to evaluate in terms of monetary compensation the injuries and pain and suffering sustained. In guiding the jury in this difficult task, the courts, including those in this state, permit counsel to suggest a "lump sum," and the "mere argumentative suggestion" of a lump sum is not error. It is proper to inform the jury of the total amount of damages sought and this technique does not seem to be questioned....

Consider a more recent statement of the law of damages.

Furr's Inc. v. Logan
893 S.W.2d 187
Court of Appeals of Texas, El Paso
1995

Larsen, J.:

* * * *

Furr's is a grocery store chain with a retail facility in Odessa, Texas. On the sidewalk outside the store, Water Vend, Inc., placed a coin-operated machine selling purified water for drinking and cooking. On Christmas Day 1989, Furr's was closed, but the Water Vend machine was accessible.

That day, plaintiff Athena Logan volunteered to purchase water to make ice [*sic*] tea for a large family dinner. She took two five-gallon bottles to the Furr's store for that purpose. Her granddaughter, Alicia, accompanied her.

Ms. Logan parked next to the Water Vend machine in the Furr's parking lot. She noticed water pooled around the machine and warned her granddaughter to stay away from it. The weather in Odessa had been cold, and the water was at least partially frozen. There had been an ice storm earlier in the week, but Christmas [Day] and the day before were clear.

Ms. Logan made several trips to the machine, filling one jug and returning with the second. She avoided the ice on the sidewalk as she made these trips, but as she carried the second empty jug to the machine, she slipped on ice in the asphalt parking lot. She testified she never saw that patch of ice before she fell.

Ms. Logan broke her ankle in the fall. She went to the emergency room Christmas afternoon and wore a cast for almost a year. She had a thyroid condition that complicated her treatment and caused the break to take almost ten times longer than normal to heal. At the time of trial, she was experiencing pain, stiffness, loss of mobility, and loss of flexibility in the ankle.

Again, pause to consider. If your team had represented the plaintiff, what would you have told the jury were the proper damages? What if your team had represented one of the defendants? What kinds of evidence would your team have offered? What would have been said in closing argument? Compare your answer with the actual result.

A jury found Furr's 60% negligent and Water Vend 40% negligent in causing the accident. It found no negligence on the part of Athena Logan. The jury awarded damages of $4,390 for past medical care, $2,200 for future medical care, $5,000 for past physical pain and mental anguish, $7,500 for past physical impairment; and $35,000 for future physical impairment.

The trial court entered judgment accordingly. Both Furr's and Water Vend appeal.

* * * *

In its Points of Error, Furr's claims there is no evidence, or insufficient evidence, to support the jury's findings on damages. In its third point of error, Water Vend challenges the jury's award of future damages.

First, we note that Furr's complains repeatedly that plaintiff did not specify dollar values for the various elements of her damage. It claims this renders defective the jury's award for Ms. Logan's future medical care, past and future pain and anguish, and past and future physical impairment. This is not the law. Personal injury damages of this sort are not capable of measurement by a specific standard, and amounts awarded are uniquely within the province of the trier of fact.... The amount awarded for future damages is necessarily subject to some guesswork, and the amount of such awards is largely within the jury's discretion....

Similarly, an award for physical pain and mental anguish, which this Court has held to be a particularly subjective non-pecuniary loss, is within the jury's broad discretion. Once the right to recover some amount for these damages is established, the amount of such award is virtually unreviewable.... There is no requirement that plaintiff place specific dollar values on elements of damage for which no mathematical formula can be set. This argument fails.

Furr's next urges that the jury's award for future medical care must be set aside because there is no evidence, based upon reasonable medical probability, as to the amount of money necessary to furnish Ms. Logan with future medical care. This is not the standard for determining future damages in personal injury cases. Texas follows the "reasonable probability" rule for future damages, including future medical expenses.... The jury may make its award for future medical care based upon the nature of plaintiff's injuries, medical care rendered before trial, and the plaintiff's condition at the time of trial. Plaintiff is not required to establish the future medical consequences of her injury by expert testimony based on reasonable medical probability.

The evidence here established that Ms. Logan sustained a serious ankle fracture, that she had a thyroid condition that complicated the healing

---

process, and that for her broken ankle to heal would take ten times longer than normal. According to her treating physician, she was still in the healing process at the time of trial, and he expected it to take another two years for her to heal completely. At the time of trial, she still had constant pain, burning sensations, swelling, stiffness, and loss of motion. She was under the care of a doctor and had already expended over $4,000 in medical costs. This was adequate evidence to support the jury's award of $2,200 in future medical care.

Furr's also complains that the evidence on future physical impairment was lacking. The evidence recited above supported this element of damage, as does the additional statement from Ms. Logan's treating physician's records that she had a 10% permanent impairment to her left foot. Furr's Points of Error ... are overruled.

Do you feel that the standard for computing damages for bodily injury is any more precise at this point?

The Difficulty in Computing Damages

From these cases, can you write down a general algorithm or principle for computing the proper amount of damages to award someone who has sustained bodily injury?

If you answered no, you are by no means alone. Most pattern jury instructions for bodily injury do no more than tell the jury to award what is fair and reasonable compensation. The translation of "fair and reasonable" into a dollar figure is a job belonging to counsel, and many cases on "damages" really are cases about the way in which counsel presented a claim for damages.[1]

Elements of a Damage Award

We could go through hundreds more cases and find that most state the same general principles. Such a review would reveal that the basic elements of an award of damage in a bodily injury case are

- medical expenses
- lost income
- pain and suffering.

Medical Expenses

Medical expenses are defined as "the costs of care and treatment, rehabilitation, surgery, medicine, prostheses and devices, therapy and similar matters." **Past medical expenses** are those that have actually been incurred up to the time of trial. Usually, it is not necessary that they have been paid. **Reasonably necessary future expenses** are reduced to present value. We'll discuss this idea in just a moment.

Lost Income

Lost income is defined as "wages or salary, commissions and benefits from job or occupation." **Past lost income** are actual amounts lost through the time of trial. **Future income losses** are reduced to present value.

Pain and Suffering

Pain and suffering are defined ... well, pretty much as the phrase sounds ... with the understanding that these are highly subjective areas left largely to the jury's discretion.

Issues to Consider

Before discussing some more controversial categories of damage, let us pause to consider some of the issues arising from what we have learned here.

First, suppose, as is usually the case, that the plaintiff has health insurance of some kind. Is the defendant allowed a deduction for medical care costs paid through such insurance? The answer almost universally has been negative. Courts call health insurance benefits, HMO coverage, workers compensation, or similar payments "collateral sources" and hold that evidence of such payments is not admissible to reduce a plaintiff's award of damages.

The theory behind the rule is straightforward enough. Not everyone has insurance to begin with, and it is impossible to measure whether benefits will continue in the future. Thus, focusing on what kind of health plan the plaintiff has often leads to nothing but confusion. Moreover, to the extent that an insurer pays benefits to an injured party, it becomes subrogated to the extent of its payments to the plaintiff's rights to recover from the alleged tortfeasor.

Subrogation is a doctrine by which an entity that pays on behalf of another obtains the injured party's right (up to the amount it has paid out) to sue the person or entity that caused the harm. The right may exist in equity or by virtue of a contract. Most insurance policies contain subrogation clauses that contractually confer this right upon an insurer that pays under its policy.

Subrogation may also come into existence by statute, as might be the case if someone received Medicaid benefits for an injury resulting from tortious conduct. Putting this kind of evidence before a jury may be so confusing or distracting that it prevents the jury from reaching a fair decision as to the plaintiff's damages.

On the other side of the street, should a plaintiff be allowed to tell the jury that the defendant has liability insurance that might cover a judgment entered in the case? You certainly can see why the plaintiff's attorney would want to do this. The jury presumably would be more willing to find against the defendant *and* to increase its award knowing that any judgment wouldn't really "count" because the defendant would not have to pay itself.

Again, the universal response is to try to minimize the jury's exposure to a defendant's insurance. (We use the word "minimize" here because it is impossible to "sterilize" this environment. Juries almost universally assume that insurance is available to defendants, especially businesses, so the question may be less keeping the existence of insurance away from them than the amount of coverage. Quixotic though this effort may be, the law generally forbids such discussions.)

A third area of concern is whether the award can be taxed. The niceties of tax law are far beyond the scope of this book, but the rule of thumb is clear. Awards to compensate a plaintiff for physical injuries or damage to tangible property necessary to restore it to a prior condition are not taxable. Awards of punitive damages, damages for lost profits, or business income are taxable.

How do you think jurors handle this information? If nothing is certain but death and taxes, isn't it logical to assume that they will increase the award to account for the tax bite?

In fact, the evidence is disputed. For many years, in cases arising under the Federal Employee Liability Act, a workers compensation statute, the United States Supreme Court has required judges to instruct juries that their awards to a prevailing plaintiff are not taxable. Some states have followed a similar course; others have not. The trend is unclear, at least as far as the author can determine, except that it remains something hotly disputed by those involved in tort litigation, especially the largest cases.

Two other issues arise over and over again in tort cases: **reasonableness** and **present value**. Each has an important role in the damage process.

Reasonableness

Suppose you were involved in a case in which the plaintiff was rendered a quadriplegic through the defendant's alleged negligence. During trial, plaintiff's counsel tries to put into evidence the cost of an annual seven-day cruise trip for the plaintiff, suggesting in response to objection that it will improve the quality of the plaintiff's life. What should the court do?

This actually happened to the author in a case many years ago. The judge promptly excluded the evidence as patently unreasonable, and the issue never came up on appeal. This example is a bit extreme, but the point is not. The reasonableness requirement protects defendants from being gouged for unnecessary treatments, phony nostrums, and absurd demands, while preserving the plaintiff's right to seek whatever treatment the plaintiff's providers deem reasonably necessary.

Present Value

The other concept, present value, is simply a function of the time value of money and the limitations on what a jury can award. Plaintiffs have every right to seek money for needed medical care in the future, but jurors must award a lump sum today. If they give plaintiff the full amount of what he needs for medical care 20 years from now, they have overcompensated him, because he can invest the money and draw interest on it until needed. In other words, to avoid overcompensation, the jury must award the sum today that will by prudent investment become the amount needed to fund the medical care (or whatever else) at the specified time in the future.

These present value computations are not as simple as this description might at first seem. Inflation must be factored in. Medical costs have risen steadily, sometimes at a level far exceeding inflation in the economy as a whole. This factor also must be taken into account.

Generally. there are three ways of accomplishing the process. First, some states hold that the long-term variations in inflation and interest rates nullify each other so that present value and future value should be **equal**. The second approach is called a "**net**" or "**real**" approach. It subtracts an average inflationary percentage from the available interest rate and uses the "net" figure as the basis for calculation. Finally, there is the so-called "**gross rate**" approach, in which real world inflation rates averaged over time and real world interest rates averaged over the same period are used.

As the foregoing summaries demonstrate, this is an abstruse area heavily dependent upon expert witnesses and economic data from government and private sources. The battle over such experts may involve *Daubert* issues or questions arising under similar state statutes or decisions. It may also involve questions of foundation, depending on how the expert chooses his or her interest rates. It definitely is an area of ongoing and intense involvement for all on the trial team.

Emotional Distress

Finally, we must pause and examine a difficult area: if, when, and how to permit damages for emotional distress. To obtain some background in this difficult area, we return to the case law:

City of Tyler v. Likes
962 S.W.2d 489
Supreme Court of Texas
1997

Phillips, C.J.:

This is a suit for flood damage brought against a municipality under the Texas Tort Claims Act, common law, and the Texas Constitution. Floodwaters flowing through a municipal culvert system constructed before the Legislature passed the Tort Claims Act damaged plaintiff's home. The primary issue is whether plaintiff may recover from the City for mental anguish resulting from the flood....

* * * *

Although mental anguish is a real and serious harm, there are two principal reasons why courts are not willing to recognize it as a compensable element of damages in every case where it occurs.

First, it is difficult to predict. The invasion of the same legal right may lead to extreme anguish in one person while causing essentially no emotional damage to another. Because of this variability in human nature, it is difficult for the law to distinguish between those instances when mental anguish is reasonably foreseeable from particular conduct and those when it is so

---

remote that the law should impose no duty to prevent it. For this reason, Texas courts at one time categorized mental anguish in most types of cases as too remote or speculative to be compensable as actual damages, holding the emotional consequences of the tort relevant only to exemplary damages....

Second, even in circumstances where mental anguish is a foreseeable result of wrongful conduct, its existence is inherently difficult to verify. For years the fear of false claims led us to require objective bodily symptoms of anguish in most types of cases. We eliminated this "physical manifestation" requirement after concluding that physical symptoms are not an accurate indicator of genuine mental anguish.... Yet even in those cases where a defendant has breached the type of duty for which mental anguish is recoverable, we frequently demand direct evidence of the nature, duration, and severity of the mental anguish, establishing a substantial disruption in the plaintiffs' daily routine.... While we recognize that such artificial evidentiary barriers as the *Parkway* standard may merely encourage exaggeration and penalize those who deal constructively with life's vicissitudes, we continue to insist on such safeguards because the law has not yet discovered a satisfactory empirical test for what is by definition a subjective injury....

Without intent or malice on the defendant's part, serious bodily injury to the plaintiff, or a special relationship between the two parties, we permit recovery for mental anguish in only a few types of cases involving injuries of such a shocking and disturbing nature that mental anguish is a highly foreseeable result. These include suits for wrongful death ... and actions by bystanders for a close family member's serious injury.

Chief Justice Phillips's analysis of this complicated issue highlights the many problems that have been associated with damages for emotional distress over the years. Historically, the idea that such damages could be awarded arose in cases involving highly sensitive situations. Misdelivery of a telegram containing distressing news, improper burial, and seeing a family member severely injured were the only three situations in which damages for emotional distress could be awarded in the absence of a contemporaneous injury.

As time went on, however, and psychiatry became more rigorous, pressure rose to permit these damages, in part because medical science recognized them as "stand alone" problems that could arise from tortious behavior, and in part because failing to do so seemed inconsistent with the broad discretion otherwise afforded juries in assessing damages for bodily injury.

Two New Areas of Damages

This same advancement in medical science has led to two controversial new areas of damage, both of which arise out of the following scenario. (Subtextual query: Does this remind you just a bit of a movie?) Suppose you and your neighbors come home one day to find notices from the state environmental protection agency on your door:

"Warning!" it reads. "You have been exposed to a known disease causing agent at unknown levels. We recommend that you seek medical attention immediately." Are you afraid? Probably. Do you want some kind of medical attention? Probably. And it is this fear and your desire for medical treatment that form our last two areas for discussion.

Fear of Exposure

An example of the kind of problems associated with this area can be found in cases involving exposure of health care personnel to HIV. In *Brown v. New York Health and Hospitals Corp.*, 225 A.D.2d 36, 648 N.Y.S.2d 880, (2d Dept. 1996), for example, the court had to confront the concerns of a nurse who was exposed to HIV virus at a hospital.

In discussing the problems associated with this field, the court stated:

> In determining the reasonableness of a plaintiff's fear of developing AIDS, courts have considered one or more of three factors:
>
> (1) the channel of transmission of the disease
> (2) whether HIV was present when the transmission occurred
> (3) the results of HIV-antibody tests.

A positive HIV-antibody test, of course, is sufficient prima facie proof that the plaintiff's fear of developing AIDS is reasonable. We are concerned here, however, with a case where the plaintiff has not tested seropositive. We conclude that, in order to maintain a cause of action for damages due to the fear of contracting AIDS, a plaintiff who has not tested seropositive must offer proof of "actual exposure," that is, proof of both a scientifically accepted method of transmission of the virus (in this case, a needle puncture) and that the source of the allegedly transmitted blood or fluid was in fact HIV-positive (in this case, the unfortunate infant).

Requiring proof of actual exposure in this manner will, we believe, insure that there is a genuine basis for the plaintiff's fear of developing the disease, that the fear is not based on public misconceptions about the disease, and that such claims are treated consistently.

Moreover, we emphasize that the existence of the channel for infection makes the threat of infection much more of a real possibility to be feared and far more than a speculative worry. Liability in the absence of a channel could provoke a flood of ill-justified litigation. Of course, it is the channel for infection, not actual HIV transmission or infection, that must be proven.

* * * *

Having determined that the reasonableness of a plaintiff's fear of contracting AIDS depends upon proof of a channel of transmission and the presence of HIV during the transmission, we address the effect of HIV antibody test results. As previously noted, tests for the presence of infection in the initial three months following exposure are not reliable, and only if there is no evidence of infection after six months can an individual be assured that exposure did not result in infection by the virus.

Thus, where there has been sufficient *prima facie* proof of actual exposure to the virus, we conclude that, for the first six months following exposure, a plaintiff need not present proof of actual infection with the virus in order to establish that the fear of developing AIDS is reasonable during that time period....

A plaintiff's initial, reasonable fear of contracting AIDS thus becomes unreasonable if more than six months have passed since exposure, and the plaintiff continues to test negative for HIV antibodies.... Of course, a

plaintiff who tests positive for HIV would not be precluded from seeking
damages for emotional distress suffered during the period of time that the
virus could remain latent before any symptoms of AIDS develop....

This is a thoughtful analysis in a difficult and potentially hysteria-filled
area. The need to balance irrational fear against objective evidence is
vital to sustaining a cause of action for "AIDS-phobia" or for
"cancerphobia," generally defined as the exposure to a known
carcinogen or similarly toxic substance.

This area of law remains unsettled, in part because these fears, no matter
how well founded, are fears that rest upon a statistically increased
chance of exposure to a condition. As noted in the opinion we have just
read, the chances of HIV exposure from a single needle stick are
approximately 0.3% to 0.5%, or three to five in one thousand. In cancerphobia cases, the change in probability of getting cancer can be as low
as one in a million or even less. None of this is to minimize the fears of
those exposed, but these figures do suggest caution in setting legal
standards.

Fear of Exposure and Future Monitoring

Most plaintiffs exposed to such substances take a different approach
from Ms. Brown, the plaintiff in our last case. They do seek some kind
of ongoing medical monitoring. There has been considerable
controversy, which still arises in many mass toxic tort cases today.
Cases such as *Redland Soccer Club Inc. v. Department of the Army and
Department of Defense of the United States,* 548 Pa. 178, 696 A.2d 137
(Pa. 1997), summarize this difficult area. These cases require, among
other factors, proof of exposure and a significantly increased risk of
contacting a disease, all proven by expert testimony.

Even with these elements of proof required, medical monitoring still
presents real issues for many courts. In most cases, the "monitoring" at
issue is nothing more than a comprehensive physical performed

regularly. The lab work obtained in such physicals may be all that is available to check for disease. Even "newfangled" tests for certain forms of cancer often do not address the health risks that may arise from toxic exposure; early detection may do little to prevent disease. Thus, the efficacy of medical monitoring as a remedial device is still hotly at issue.

But the fight also goes to a second level. If a plaintiff can go to court to get damages for medical monitoring and emotional distress, should he of she be allowed to come back to court years, possibly decades, later, to seek damages for cancer or some other disease? One bedrock of the common law is the idea that matters should be litigated once and once only, as you will see in your class on civil procedure. The concepts of collateral estoppel and *res judicata*, sometimes called issue and claim preclusion, are high barriers to relitigation of issues once decided in a court.

And, as we learned before, if these same plaintiffs had suffered a condition with a faster onset, they would be able to recover their past medical expenses, their pain and suffering, and likely their emotional distress. This question remains open and hotly debated.

Fears Later Proven Unfounded

The final area of controversy here is the most difficult. Suppose a court awards medical monitoring damages for persons exposed to a chemical, only to find that later scientific advances prove the substance to be harmless.[2] Or what if we discover that it was not the suspect chemical at all but something else occurring naturally that caused the problem? Should the award be dissolved?

These questions force us to recognize that much of what we use as legal standards in this area rests upon incomplete knowledge, misconception and no small amount of ignorance. Given the "lag time" inherent in development of the common law, this problem is not likely to be remedied any time soon.

We have made an overview of the significant issues in the law of damages. The field remains alive, changing, and one that is more susceptible than any other to the ingenuity of the legal team.

Key Words and Phrases

compensatory damages
damages for bodily injuries
damages to chattels
damages to personal property
emotional distress
fear of exposure
fears later proven unfounded
future monitoring
lost income
making whole
medical expenses
nominal damages
pain and suffering
past medical expenses
present value
reasonableness
reasonably necessary future expenses
subrogation

Review Questions

1. List the relevant factors considered when setting damages for loss of real property. Give an example of each.

2. Find the section in the *Farmers* excerpt where Judge Hathaway cites *Restatement (Second)*, which in turn quotes from Dobbs' *Remedies*. Apply this information to the losses of chattel described in *Likes*. What may Likes have reasonably expected to receive as damages for her personal property loss?

3. On page 183, you were asked to pause and answer three questions about *Graeff*. Now that you have finished the entire chapter, how (if at all) would you change the answers you originally gave to these questions?

4. If you were working for the defense in *Furr's*, what points might you have made concerning plaintiff Logan and her actions? Could you argue that any of her actions contributed to her injury?

5. Note that the incident in *Brown* occurred in 1990, and the opinion was written in 1996. Do you think the same verdict would have been rendered if the case had been brought today? Why, or why not?

---

[1] For example, most of the *Graeff* opinion we have read covered whether it was permissible for plaintiff's counsel to make a "per diem" argument (*i.e.*, one in which a total award of damages is calculated as though it were a series of equal daily payments made over the plaintiff's actuarial life expectancy). Another example for this is the "golden rule" argument, in which counsel asks each juror to award to plaintiff what he or she would expect to receive in the plaintiff's place. Other arguments are based upon the plaintiff's poverty ("Plaintiff is too poor to afford the treatments necessary to get better....") or the defendant's wealth (if punitive damages are not involved). Each of these three arguments are almost universally condemned. Counsel may also make comments on the income tax consequences of an award. These examples barely scratch the surface of the bar's creativity in arguing about damages.

[2] The harmless part of the hypothetical has occurred several times.

Chapter Nine

"OOOOH ... GROSS!"
AGGRAVATED NEGLIGENCE, FAULT, AND PUNITIVE DAMAGES

In our prior discussions concerning breaches of obligation and damages, we have more or less assumed that the person who had breached an obligation was, at most, just oblivious — clueless possibly, but certainly no more than that.

We also limited our theorizing on the law of damages to what was meant as redress for value of the injury as opposed to the value of the promise. At the same time, however, we all know of situations where one person intentionally harms another or acts in conscious disregard of the safety of others. The case reports are replete with situations where someone fires a gun into a crowd[1] or deliberately rams another car,[2] and other such situations too numerous to mention. In this chapter, we address these situations and the way tort law accounts for them. As we shall see, it all is a question of attitude.

The study of aggravated fault or intent also is a matter of considerable controversy, because some level of aggravation must exist before a jury can award punitive damages in a tort action. As the name implies, punitive damages exist to punish persons who engage in intentional or grossly negligent tortious conduct. Punitive damages also serve as a warning or deterrent to others who would engage in similar conduct. The Texas Supreme Court has aptly summarized the controversy that underlies the law of punitive damages and aggravated fault:

> Punitive (or exemplary) damages are levied against a defendant to punish the defendant for outrageous, malicious, or otherwise morally culpable conduct. *Id.*; Texas Civil Practice & Remedies Code Annotated

§ 41.001(3) (Vernon Supp. 1994) (defining "exemplary damages" as "any damages awarded as an example to others, as a penalty, or by way of punishment"). The legal justification for punitive damages is similar to that for criminal punishment, and like criminal punishment, punitive damages require appropriate substantive and procedural safeguards to minimize the risk of unjust punishment.

Although punitive damages are levied for the public purpose of punishment and deterrence, the proceeds become a private windfall.... In contrast, criminal fines are paid to a governmental entity and used for a public benefit. Our duty in civil cases, then, like the duty of criminal courts, is to ensure that defendants who deserve to be punished in fact receive an appropriate level of punishment, while at the same time preventing punishment that is excessive or otherwise erroneous.[3]

These concerns have led courts to define with increasing precision the kinds of conduct necessary to support findings of aggravated fault. The field is by no means closed, and there will be much to say on this subject in the years ahead.

With that controversy in mind, it is possible to think of aggravated fault in terms of a ladder, with each rung representing a higher degree of improper or bad intent.

Breach of Obligation

Ground level on our ladder represents **"plain" negligence**—a breach of obligation without anything more.

Gross Negligence

The next step, usually called **gross negligence** or **recklessness**, involves something more, as our next excerpt demonstrates.

Gross negligence. A conscious act or omission that recklessly disregards a legal duty, resulting in harm to another.

Burk Royalty Co. v. Walls
616 S.W.2d 911
Supreme Court of Texas
1981

SPEARS, Justice:

* * * *

This suit for exemplary damages was brought by ... Sally Walls, individually and as next friend and guardian of Jeffery Paul Walls, Jr., her minor son, against the employer of her deceased husband, Jeffery Paul Walls. Mrs. Walls alleged that both the employer, Burk Royalty Company and its district superintendent, Kenneth Sweetnam, were grossly negligent.

* * * *

The deceased, Jeff Walls, was an employee of Burk Royalty on November 8, 1974, when he was burned to death at an oil well site in Rusk County. The fatal fire occurred while he was working as a member of a four-man crew pulling wet tubing from an oil well so that the pump at the bottom could be replaced and production restored. Walls was working on the tubing board or derrick board about 25 feet up in the derrick, above the floor of the well.

Before work had begun that day, Billy Lay, Burk's operator in charge of the well, had intended to get in his truck and look for Boyd ECL, the toolpusher in charge of the crew, to find out how they should remove the fluid that would be trapped in the tubing (wet tubing) held in by the standing valve at the bottom of the tubing. In the meantime, Sweetnam drove up to deliver the crew's paychecks, and Lay asked him instead.

* * * *

Lay suggested that an explosive charge be dropped in the well to blow a hole in the tubing and let the fluid drain out the bottom, a process called "shooting the tube." However, Sweetnam told Lay not to use that method, but rather to pull the tubing until they reached fluid, then "swab" the remainder of the tubing in the hole into the "cellar" from which it was to be hauled off by truck. During the conversation, Sweetnam said nothing about safety. He remained in his car and did not check for fire extinguishers or any other safety equipment.

After Sweetnam left, the crew began pulling tubing. Walls' job up on the tubing board was to take the 30-foot sections ("joints") of pipe as they were pulled up and place them in a rack. He had a safety belt strapped around his shoulders and waist and attached to the derrick to prevent his falling....

The tubing closest to the surface contained no fluid. Shortly before noon after pulling approximately 20 dry joints, the crew reached wet tubing, (i.e., full of fluid). Before the next joint could be pulled, some pressurized gas escaped, causing oil to spew out of the tubing up into the derrick, covering Walls' body with oil. Somehow the gas ignited and shot flames like a torch to the top of the derrick, igniting the oil on Walls' body.... Some of the crew tried unsuccessfully to extinguish the fire on Walls by throwing buckets of water at him. There were no fire extinguishers on the rig. After the fire, Walls' body hung in mid-air, suspended by his safety belt, until taken down two hours later.

* * * *

The development of the concept of gross negligence in Texas has been somewhat confusing. Various definitions have been approved by the courts depending on the type of case involved. A discussion of the concept's historical development and the gross negligence definitions used by the Courts will be helpful in arriving at the correct definition of gross negligence....

* * * *

In 1869, the Texas Constitution ... added the allowance of a recovery for exemplary damages for a "homicide through willful act or omission," regardless of the existence of any criminal proceeding arising from the homicide.... Most of the definitions of gross negligence used today come from this period, which can be termed the "Texas Railroad Statute Period."[4]

During the Texas Railroad Statute period, there were at least four attempts by this court to define gross negligence. The first ... [stated]:

Gross negligence, to be the ground for exemplary damages, should be that entire want of care which would raise a presumption of a conscious indifference to consequences. Such indifference is morally criminal, and if it leads to actual injury may well be regarded as criminal in law.... A mere act of omission or non-feasance, to be punishable by exemplary damages, should reach the borderline of a quasi-criminal act of commission or malfeasance....

Next came ... the following:

[T]he road was unsafe, and for a long time prior to the injury was known to be so to the [railroad], who, notwithstanding such knowledge, with a conscious and criminal indifference to the safety of passengers, continued to run trains without repairing its road....

[The Court's] next discussion of gross negligence ... was:

Negligence cannot be considered 'gross' unless evidenced by an entire failure to exercise care, or by the exercise of so slight a degree of care as to justify the belief that the person on whom care was incumbent was indifferent to the interest and welfare of others....

By 1888, the court ... defines gross negligence as follows:

While in a given case, 'ordinary care' may not exist, yet there may exist, at least, slight care .... Gross negligence, to be the ground for exemplary damages, should be that entire want of care which would raise the belief that the act of omission complained of was the result of a conscious indifference to the right or welfare of the person or persons to be affected by it....

* * * *

The next major legislation to influence the definition of gross negligence ... was the passage of the Workmen's Compensation Act in 1913.... Section 5 of that original act preserved the right of a deceased worker's surviving spouse and heirs to recover exemplary damages when the employee's death is occasioned by homicide, through "the wilful [*sic*] act or omission or gross negligence" of the employer....

[In 1935], the court added a requirement to the by holding that gross negligence is positive or affirmative rather than merely passive or negative as ordinary negligence often is. The court focused on the phrase "conscious indifference" and stressed that the key to gross negligence was the mental attitude of the person charged. The court quoted with approval that statement, "The rule is that recovery is permitted in, and confined to, cases where the negligence is wilful, [*sic*] or where it is so gross as to indicate wantonness or malice. The court holds ... :"

> Mere indifference is not enough. The indifference must be conscious. The indifference is to the rights or welfare of the person or persons who may be affected by the act or omission. Thus the doctrine of foreseeableness becomes important....

The last of the cases applying the active/passive test to gross negligence also introduced the "some care" test into ... gross negligence....

The rationale of the "some care" cases is that there cannot be degrees of entire want of care; there is either an entire want of care or there is not. If there is any care (i.e., "some" care) then there cannot be an entire want of care....

In 1931, the legislature enacted the Texas Guest Statute ... prohibiting a guest in a motor vehicle from recovering from the owner or operator of the vehicle "unless such accident shall have been intentional on the part of said owner or operator, or caused by his heedlessness or his reckless disregard of the rights of others." ... Rather than an active/passive of "some care" test, the meaning of gross negligence in guest statute cases was accomplished by examining the record for some evidence of an entire want of care, looking to all of the surrounding facts and circumstances, not just individual elements or facts....

> All roads lead us back to the acceptance of the ... definition which reads:
>
> > Gross negligence, to be the ground for exemplary damages, should be that entire want of care which would raise the belief that the act or omission complained of was the result of a conscious indifference to the right or welfare of the person or persons to be affected by it.
>
> .   * * * *
>
> "Heedless and reckless disregard" means more than momentary thoughtlessness, inadvertence or error of judgment. It means such an entire want of care as to indicate that the act or omission in question was the result of conscious indifference.

Now that is a loaded excerpt, but it is loaded with just about every stab that most state courts have taken in trying to deal with gross negligence.

What Identifies Gross Negligence?

Two issues arise from the foregoing excerpt. The first is whether gross negligence depends upon the degree of risk associated with the conduct, the tortfeasor's mental attitude, or both. The second is whether mental intent can be shown by objective proof — whether an objective person in the shoes of the defendant would have the required degree of indifference — or whether the actor's actual intent must be shown.

Texas courts have adopted a two-part analysis to resolve such issues:

> [T]he test for gross negligence contains both an objective and a subjective component. Subjectively, the defendant must have actual awareness of the extreme risk created by his or her conduct. Objectively, the defendant's conduct must involve an extreme degree of risk, a threshold significantly higher than the objective reasonable person test for negligence. Extreme risk is a function of both the magnitude and the probability of

the anticipated injury to the plaintiff.... [T]he "extreme risk" prong is not satisfied by a remote possibility of injury or even a high probability of minor harm, but rather the likelihood of serious injury to the plaintiff. An act or omission that is merely thoughtless, careless, or not inordinately risky cannot be grossly negligent. Only if the defendant's act or omission is unjustifiable and likely to cause serious harm can it be grossly negligent.[5]

Other states have taken different positions, but when they are distilled, the definition of gross negligence always involves some combination of **heightened degree of risk** and **awareness of that risk**.

The Element of Intent

At the same time, the existence of a heightened risk or actual awareness of risk does not necessarily mean that an intent to cause harm or some other wrongful motive exists. We can easily think of situations that confirm this general idea: hot-rodders drag racing on a public street, people who disable safety interlocks on machinery to speed production, or people who keep firearms within reach of a minor. These and many others may act with knowledge of risk but without an intent to cause harm.

The intrinsic difficulty of imposing punitive or exemplary damages in this situation is that there is no easy bright line of heightened risk or heightened awareness that distinguishes gross negligence from ordinary negligence. It is because of this problem — this potential clash between our intuitive sense of fairness and justice and the legal definitions embodied in jury instructions — that the area of gross negligence remains such a fertile field for analysis by courts and commentators.

Malice

There usually is less difficulty in reconciling our intuitive sense of fairness and definitions in jury instructions once we reach the next levels of aggravation on our ladder of fault.

In these levels we encounter the concept of **malice**, which is discussed in the next excerpt.

> *Malice.* The intent to commit a wrongful act.

Sanders v. Daniel International Corp.[6]
682 S.W.2d 803
Supreme Court of Missouri
1984

Welliver, Judge:

This case involves a malicious prosecution action[7] brought by ... Robert A. Sanders.... The criminal prosecution forming the basis for this malicious prosecution action was a misdemeanor case in which [Sanders] was charged with the attempted theft of tools and gauges valued over fifty dollars. [Sanders] was one of seven persons charged with that crime. The information[8] was sworn to by the prosecutor following a conversation in his office with agents of ... Daniel International Corporation. The prosecutor dismissed the information because he believed that insufficient information existed to proceed with the trial. Respondent then filed this action.

* * * *

A person suing on a theory of malicious prosecution must plead and prove [among other things that] the defendant's conduct was actuated by malice....

The word "malice" connotes a culpable mental state, but the term lacks any uniform definition. In a well-researched opinion in 1917, the Arizona Supreme Court observed that "[t]here are different kinds and degrees of malice as well as the nature of the evidence going to prove its existence...." Indeed, one eminent scholar commented that the term is so "slippery" that it should be banished from the law.... We have retained the term and, not surprisingly, the different kinds and degrees of malice have often been confused throughout the development of the law....

In general, the law recognizes three degrees of malice. First, there is malice in its universal sense as understood in the popular mind which means ill will, spite, personal hatred, or vindictive motives.... Such malicious conduct is founded in ill will, and is evidenced by an attempt to vex, injure or annoy another.... This type of malice is commonly referred to as "malice in fact" or "actual malice."

A second degree of malice is malice in its legal sense. The definition of legal malice has a broader meaning than the popularly understood definition of malice in fact. Malice in its enlarged legal sense embraces any improper or wrongful motive—that is, *malo animo*.... Some courts have also included within legal malice conduct that is so reckless or wantonly and willfully in disregard of one's rights that a trier of fact could infer from such conduct bad faith or *malo animo*.... Although he incorrectly termed it "malice in law," Newell aptly defined this kind of malice as something less than malice in fact and "simply ... a general wickedness or intent on the part of a person; a depraved inclination to do harm, or to disregard the rights or safety of mankind generally...."

Third, there is "malice in law." This degree of malice is properly defined as a wrongful act done intentionally without just cause or excuse.... The law imputes malice to a wrongdoer from the mere intentional doing of a wrongful act to the injury of another without legal justification or excuse .... For example, [i]f one gives a perfect stranger a blow with a deadly weapon likely to produce death, he does it of malice, because he does it intentionally without just cause or legal excuse. This is the malice of the law—a malice of pleading and proof made necessary by definitions of offenses against the law or the exigencies of the case. It is established by a conclusive legal presumption, and proof of malice in fact is not required.

An all-too-often unrecognized difference exists between this type of malice in law and malice in its legal sense. The former rests upon a legal presumption independent of any proof concerning a defendant's mental state, while the latter requires either direct or indirect proof of a mental state somewhat less culpable than malice in fact....

As some reflection suggests, adding these three degrees or levels of malice to the obliviousness of negligence and the heightened risk and awareness of gross negligence gives us a complete spectrum of intents from which to select as we determine whether punitive damages should be allowed. Just about every kind of bad intent or improper motive can be put into one of these pigeonholes.

Punitive Damages

Questions associated with punitive damages are likely to remain lively — even incendiary — for many years to come. Lawyers who represent the interests of consumers often argue that punitive damages have been a vitally important way of ensuring that "corporate America" acts responsibly. Lawyers who represent the interests of defendants and businesses argue with equal shrillness that the imposition of punitive damages costs Americans huge sums of money every year, thereby driving up the cost of everything one way or another and impeding the legitimate development of business.[9]

As always, the truth — and the proper solution in this matter — probably lies somewhere in between the opposing views. There most assuredly are situations in which the threat of a lawsuit or punitive damages causes some business to do something differently, something that prevents later trouble or cures an existing problem. There also are situations in which astronomical punitive damage awards have emerged from jury rooms; think back to the Texaco/Penzoil litigation, which involved a jury award of punitive damages in the billions. Neither side truly has the better of this argument, but as this book is written, it seems clear that those who favor the restrictions on punitive damages have carried the day.

Legislatures, state appellate courts, and the United States Supreme Court all have jumped into the fray over punitive damages, and each has added spin to the field. A brief survey of what has happened will allow you to understand better what is at issue in cases you undertake.

In a series of cases, the United States Supreme Court has considered whether or not awards of punitive damages are constitutional under the "excessive fines" clause of the Eighth Amendment of the United States Constitution, and whether the procedure used in state courts for awarding punitive damages meets the standards contained in the due process clause of the Fourteenth Amendment.

The Supreme Court understandably has been reluctant to invoke the Eighth Amendment's protections (which run to criminal cases) in civil lawsuits, but it has held that due process protections do apply to the process by which punitive damages are awarded. To date, the Supreme Court's most significant holdings in the field have limited the extent that one state's courts can impose punitive damages based upon conduct in another state.[10]

Regulation of Punitive Damages

Partly because of the Supreme Court rulings and partly for their own reasons, state legislatures and judges have taken numerous steps to limit or regulate punitive damages. These take the following general forms:

Higher Burdens of Proof

As you may recall, plaintiffs in a tort case will prevail if they prove their case by a preponderance of the evidence. As we discussed previously in Chapter Six (*see* p. 124), this concept means that the plaintiff prevails if its evidence is even slightly more persuasive than that offered by the defendant. It is not a difficult standard to meet.

In order to make punitive damages more difficult to obtain, some states have required plaintiffs seeking such damages to prove that portion of their case "beyond a reasonable doubt," the same standard used in criminal cases, or "by the great weight of the evidence," something more than a preponderance of the evidence but less than beyond a reasonable doubt. Proponents of this approach argue that it ensures that punitive damages do not serve as a form of supplementary compensation for aggrieved plaintiffs.

Limits on the Recoverable Amount

In order to prevent punitive damages from becoming a windfall, some states have limited the amount of punitive damages that any single plaintiff may recover. In Texas, for example, the Texas Civil Practice and Remedies Code provides that an award of punitive damages generally may not exceed four times the amount of compensatory damages awarded in most situations. Other states have similar limitations.

Special Trial Procedures

One of the most common complaints made by defendants was that evidence relevant to questions of aggravated fault or punitive damages, which often was highly inflammatory, could be heard by the jury before they had decided whether the defendant was liable in the first place. This evidence, which usually showed that the plaintiff was poor and the defendant was a rich business or that there had been other similar accidents, allegedly could cause the jury to put aside its impartiality and find in favor of the poor little guy.[11]

To avoid such problems, courts and legislatures have used bifurcated trials or required plaintiffs to make a *prima facie* showing outside the jury's presence that punitive damages should be awarded.

Jury Instructions

In response to criticism from scholars and the United States Supreme Court, most states have rewritten the instructions given to juries in cases where punitive damages are sought. Such instructions are necessary to prevent the punitive damage process from becoming a "roving commission," lawyerese for situations where the jury is free to do whatever it wants without any restraint from the court.

Despite — or because of — these efforts, the whole question of punitive damages remains an open one. There will be more swings and developments in this field in the future. As you watch and participate in them, don't forget that the levels of aggravated intent we have discussed in this chapter play a significant role in many of the torts we are about to study, whether or not punitive damages can be awarded.

Key Words and Phrases

breach of obligation
by the great weight of the evidence
degree of risk
exemplary damages
gross negligence
intent
malice in law
malo amino
plain negligence
preponderance of the evidence
punitive damages
recklessness

Review Questions

1. Using the discussion found in *Burk* and other resources, explain the difference between

    a. negligence and gross negligence
    b. gross negligence and malice

2. Locate and read the Eighth and Fourteenth Amendments to the U.S. Constitution. Do you agree with court rulings that have linked them to the issue of excessive punitive damages? Why or why not? Explain your thinking.

3. Suppose you are on Kenneth Sweetnam's defense team in *Burk.* What arguments or legal theories might be advanced on Mr. Sweetnam's behalf?

   Now suppose you are on Mrs. Wall's legal team in *Burk.* What arguments or legal theories might be advanced on her behalf?

---

[1] *Misle v. State Farm Fire & Cas. Co.,* 908 S.W.2d 289 (Tex. App.–Austin 1996, no writ).

[2] *Southern Farm Bureau Ins. Co. v. Brock,* 659 S.W.2d 165 (Tex. App.– Amarillo 1983, writ ref'd n.r.e.).

[3] *Transportation Ins. Co. v. Moriel,* 879 S.W.2d 10 (Tex. 1994).

[4] As a historical aside, early railroading was extraordinarily dangerous. The idea of exemplary damages in railroad cases sprang generally from a desire to regulate the railroads and make them safer for passengers and workers alike.

[5] *Moriel, supra note 3,* at 21–22.

[6] Internal quotations and citations omitted.

[7] We discuss the tort of malicious prosecution more fully in Chapter Thirteen. For now, it is sufficient to say that the tort involves the damages that may result from the wrongful filing of a criminal charge or a civil action.

[8] For those not familiar with the term, an "information" is a formal pleading filed to institute criminal charges. The difference between an information and an indictment, the more familiar term, is that the former is signed and filed only by a prosecutor, while a grand jury submits the latter.

[9] A few states do not permit the award of punitive damages in any situation, thereby avoiding all of the ruckus!

[10] The ruling is very significant to businesses who sell or distribute products in more than one state. Assume that XYZ Company makes a defective widget and distributes it in all 50 states. It faces the risk of different awards of punitive

damages in each state, and, if each state's law permits such damages to be imposed for conduct outside of the state, XYZ Company can be penalized 50 times for the same conduct. Such a result hardly is fair, even if awards of punitive damages otherwise would be justifiable.

[11] Having offered and objected to this kind of evidence in different trials over the years, the author has come to the unscientific, and probably grossly presumptuous, conclusion that this issue is more in the minds of lawyers than any other. There certainly can be evidence so prejudicial that merely stating it is enough to poison the minds of jurors, but it strains credulity to suppose that jurors *don't* assume that the average plaintiff is a good deal poorer than a large corporation, that insurance isn't involved in the case somehow, and so on. Similarly, it doesn't take a lot of time in voir dire to conclude that there are a good number of people who do feel that large corporations should be stuck, that it doesn't matter what they do because insurance will cover it anyway and soon. The distinction is between thinking that our evidence drives people to the conclusions, when in fact they arrive for jury duty with them.

Chapter Ten

TORT LIABILITY FOR
DEFECTIVE PRODUCTS

By the early twentieth century, the concept of negligence was firmly rooted in the law of torts. Yet again, however, the world had rendered the law obsolescent.

New large and very impersonal industries turned out huge quantities of mass produced products sold through chain stores and catalogue outlets. People no longer bought goods from other people. Privity — that old-fashioned concept of face-to-face dealing based upon contractual concepts of offer and acceptance, bargain and consideration — had given way to impersonal levels of wholesalers, jobbers, drummers, and manufacturers.

As people began to be injured by these new mass produced products (or by making them, the problem that gave rise to modern workers' compensation laws), the lawsuits followed, and lawyers began to deal with the issues associated with this change in the world.

Contract Law

Historically, the first efforts to address the problems caused by mass produced products arose from contract law. This was natural because issues of product quality and durability — and safety, to the extent that it was an issue — were issues of negotiation between direct buyers and sellers, and thus a part of a contract.

(For those who have not yet taken a course in contract law, these issues came to be known as **warranties**, representations by the maker or seller about some aspect of a product that could be the basis for a lawsuit if breached.)[1]

Warranties, like so much else in the law of contracts, depended on privity, the face-to-face relationship of the parties to the contract, and that certainly did not exist in most transactions involving mass produced goods. The response of contract law was two related concepts, the implied warranty, and "transparency" for privity purposes of the wholesalers and jobbers and distributors between maker and buyer.

The Concept of Transparency

Every time a buyer fills out a manufacturer's warranty registration card, that buyer demonstrates the transparency concept. Even though the product passes from its hands through a chain of wholesalers and retailers, the manufacturer is the one giving the warranty. Filling out the card—in most cases, simply using the product—creates the contract. Even though maker and user never actually talk face-to-face, the law implies the privity. It assumes the "middlemen" did not exist.

The Concept of Implied Warranty

Implied warranties, the other concept developed from contract law, are somewhat more complex. Everyone has heard the adage *caveat emptor,* meaning "Let the buyer beware." Under this doctrine, any product defects or any deviations in quality or durability from what the buyer wanted or needed were not the seller's responsibility. The buyer, after all, could examine the goods and pick what he or she wanted.

This may have worked well in ancient times, but by the time of the Industrial Revolution, it was a "lemon." The response of contract law was to develop certain warranties that would be assumed to exist in every transaction. Some of these implied warranties can wait for a course in contract law, but the implied warranty of **merchantability** is important to this chapter.

Under the implied warranty of merchantability, every item sold is impliedly warranted by the manufacturer or seller to be **fit for the ordinary purposes for which such goods are used**.

As can be seen, this standard is a "floor," and not much of one at that. So long as a product is "as good as" the ordinary run of similar products, it is merchantable. Moreover, the idea of an implied warranty does not solve all of the privity problems. We have little trouble with implying a warranty in favor of the buyer of a product, but what if he or she loans it out? How does one deal with the proverbial used car?

From Contract Law to Tort Law

Implied warranties were not entirely satisfactory solutions to this issue, and by the beginning of the 20th century the law had turned to tort concepts, which involved public duties as a way of solving the problem.

The first, and still the most important, case in this field involved a wooden automobile wheel that broke. The opinion in this case was written by Justice Cardozo, who would later write the majority opinion in the *Palsgraf* case we have already read. Let us see how he addressed the legal issues associated with a mass-produced world:

MacPherson v. Buick Motor Co.
217 N.Y. 382, 111 N.E. 1050
Court of Appeals of New York
1916

Cardozo, J.:

The defendant is a manufacturer of automobiles. It sold an automobile to a retail dealer. The retail dealer resold to the plaintiff. While the plaintiff was in the car, it suddenly collapsed. He was thrown out and injured. One of the wheels was made of defective wood, and its spokes crumbled into fragments. The wheel was not made by the defendant; it was bought from another manufacturer. There is evidence, however, that its defects could have been discovered by reasonable inspection, and that inspection was omitted. There is no claim that the defendant knew of the defect and willfully concealed it.... The charge is one, not of fraud, but of negligence. The question to be determined is whether the defendant owed a duty of care and vigilance to any one but the immediate purchaser.

The foundations of this branch of the law, at least in this state, were laid in *Thomas v. Winchester* (6 N.Y. 397). A poison was falsely labeled. The sale was made to a druggist, who in turn sold to a customer. The customer recovered damages from the seller who affixed the label. "The defendant's negligence," it was said, "put human life in imminent danger." A poison falsely labeled is likely to injure any one who gets it. Because the danger is to be foreseen, there is a duty to avoid the injury....

[I]n *Devlin v. Smith* (89 N.Y. 470)[, t]he defendant, a contractor, built a scaffold for a painter. The painter's servants were injured. The contractor was held liable. He knew that the scaffold, if improperly constructed, was a most dangerous trap. He knew that it was to be used by the workmen. He was building it for that very purpose. Building it for their use, he owed them a duty, irrespective of his contract with their master, to build it with care.

From *Devlin v. Smith* we pass over intermediate cases and turn to the latest case in this court in which *Thomas v. Winchester* was followed. That case is *Statler v. Ray Mfg. Co.* (195 N.Y. 478, 480). The defendant manufactured a large coffee urn. It was installed in a restaurant. When heated, the urn exploded and injured the plaintiff. We held that the manufacturer was liable. We said that the urn "was of such a character inherently that, when applied to the purposes for which it was designed, it was liable to become a source of great danger to many people if not carefully and properly constructed." It may be that *Devlin v. Smith* and *Statler v. Ray Mfg. Co.* have extended the rule of *Thomas v. Winchester*. If so, this court is committed to the extension. The defendant argues that things imminently dangerous to life are poisons, explosives, deadly weapons—things whose normal function it is to injure or destroy. But whatever the rule in *Thomas v. Winchester* may once have been, it has no longer that restricted meaning. A large coffee urn (*Statler v. Ray Mfg. Co., supra*) may have within itself, if negligently made, the potency of danger, yet no one thinks of it as an implement whose normal function is destruction....

Devlin v. Smith was decided in 1882. A year later a very similar case came before the Court of Appeal in England (*Heaven v. Pender, L.R.,* 11 Q.B.D. 503). We find in the opinion of Brett, M. R., afterwards Lord Esher (p. 510), the same conception of a duty, irrespective of contract, imposed upon the manufacturer by the law itself: "Whenever one person supplies goods, or machinery, or the like, for the purpose of their being used by another person under such circumstances that every one of ordinary sense would, if he thought, recognize at once that unless he used ordinary care and skill with regard to the condition of the thing supplied or the mode of supplying it, there will be danger of injury to the person or property of him for whose use the thing is supplied, and who is to use it, a duty arises to use ordinary care and skill as the condition or manner of supplying such thing." He then points out that for a neglect of such ordinary care or skill whereby injury happens, the appropriate remedy is an action for negligence. The right to enforce this liability is not to be confined to the immediate buyer. The right, he says, extends to the persons or class of persons for whose use the thing is supplied. It is enough that the goods "would in all probability be used at once ... before a reasonable opportunity for discovering any defect which might exist," and that the thing supplied is of such a nature "that a neglect of ordinary care or skill as to its condition or the manner of supplying it would probably cause danger to the person or property of the person for whose use it was supplied, and who was about to use it." On the other hand, he would exclude a case "in which the goods are supplied under circumstances in which it would be a chance by whom they would be used or whether they would be used or not, or whether they would be before there would probably be means of observing any defect," or where the goods are of such a nature that "a want of care or skill as to their condition or the manner of supplying them would not probably produce danger of injury to person or property...." His opinion has been criticized "as requiring every man to take affirmative precautions to protect his neighbors as well as to refrain from injuring them...." But its tests and standards, at least in their underlying principles, with whatever qualifications may be called for as they are applied to varying conditions, are the tests and standards of our law.

We hold, then, that the principle of *Thomas v. Winchester* is not limited to poisons, explosives, and things of like nature, to things which in their normal operation are implements of destruction. If the nature of a thing is such that it is reasonably certain to place life and limb in peril when negligently made, it is then a thing of danger. Its nature gives warning of the consequences to be expected. If to the element of danger there is added knowledge that the thing will be used by persons other than the purchaser, and used without new tests then, irrespective of contract, the manufacturer of this thing of danger is under a duty to make it carefully.
That is as far as we are required to go for the decision of this case. There must be knowledge of a danger, not merely possible, but probable. It is possible to use almost anything in a way that will make it dangerous if defective. That is not enough to charge the manufacturer with a duty independent of his contract. Whether a given thing is dangerous may be sometimes a question for the court and sometimes a question for the jury. There must also be knowledge that in the usual course of events the danger will be shared by others than the buyer. Such knowledge may often be inferred from the nature of the transaction. But it is possible that even knowledge of the danger and of the use will not always be enough. The proximity or remoteness of the relation is a factor to be considered. We are

dealing now with the liability of the manufacturer of the finished product, who puts it on the market to be used without inspection by his customers. If he is negligent, where danger is to be foreseen, a liability will follow....

From this survey of the decisions, there thus emerges a definition of the duty of a manufacturer which enables us to measure this defendant's liability. Beyond all question, the nature of an automobile gives warning of probable danger if its construction is defective. This automobile was designed to go fifty miles an hour. Unless its wheels were sound and strong, injury was almost certain. It was as much a thing of danger as a defective engine for a railroad. The defendant knew the danger. It knew also that the care would be used by persons other than the buyer. This was apparent from its size; there were seats for three persons. It was apparent also from the fact that the buyer was a dealer in cars, who bought to resell. The maker of this car supplied it for the use of purchasers from the dealer just as plainly as the contractor in *Devlin v. Smith* supplied the scaffold for use by the servants of the owner. The dealer was indeed the one person of whom it might be said with some approach to certainty that by him the car would not be used. Yet the defendant would have us say that he was the one person whom it was under a legal duty to protect. The law does not lead us to so inconsequent a conclusion. Precedents drawn from the days of travel by stagecoach do not fit the conditions of travel today. The principle that the danger must be imminent does not change, but the things subject to the principle do change. They are whatever the needs of life in a developing civilization require them to be....

*   *   *   *

We think the defendant was not absolved from a duty of inspection because it bought the wheels from a reputable manufacturer. It was not merely a dealer in automobiles. It was a manufacturer of automobiles. It was responsible for the finished product. It was not at liberty to put the finished product on the market without subjecting the component parts to ordinary and simple tests (*Richmond & Danville R.R. Co. v. Elliot*, 149 U.S. 266, 272). Under the charge of the trial judge, nothing more was required of it. The obligation to inspect must vary with the nature of the thing to be inspected. The more probable the danger, the greater the need of caution.

*   *   *   *

The judgment should be affirmed.

Notice the language in this opinion: "It was a manufacturer of automobiles. It was responsible for the finished product. It was not at liberty to put the finished product on the market without subjecting the component parts to ordinary and simple tests...."

This is a statement of economic policy, pure and simple. The burden of testing — really, the cost of conducting "ordinary and simple tests" — is on the manufacturer of the finished product. Perform the tests, says the court, and avoid the costs associated with injuries from defective products. Fail to do the tests at the risk of being liable to any reasonably foreseeable user of the goods, not just the person with whom the manufacturer has contracted.

Liability for Defective Products

But letting a manufacturer off the hook simply by conducting tests or inspecting a product doesn't really go very far to ensure a product's safety. "Reasonable" tests may not reveal latent defects or account for unintended or unforeseen product uses. And so, the doctrine of liability for defective products evolved, as the next cases show.[2]

Greenman v. Yuba Power Products, Inc.
59 Cal.2d 57, 377 P.2d 897, 27 Cal.Rptr. 697
Supreme Court of California, *En Banc*
1963

Traynor, J.

Plaintiff brought this action for damages against the retailer and the manufacturer of a Shopsmith, a combination power tool that could be used as a saw, drill, and wood lathe. He saw a Shopsmith demonstrated by the retailer and studied a brochure prepared by the manufacturer. He decided he wanted a Shopsmith for his home workshop, and his wife bought and gave him one for Christmas in 1955.

In 1957 he bought the necessary attachments to use the Shopsmith as a lathe for turning a large piece of wood he wished to make into a chalice. After he had worked on the piece of wood several times without difficulty, it suddenly flew out of the machine and struck him on the forehead, inflicting serious injuries. About ten and a half months later, he gave the retailer and the manufacturer written notice of claimed breaches of warranties and filed a complaint against them alleging such breaches and negligence.

After a trial before a jury, the court ruled that there was no evidence that the retailer was negligent or had breached any express warranty and that the manufacturer was not liable for the breach of any implied warranty. Accordingly, it submitted to the jury only the cause of action alleging breach of implied warranties against the retailer and the causes of action alleging negligence and breach of express warranties against the manufacturer. The jury returned a verdict for the retailer against plaintiff and for plaintiff against the manufacturer in the amount of $65,000.

The trial court denied the manufacturer's motion for a new trial and entered judgment on the verdict. The manufacturer and plaintiff appeal. Plaintiff seeks a reversal of the part of the judgment in favor of the retailer, however, only in the event that the part of the judgment against the manufacturer is reversed.

Plaintiff introduced substantial evidence that his injuries were caused by defective design and construction of the Shopsmith. His expert witnesses testified that inadequate set screws were used to hold parts of the machine together so that normal vibration caused the tailstock of the lathe to move away from the piece of wood being turned, permitting it to fly out of the lathe. They also testified that there were other more positive ways of fastening the parts of the machine together, the use of which would have prevented the accident. The jury could therefore reasonably have concluded that the manufacturer negligently constructed the Shopsmith. The jury could also reasonably have concluded that statements in the manufacturer's brochure were untrue, that they constituted express warranties, and that plaintiff's injuries were caused by their breach.

* * * *

[T]o impose strict liability on the manufacturer under the circumstances of this case, it was not necessary for plaintiff to establish an express warranty.... A manufacturer is strictly liable in tort when an article he places on the market, knowing that it is to be used without inspection for defects, proves to have a defect that causes injury to a human being. Recognized first in the case of unwholesome food products, such liability has now been extended to a variety of other products that create as great or greater hazards if defective....

Although in these cases strict liability has usually been based on the theory of an express or implied warranty running from the manufacturer to the plaintiff, the abandonment of the requirement of a contract between them, the recognition that the liability is not assumed by agreement but imposed by law ... and the refusal to permit the manufacturer to define the scope of its own responsibility for defective products [citations omitted] make clear that the liability is not one governed by the law of contract warranties but by the law of strict liability in tort. Accordingly, rules defining and governing warranties that were developed to meet the needs of commercial transactions cannot properly be invoked to govern the manufacturer's liability to those injured by their defective products unless those rules also serve the purposes for which such liability is imposed.

We need not recanvass the reasons for imposing strict liability on the manufacturer. They have been fully articulated .... The purpose of such liability is to insure that the costs of injuries resulting from defective products are borne by the manufacturers that put such products on the market rather than by the injured persons who are powerless to protect themselves. Sales warranties serve this purpose fitfully at best. (*See* Prosser, "Strict Liability to the Consumer," 69 Yale L.J. 1099, 1124–1134.)

In the present case, for example, plaintiff was able to plead and prove an express warranty only because he read and relied on the representations of the Shopsmith's ruggedness contained in the manufacturer's brochure. Implicit in the machine's presence on the market, however, was a representation that it would safely do the jobs for which it was built. Under these circumstances, it should not be controlling whether plaintiff selected the machine because of the statements in the brochure, or because of the machine's own appearance of excellence that belied the defect lurking beneath the surface, or because he merely assumed that it would safely do the jobs it was built to do. It should not be controlling whether the details of the sales from manufacturer to retailer and from retailer to plaintiff's wife were such that one or more of the implied warranties of the sales act arose. "The remedies of injured consumers ought not to be made to depend upon the intricacies of the law of sales." (*Ketterer v. Armour & Co.*, D.C., 200 F. 322, 323; *Klein v. Duchess Sandwich Co.*, 14 Cal.2d 272, 282, 93 P.2d 799.)

To establish the manufacturer's liability, it was sufficient that plaintiff proved that he was injured while using the Shopsmith in a way it was intended to be used as a result of a defect in design and manufacture of which plaintiff was not aware that made the Shopsmith unsafe for its intended use.

* * * *

The judgment is affirmed.

More than any other jurist after Cardozo, Roger Traynor, author of the *Greenman* opinion, was responsible for coalescing the law of defective products into a cohesive whole. Traynor's single sentence explaining and defining the principle — "A manufacturer is strictly liable in tort when an article he places on the market, knowing that it is to be used without inspection for defects, proves to have a defect that causes injury to a human being." — became the basis for almost all further development in the field and for a famous section of the *Restatement of Torts (Second)*, section 402A, that sought to be a comprehensive statement of this principle. *Greenman* and *Restatement* § 402A found homes almost everywhere, as the next case shows:

Keener v. Dayton Electric Manufacturing Co.
445 S.W.2d 362
Supreme Court of Missouri, Division 2
1969

Donnelly, J.

This is a products liability case. Plaintiff, widow of Harold Keener, sued for his wrongful death and received a verdict against Dayton Electric Manufacturing Company in the amount of $20,000. The product in question is a sump pump sold by Dayton as a wholesale distributor. In 1964, L. E. Whittaker, a handyman electrician, installed the pump in the basement of Joy Hollan's house. It rested in a sump in the basement floor and served to pump water out of the basement. Whittaker did not ground the pump when he installed it.

On September 21, 1965, after several days of rain, Joy Hollan went to her basement and found it flooded to a depth described as "ankle deep." She called upon her friends, the Keeners, for assistance. After attempting unsuccessfully to empty the basement with a rented gasoline-powered pump, Harold Keener went to work on the Dayton pump. With the pump plugged into an electric outlet, standing ankle deep in water with no rubber gloves or rubber boots, he stooped over and lifted the pump from the sump. When the pump cleared the floor of the sump, Keener received an electric shock which resulted in his death.

The pump, when sold by Dayton, was not equipped with a ground wire or a overload protector. Plaintiff alleges the pump was defective in these respects and seeks on appeal to sustain her recovery under a theory of strict liability in tort.

The law involving products liability has undergone dramatic change in recent years.... In *Morrow v. Caloric Appliance Corporation*, Mo. Sup., 372 S.W.2d 41, this Court *en banc* held that privity of contract was not necessary in order for the purchasers of a gas range to recover on implied warranty for fire damage against the manufacturer.... We now adopt the rule of strict liability in tort stated in 2 *Restatement, Law of Torts*, Second, § 402A, as follows:

(1)   One who sells any product in a defective condition reasonably dangerous to the user or consumer or to his property is subject to liability for physical harm thereby caused to the ultimate user or consumer, or to his property, if

(a)   the seller is engaged in the business of selling such a product, and
(b)   it is expected to and does reach the user or consumer without substantial change in the condition in which it is sold.

(2)   The rule stated in Subsection (1) applies although

(a)   the seller has exercised all possible care in the preparation and sale of his product, and
(b)   the user or consumer has not bought the product from or entered into any contractual relation with the seller.

We adopt this rule of strict liability in tort for at least three reasons:

(1) "* * * The purpose of such liability is to insure that the costs of injuries resulting from defective products are borne by the manufacturers (and sellers) that put such products on the market rather than by the injured persons who are powerless to protect themselves." *Greenman v. Yuba Power Products, Inc.*, 59 Cal.2d 57, 27 Cal.Rptr. 697, 377 P.2d 897, 901, 13 A.L.R.2d 1049.

(2) "* * * The main advantage to Missouri courts in fully adopting the *Restatement* theory could be release from the shackles of warranty language. Whether the words 'strict liability' or 'implied warranty' or both combined are used, the difference in Missouri would not be one of substance since our courts are clearly recognizing the tort nature of the liability imposed. However, using the language of the *Restatement* would avoid innumerable vexing problems that have arisen in other jurisdictions where the device of warranty is used to impose strict liability." Krauskopf, "Products Liability," 32 Mo.L.Rev. 459, 469.

(3) It is essential now that the Bench and Bar of Missouri be given some sense of direction in products liability cases.

We turn then to the questions raised on this appeal:

* * * *

Should May Dayton, a wholesale distributor, be held liable? We hold that it may. The *Restatement* position is that § 402A, *supra*, "applies to any person engaged in the business of selling products for use or consumption." 2 *Restatement, supra*, § 402A, p. 350.

Was Harold Keener a "user or consumer" and, therefore, entitled to the protection afforded under § 402A, *supra*? The *Restatement* position is that "user" includes "those who are utilizing ... (the product) for the purpose of doing work upon it." 2 *Restatement, supra*, § 402A, p. 354. We hold that Harold Keener was a "user" under § 402A, *supra*....

Was Harold Keener guilty of "contributory negligence as a matter of law," as asserted by Dayton? We hold he was not. Contributory negligence, as we ordinarily apply it, is not a defense to strict liability. The "defense which consists of voluntarily and unreasonably encountering a known danger * * * will, in general, relieve the defendant of strict liability...." The *Restatement* position is that if the user "discovers the defect and is aware of the danger, and nevertheless proceeds unreasonably to make use of the product and is injured by it, he is barred from recovery." 2 *Restatement, supra*, § 402A, p. 356. In 3 *Restatement, Law of Torts*, First, § 524, this defense is referred to as "contributory fault."

Dayton urges that Harold Keener must be convicted of "contributory negligence as a matter of law" because he lifted the pump out of the sump while standing ankle deep in water, with no rubber gloves or rubber boots, and with the pump plugged into an electric outlet. Dayton argues that this "was a voluntary exposure to a known danger."

In a sense, the argument is of some persuasion. However, it misses the mark in this case involving strict liability in tort. There is no evidence, direct or circumstantial, on this record on this appeal that Harold Keener had knowledge that the pump was not equipped with a ground wire or an overload protector. Therefore, there is no evidence justifying a finding that

Harold Keener became chargeable with knowledge of the "dangerous potentialities" of the pump by reason of such defects. *Morrow v. Caloric Appliance Corporation,* supra, 372 S.W.2d 41, 57. We agree that Harold Keener voluntarily exposed himself to a dangerous situation if he knew the pump was defective. However, there is no evidence to show that he knew the pump was defective. In these circumstances, plaintiff is not barred from recovery under a theory of "contributory fault."

In order to establish Dayton's liability, must the jury be required to find that Harold Keener was killed while using the pump in a way it was intended to be used? We hold that it must. The *Restatement* position is that a "product is not in a defective condition when it is safe for normal handling and consumption. If the injury results from abnormal handling, * * *, the seller is not liable." *2 Restatement, supra,* § 402A, p. 351.

* * * *

If the evidence supports it on re-trial, an instruction in substantially the following form should be used:

> Your verdict must be for plaintiff if you believe:
>
> First, plaintiff was (here insert statutory qualification required to bring wrongful death action), and
>
> Second, defendant sold the sump pump, and
>
> Third, the sump pump, as sold by defendant, was defective and therefore dangerous when put to a use reasonably anticipated, and
>
> Fourth, when Harold Keener used the sump pump it was in substantially the same condition as when sold by defendant, and
>
> Fifth, Harold Keener used the sump pump in a manner reasonably anticipated and, as a direct result of the sump pump being defective, died (unless you believe plaintiff is not entitled to recover by reason of Instruction No. ___ (here insert number of affirmative defense instruction)....

Dayton will then be entitled to a converse of plaintiff's verdict-directing instruction. MAI No. 29.01. This will enable Dayton to argue that Harold

Keener, when he lifted the pump from the sump under the circumstances in evidence, put the pump to an abnormal use, did not use the pump in a manner reasonably anticipated, and did not use it in a way it was intended to be used.

If the evidence supports it on retrial, Dayton may also submit the affirmative defense of "contributory fault." Harold Keener's knowledge of the defective and dangerous condition of the pump may be proved by circumstantial evidence. But the circumstances must be such that the necessary fact may be inferred therefrom and must reasonably follow, so that the conclusion so reached is not the result of guesswork, conjecture or speculation....

The judgment is reversed and the cause remanded.

After cases like *Greenman* and *Keener*, liability for defective products has grown considerably. Notice first that "reasonably anticipated use" in the foregoing definition includes misuse. In other words, if a person used a product in a way different from the way the manufacturer intended the product to be used, liability would still attach if the misuse involved was something that reasonably should have been foreseen by the seller or manufacturer of the product.

Second, if the manufacturer made one million widgets and only one of them caused harm, it could be liable for it regardless of the quality of the other 999,999!

And third, the user's negligence — his or her failure to read the instruction book, for example — was not a defense. The defense of contributory fault — not to be confused with more recent statutory or common-law concepts of fault that include negligence — required the user to have actual awareness of the defect and to misuse the product with that knowledge.

So, if you manufacture a product that has some risk associated with it, even if it is manufactured safely — power tools or chemicals immediately come to mind — what can you do to avoid liability? The obvious answer, and the one upon which the legal system relied, was the concept of **warning**.

The Concept of Warning

If the manufacturer gave an effective warning of the dangers associated with use or misuse of the product in such a way as to be visible and understood by a reasonable user, it would not be liable for injuries against which it had warned.

The key word here is "effective," and defining it has raised as many questions as it has solved. Is a warning in English effective if the user speaks only Spanish, as is quite possible in certain parts of the United States? What if the user speaks only Vietnamese? Or Ibo? Is a textual warning sufficient if pictures or pictographs would better convey the danger? What priority should be given to multiple warnings?[3] Is it enough to say, "Misuse of this product may result in serious injury or death"? Must specific possible injuries be listed? What if the actual injury sustained is not on the list?

As you can see from this series of questions, all of which have arisen in actual cases involving warnings, and many of which the author has confronted in his own practice, this is hardly a precise science. Issues associated with warnings are extremely fact-intensive, and rarely can be resolved on a general basis. The product, the magnitude of the risk, the likelihood of its occurrence, and the extent to which the harm can occur through "normal" or reasonably foreseeable use of the product all enter into play.

Effects of the Warning Concept on the Legal Team

Now consider what these product liability standards mean to practitioners. These standards are expert-intensive. Showing that a product is unreasonably dangerous means finding an engineer or other expert who could show that there existed a manufacturing defect — a bad weld or weak structure, to give two examples — or a design defect such as the lack of a ground wire or overload protector, as in *Keener*.

Plaintiffs attempt to show the existence of a manufacturing defect or that a feasible alternative design would have prevented the accident at little or no cost. Defendants hire experts to explain why the products were not defective or that the purported redesign is not feasible. In some situations, these experts become almost a traveling road show, choosing up sides and testifying in many different states about the same products or designs.[4]

There are experts who testify — pro and con — on all manner of products, making themselves and their credibility the focus of many cases. Similarly, the manufacturer who uses its own employee, no matter how qualified, to opine on a product's safety or quality runs grave risks of the testimony being tainted because of the witness's supposed bias in favor of his or her employer. Warning cases generate the same kinds of issues.

Another issue for practitioners concerns the product itself. Suppose a manufacturer made modifications to an existing and allegedly defective product. Should the fact of those modifications be admissible? What about other incidents involving the same or similar products?

The problems are fairly obvious. If every improvement in a product could be used as evidence to show that prior versions of it were faulty, manufacturers would be tempted not to improve their products in order to avoid liability. Plaintiffs would want to show the modifications to demonstrate that design changes and improvements were feasible.

Similar concerns existed with respect to "other incident" evidence — evidence of other problems with or injuries from the product. User modification of products also adds difficulties. For example, in one case involving safety rigging used by construction workers, the workers would remove the device that locked the safety snap hook in place because it slowed them down as they moved across the structure they were building. It was common knowledge that this was done. The locking snap worked well *unless* it was disabled, but there did exist alternative designs that made modification of the hook more difficult. Query: Does the removal by the user constitute an abnormal use of the product or a foreseeable misuse of the snap hook that the manufacturers should have accounted for?

Try this one: XYZ Corp. has a catalog full of safety equipment that works very well when used in accord with the description in the catalogue. But everyone knows that people buy things from catalogues and use them for purposes other than those for which they are intended. If the buyer does this, is it an abnormal use, or should the manufacturer be responsible?

In short, the question reduces to a single enduring issue: to what extent is the manufacturer or seller of a product responsible for the conduct, misconduct, forgetfulness, laziness, or downright stupidity of the user?

Vaccine Cases

The Section 402A approach creates a relatively heavy burden on product manufacturers and sellers in this area, on the theory that they get the profits from products and should be responsible at least for avoiding the shoddiest and least safe approaches to manufacture.

By the 1970s, another limitation on the doctrine came to light through problems with vaccines, particularly those for swine flu and DPT, and certain drugs. Those of a certain age may remember the dreadful diseases diphtheria, whooping cough, and tetanus, and how medical science eradicated them through mass immunization programs. Surely all would agree that these are important, even vital, societal goals.

But what was less well known was that a very small percentage of those given the vaccines reacted to them. A small number of individuals who received DPT vaccine contracted a seizure disorder. Small numbers of individuals who received other vaccines also had serious complications. These individuals, often children, and their families, brought lawsuits to recover for the injuries they received from these products. Companies that manufactured vaccines faced extremely high litigation costs and the loss of insurance coverage; many believed that they would be unable to continue manufacturing vaccines unless they received some protection.

Congress responded to these issues by passing the National Childhood Vaccine Injury Act, 42 U.S.C. §§ 300aa-1 to 300aa-34, which provided special methods for dealing with vaccine-related injuries. But the real problem was still in the idea of "unreasonable danger" contained in the definition of strict liability: In assessing danger, does one look only to the injured plaintiff or to all who receive the product? If the benefits of using a product like a vaccine or drug are substantial, do these count as an offset to risks that may be associated with the product?

Here, of course, the recipients of the vaccine have little choice. They cannot choose between competing brands, and in many cases cannot even forego the inoculation, as is the case where school districts impose immunization requirements on entering students. But the problem still exists and changes very little even in these unusual circumstances. How much danger are we willing to accept?

The next case excerpt examines some of these issues as they have developed, and it also shows what has become of the idea of warning.

Uniroyal Goodrich Tire Co v. Martinez
977 S.W.2d 328
Supreme Court of Texas
1998

Phillips, C.J.:

We must decide whether a manufacturer who knew of a safer alternative product design is liable in strict products liability for injuries caused by the use of its product that the user could have avoided by following the product's warnings. The court of appeals held that the mere fact that a product bears an adequate warning does not conclusively establish that the product is not defective.... Because we agree, we affirm the judgment of the court of appeals.

I.

Roberto Martinez, together with his wife and children, sued Uniroyal Goodrich Tire Company ("Goodrich"), The Budd Company, and Ford Motor Company for personal injuries Martinez suffered when he was struck by an exploding 16" Goodrich tire that he was mounting on a 16.5-inch rim. Attached to the tire was a prominent warning label containing yellow and red highlights and a pictograph of a worker being thrown into the air by an exploding tire. The label stated conspicuously:

DANGER

NEVER MOUNT A 16" SIZE DIAMETER TIRE ON A 16.5" RIM.
Mounting a 16" tire on a 16.5" rim can cause severe injury or death.
While it is possible to pass a 16" diameter tire over the lip or flange
of a 16.5" size diameter rim, it cannot position itself against the rim
flange. If an attempt is made to seat the bead by inflating the tire, the
tire bead will break with explosive force.

* * * *

NEVER inflate a tire which is lying on the floor or other flat surface.
Always use a tire mounting machine with a hold-down device or
safety cage or bolt to vehicle axle.

NEVER inflate to seat beads without using an extension hose with
gauge and clip-on chuck.

NEVER stand, lean or reach over the assembly during inflation.

* * * *

Failure to comply with these safety precautions can cause the bead to
break and the assembly to burst with sufficient force to cause serious
injury or death.

Unfortunately, Martinez ignored every one of these warnings. While leaning
over the assembly, he attempted to mount a 16" tire on a 16.5" rim without a
tire mounting machine, a safety cage, or an extension hose. Martinez
explained, however, that because he had removed a 16" tire from the 16.5"
rim, he believed that he was mounting the new 16" tire on a 16" rim.
Moreover, the evidence revealed that Martinez' employer failed to make an
operable tire-mounting machine available to him at the time he was injured,
and there was no evidence that the other safety devices mentioned in the
warning were available.

In their suit, the Martinezes did not claim that the warnings were inadequate
but instead alleged that Goodrich, the manufacturer of the tire, Budd, the
manufacturer of the rim, and Ford, the designer of the rim, were each

negligent and strictly liable for designing and manufacturing a defective tire and rim. Budd and Ford settled with the Martinezes before trial, and the case proceeded solely against Goodrich.

At trial, the Martinezes claimed that the tire manufactured by Goodrich was defective because it failed to incorporate a safer alternative bead design that would have kept the tire from exploding. This defect, they asserted, was the producing cause of Martinez' injuries. Further, they alleged that Goodrich's failure to adopt this alternative bead design was negligence that proximately caused Martinez' injury.

The bead is the portion of the tire that holds the tire to the rim when inflated. A bead consists of rubber-encased steel wiring that encircles the tire a number of times. When the tire is placed inside the wheel rim and inflated, the bead is forced onto the bead-seating ledge of the rim and pressed against the lip of the rim, or the wheel flange. When the last portion of the bead is forced onto this ledge, the tire has "seated," and the air is properly sealed inside the tire. The bead holds the tire to the rim because the steel wire, unlike rubber, does not expand when the tire is inflating.

The tire in this case was a 16" bias-ply light truck tire with a 0.037" gauge multi-strand weftless bead, or tape bead, manufactured in 1990. A tape bead consists of several strands of parallel unwoven steel wires circling the tire with each layer resting on top of the last, similar to tape wound on a roll. After a number of layers have been wound, the end of the bead is joined, or spliced, to the beginning of the same bead to form a continuous loop.

The Martinezes' expert, Alan Milner, a metallurgical engineer, testified that a tape bead is prone to break when the spliced portion of the bead is the last portion of the bead to seat. This is commonly called a hang-up. Milner testified that an alternative bead design, a 0.050" gauge single-strand programmed bead, would have prevented Martinez' injuries because its strength and uniformity make it more resistant to breaking during a hang-up. Milner explained that the 0.050" single-strand programmed bead is stronger because it is 0.013" thicker and that it is uniform because it is wound, or programmed, by a computer, eliminating the spliced portion of the bead that can cause the tire to explode during a hang-up.

According to Milner, Firestone was the first to document that tape beads were prone to break during hang-ups in a 1955 patent application. This application, which was granted three years later, stated in part:

It has developed that in tires of the type now in common use that the grommet of wire used becomes ruptured or broken too frequently at or near the end of the wire splice when the tire bead is forced onto the rim bead seat during mounting of the tire. Applicant has discovered that such breaking of the bead wire occurs most frequently when the spliced portion of the bead wire grommet is located in the last portion of the tire bead to be seated on the rim, and they have noted that when an end of the said wire ribbon was disposed on the radial inner surface of the bead grommet that the break started at or adjacent to that point.

Milner testified that the design of the bead in the Goodrich tire in question was the same design criticized in the patent. Milner also testified, relying on an internal memorandum that was admitted into evidence, that in 1971 General Tire, one of Goodrich's competitors, knew its tape bead design was prone to break during hang-ups.

In 1966, 16.5" wheel rims were first introduced into the American market. Milner testified that Uniroyal, Inc. and B.F. Goodrich Company, who in 1986 merged to form Goodrich, soon became aware that mismatching their 16" tires with the new wheel rims often caused hang-ups that resulted in broken beads. The minutes of a 1972 meeting of the Rubber Manufacturers Association ("RMA"), of which both Uniroyal, Inc. and B.F. Goodrich were members, provided:

Mounting of LT [light truck] tires. Attention was drawn to reports that there have been instances where 16" LT tires have been mounted on 16.5" rims and 14" tires on 14.5" rims. It was proposed and approved to request the Service Managers Committee to add a cautionary statement to RMA documents.

Similarly, the minutes from a 1972 meeting of the Tire and Rim Association, of which Uniroyal, Inc. and B.F. Goodrich were both members, provided:

It was reported that there have been incidents where 14" and 16" tires have been mounted on 14.5" and 16.5" rims that have resulted in broken beads. The Rim Subcommittee of the Technical Advisory

Committee was requested to consider some method of marking 15" Drop Center rims and wheels to avoid this practice.

Finally, Milner testified that B.F. Goodrich's own testing department was aware by at least 1976 that a 16" tire mounted on a 16.5" rim would explode during a hang-up. A B.F. Goodrich "test request" of that year was entered into evidence indicating that a 16" tire would explode when mounted on a 16.5" rim at 73 psi (pounds of pressure per square inch). The test request further indicated that "inspection revealed break was at [illegible] ends of bottom layer of [bead] wires as anticipated." The stated "Object of Test" was: "To develop demonstrative evidence & data for use in lawsuits involving broken beads."

Milner explained that the computer technology required to manufacture the programmed bead was developed in 1972 and widely available by 1975. Milner testified that Goodyear began using a 0.051" gauge single-strand programmed bead in its radial light truck tires in 1977, and that Yokohama began using a single-strand programmed bead in its radial light truck tires in 1981. Milner also testified that General Tire began using a single-strand programmed bead in its bias-ply light truck tires in 1982. Finally, Milner testified that Goodrich itself began using the single-strand programmed bead in its 16" radial light truck tires in 1991.

Based upon this evidence and his expert opinion, Milner testified that the tire manufactured by Goodrich with a tape bead was defective and unreasonably dangerous. Because Goodrich had also been sued in 34 other lawsuits alleging accidents caused by mismatching Goodrich tires, Milner asserted that Goodrich was grossly negligent in failing to adopt the 0.050" single-strand programmed bead in it bias-ply 16" light truck tires.

Milner also testified that the rim designed by Ford and manufactured by Budd was defective because its size was not clearly marked on it and because it could have been redesigned to prevent a 16" tire from passing over its flange.

The jury found that Goodrich's conduct was the sole proximate cause of Martinez' injuries and that Goodrich was grossly negligent. Furthermore, the jury found that the tire manufactured by Goodrich was defective, while the wheel rim designed by Ford and manufactured by Budd was not defective. The jury allocated 100% of the producing cause of Martinez' injuries to the acts and omissions of Goodrich.

The jury awarded the Martinezes $5.5 million in actual damages and $11.5 million in punitive damages. After reducing the award of actual damages by $1.4 million pursuant to a settlement agreement between the Martinezes, Ford, and Budd, reducing the punitive damages to the amount of actual damages pursuant to a pretrial agreement between Goodrich and the Martinezes, and awarding prejudgment interest, the trial court rendered judgment for the Martinezes for $10,308,792.45.

The court of appeals affirmed the award of actual damages, holding that there was legally sufficient evidence to support the finding of a design defect based upon its examination of the following factors:

(1) the availability of safer design alternatives;
(2) similar accidents involving the same product;
(3) subsequent changes or modifications in design;
(4) out-of-court experiments indicating Goodrich's knowledge of a design defect; and
(5) expert testimony claiming a design defect.

The court rejected Goodrich's argument that Martinez' failure to heed the product's warnings was a complete defense to the product defect claim. However, the court of appeals reversed and rendered the award of punitive damages, holding that there was no evidence to support the jury's finding of gross negligence.

Only Goodrich applied to this Court for writ of error. As in the court of appeals, Goodrich's principal argument here is that no evidence supports the jury finding that the tire was defective because "the tire bore a warning which was unambiguous and conspicuously visible (and not claimed to be inadequate); the tire was safe for use if the warning was followed; and the cause of the accident was mounting and inflating a tire in direct contravention of those warnings."

* * * *

II.

A.

This Court has adopted the products liability standard set forth in section 402A of the *Restatement (Second) of Torts*. Section 402A states:

(1) one who sells any product in a defective condition unreasonably dangerous to the user or consumer or to his property is subject to liability for physical harm thereby caused to the ultimate user or consumer, or to his property, if

   (a)   the seller is engaged in the business of selling such a product, and

   (b)   it is expected to and does reach the user or consumer without substantial change in the condition in which it is sold.

A product may be unreasonably dangerous because of a defect in manufacturing, design, or marketing.... To prove a design defect, a claimant must establish, among other things, that the defendant could have provided a safer alternative design. [I]f there are no safer alternatives, a product is not unreasonably dangerous as a matter of law. Implicit in this holding is that the safer alternative design must be reasonable, *(i.e.,* that it can be implemented without destroying the utility of the product). Texas law does not require a manufacturer to destroy the utility of his product in order to make it safe.

The newly released *Restatement (Third) of Torts: Products Liability* carries forward this focus on reasonable alternative design. *See Restatement (Third) Of Torts: Products Liability* § 2(b). Section 2(b) provides:

A product ... is defective in design when the foreseeable risks of harm posed by the product could have been reduced or avoided by the adoption of a reasonable alternative design by the seller or other distributor, or a predecessor in the commercial chain of distribution, and the omission of the alternative design renders the product not reasonably safe.

To determine whether a reasonable alternative design exists, and if so whether its omission renders the product unreasonably dangerous (or in the words of the new *Restatement*, not reasonably safe), the finder of fact may weigh various factors bearing on the risk and utility of the product.... One of these factors is whether the product contains suitable warnings and instructions.... The new *Restatement* likewise carries forward this approach:

A broad range of factors may be considered in determining whether an alternative design is reasonable and whether its omission renders a product not reasonably safe. The factors include, among others, the magnitude and probability of the foreseeable risks of harm, the instructions and warnings accompanying the product, and the nature and strength of consumer expectations regarding the product, including expectations arising from product portrayal and marketing.... The relative advantages and disadvantages of the product as designed and as it alternatively could have been designed may also be considered. Thus, the likely effects of the alternative design on production costs; the effects of the alternative design on product longevity, maintenance, repair, and esthetics; and the range of consumer choice among products are factors that may be taken into account.... *Restatement (Third) Of Torts: Products Liability* § 2 cmt. f

Goodrich urges this Court to depart from this standard by following certain language from Comment j of the *Restatement (Second) of Torts*. Comment j provides in part:

Where warning is given, the seller may reasonably assume that it will be read and heeded; and a product bearing such a warning, which is safe for use if it is followed, is not in defective condition, nor is it unreasonably dangerous. *Restatement (Second) Of Torts* § 402A cmt. j (1965).

The new *Restatement*, however, expressly rejects the Comment j approach:

Reasonable designs and instructions or warnings both play important roles in the production and distribution of reasonably safe products. In general, when a safer design can reasonably be implemented and risks can reasonably be designed out of a product, adoption of the safer design is required over a warning that leaves a significant residuum of such risks. For example, instructions and warnings may be ineffective because users of the product may not be adequately reached, may be likely to be inattentive, or may be insufficiently motivated to follow the instructions or heed the warnings. However, when an alternative design to avoid risks cannot reasonably be implemented, adequate instructions and warnings will normally be sufficient to render the product reasonably safe.... Warnings are not, however, a substitute for the provision of a reasonably safe design. *Restatement (Third) Of Torts: Products Liability* § 2 cmt. l.

The Reporters' Notes in the new *Restatement* refer to Comment j as "unfortunate language" that "has elicited heavy criticism from a host of commentators." *Restatement (Third) Of Torts: Products Liability* § 2, Reporters' Note, cmt. l....

Similarly, this Court has indicated that the fact that a danger is open and obvious (and thus need not be warned against) does not preclude a finding of product defect when a safer, reasonable alternative design exists.... .

The drafters of the new *Restatement* provide the following illustration for why courts have overwhelmingly rejected Comment j:

> Jeremy's foot was severed when caught between the blade and compaction chamber of a garbage truck on which he was working. The injury occurred when he lost his balance while jumping on the back step of the garbage truck as it was moving from one stop to the next. The garbage truck, manufactured by XYZ Motor Co., has a warning in large red letters on both the left and right rear panels that reads "DANGER—DO NOT INSERT ANY OBJECT WHILE COMPACTION CHAMBER IS WORKING—KEEP HANDS AND FEET AWAY." The fact that adequate warning was given does not preclude Jeremy from seeking to establish a design defect under Subsection (b). The possibility that an employee might lose his balance and thus encounter the shear point was a risk that a warning could not eliminate and that might require a safety guard. *Restatement (Third) Of Torts: Products Liability* § 2 cmt. l, illus. 14.

In fact, Goodrich recognized at trial that warnings are an imperfect means to remedy a product defect. In response to a question posed by the Martinezes' attorney, Goodrich engineer Stanley Lew answered:

> Q: Is that why designs of a product are more important than warnings on a product because people may not see warnings but they are always going to encounter the design?
> A: Yes, that's correct. It's the products they deal with.

For these reasons, we refuse to adopt the approach of Comment j of the superseded *Restatement (Second) of Torts* section 402A.

To determine whether a reasonable alternative design exists, and if so whether its omission renders the product unreasonably dangerous (or in the words of the new *Restatement*, not "reasonably safe"), the finder of fact may weigh various factors bearing on the risk and utility of the product.... One of these factors is whether the product contains suitable warnings and instructions.... The new *Restatement* likewise carries forward this approach:

A broad range of factors may be considered in determining whether an alternative design is reasonable and whether its omission renders a product not reasonably safe. The factors include, among others, the magnitude and probability of the foreseeable risks of harm, the instructions and warnings accompanying the product, and the nature and strength of consumer expectations regarding the product, including expectations arising from product portrayal and marketing.... The relative advantages and disadvantages of the product as designed and as it alternatively could have been designed may also be considered. Thus, the likely effects of the alternative design on production costs; the effects of the alternative design on product longevity, maintenance, repair, and esthetics; and the range of consumer choice among products are factors that may be taken into account.... *Restatement (Third) Of Torts: Products Liability* § 2 cmt. f.

Is the new *Restatement* standard for products liability a remedy for the problems with the older Section 402A test? In one area, at least, it does offer some prospect for improvement: In the past, too often "alternative designs" offered in the courtroom to show a product defect were purely theoretical constructs impractical in the real world or, even worse, simply "cures" for particular problems often of dubious function or value compared to the product's utility.

But does the new formulation of utility and reasonableness really change anything except the buzz words? Those critical of products liability law under the *Second Restatement* would certainly argue that it does not and that *Martinez* is just another example of how the wheels had come off. After all, if someone can prevail in a lawsuit by doing precisely the things he was clearly warned not to do, it would seem that there would be no way that a manufacturer or seller of a product ever could escape from liability for injuries caused by its products.

A Look from the Defense's Angle

But before we go condemning this rule too quickly, approach it from the other side. Suppose that a business produces a product that has clear and demonstrable links to numerous long-term serious or fatal health problems — even cancer or other similarly catastrophic disease — in large numbers of its users. Suppose further that the manufacturers place a warning on its package that says, "Use of this product may be dangerous to your health." (Compare that with the warnings in *Martinez*.) Is it fair to allow the maker or distributor of the product to escape liability just because of the warning?

Obviously, this isn't really a hypothetical; it is a quick paraphrase of a central issue in the ongoing litigation over the use of cigarettes, as you probably guessed. But it does put the issue in perspective in a more realistic way.

With almost every legal rule or principle it is possible to find situations in which it operates harshly or absurdly. Much of the growth of the common law has been an effort to ease or amend rules to avoid such results while keeping the "good parts." Also, because rules of law ultimately are forged on the basis of a trial record (in which the strategy or demeanor of lawyers and parties, composition of the jury, perceptions of what is morally right and wrong and even seemingly trivial matters can have a profound influence on the outcome and what a court is willing to do) rules or rulings that seem unduly harsh or ill-considered in an appellate reporter may look a great deal different when viewed in light of additional information.

It is also too easy to forget that standards like "reasonable care" and "unreasonably dangerous" ultimately are *community* standards that rest in no small measure upon shared perceptions of the amount of risk that a community is willing to bear.

There is no bright-line test here, but each decision bears its own price. The society that demands vaccines free from side effects, for example, may face outbreaks of dangerous disease, and those who adhere inflexibly to *caveat emptor* may face shoddy, dangerous products.

But this evolving consensus, expressed by lawyers and juries and appellate courts, has now endured for almost a century, a sign that society at large does seek in some form the protections that judges Cardozo, Traynor, and others sought to embody in this area of the law.

Key Words and Phrases

caveat emptor
contributory fault
design defect
fit for ordinary purposes
implied warranty
manufacturing defect
merchantability
other incident evidence
privity
reasonable care
Restatement (Second) of Torts, Section 402
transparency
unreasonable danger
warning
warranties

Review Questions

1.   List examples from your personal experience of these concepts:

    a.   face-to-face privity
    b.   transparency
    c.   implied warranty

2.   In his 1916 *MacPherson* opinion, Justice Cardozo wrote, "The obligation to inspect must vary with the nature of the thing to be inspected. The more probable the danger, the greater the need of caution." Do you feel this dictum is applicable in the 21st century? Why, or why not?

3.   At this point in the semester, when it's probably too late to drop the course, levity is needed. Bring to class the most ridiculous

example you can find of a written warning about using a product. If you can't find such a written warning, share (if you can remember it) your last experience of purchasing something that worked right the first time.

---

[1] The concept of warranty really is closest to the idea of a material representation, a statement so important to the transaction or contract that the contract is breached if the statement is false. Warranties can relate to many different issues, ranging from quality or durability to a party's ability to "do the deal." Warranties are an important part of many business transactions, and lawyers often spend seemingly endless amounts of time dickering over warranty language in large transactions.

[2] They also show some of the problems with contract-based claims for defective products.

[3] As an example, in a case involving a swimming pool injury in which the author represented the pool manufacturer, the plaintiff's expert opined that there should be warnings about drowning, spinal cord injuries from diving, swimming while intoxicated, chlorine from the purification system, swimming during electrical storms, and several other mishaps. Each of these may well be worth warnings, but how to place them so that all are effective is by no means a science.

[4] A good example in the author's own experience involved claims that cotton flannel nightgowns were unreasonably dangerous because they presented an unreasonable risk of fire. (The nap of the fabric permitted any flame to spread catastrophically, said the plaintiffs.) The same experts traveled the country to testify in case after case for each side!

Chapter Eleven

STICKS AND STONES:
THE LAW OF DEFAMATION,
LIBEL, AND SLANDER

Previously, our focus has been on the tangible: bodily injury and property damage. Now we must shift our focus to intangible things: reputation, and privacy. We start by looking at the related concepts of **libel, slander,** and **defamation.**

In his book *The Common Law,* Justice Oliver Wendell Holmes devoted only a page to libel, slander, and defamation, focusing on the intent required before recovery was possible. Nonetheless, the concept of defamation has a relatively long history.

In the older common law, and in states that still recognize it today, libel involved false and damaging statements in written publications, while slander related to such statements when made orally. Libel was a more serious offense than slander because the printed media allowed libelous statements to be spread over a larger area (by mail or distribution of copies) and to be preserved so that they might be viewed by others long after initially being made.

Before the advent of radio, telephone, television, and now the Internet, slander's range was limited to earshot. Oral statements traveled no farther than the speaker could be heard. Moreover, the law reasoned, perhaps somewhat dubiously, that slanderous statements would fade from memory sooner than libelous ones. Thus, slander had relatively strict requirements for proof of damages, stricter than those of libel.

The Concept of Defamation

What exactly is defamation? Our first case excerpt defines the rather universally accepted elements of defamation, whether oral or written, and it introduces some peculiarities of defamation law.

Bryson v. News America Publications, Inc.
174 Ill.2d 77, 672 N.E.2d 1207, 220 Ill. Dec. 195
Supreme Court of Illinois
1996

Bilandic, C.J.:

The plaintiff, Kimberly Bryson, brought an action against the defendants, News America Publications, Inc., and Lucy Logsdon. The plaintiff's two-count complaint alleged that she was defamed by the publication of an article entitled "Bryson," which was written by defendant Logsdon and published by defendant News America in the March 1991 edition of *Seventeen* magazine.

* * * *

The plaintiff subsequently filed a second amended complaint, which was dismissed by the trial court and is the subject of this appeal. Each count of the second amended complaint alleged that an article appeared in the March 1991 edition of *Seventeen* magazine that referred to the plaintiff as a "slut" and implied that she was an unchaste individual. The complaint alleged that this language and implication were false. Counts I through IV of the second amended complaint sought damages for defamation....

The defendants filed a motion to dismiss counts I through IV of the second amended complaint ... for failure to state a cause of action for defamation.... The trial court granted the defendants' motions and dismissed the second amended complaint. The appellate court affirmed.... We granted the plaintiff's petition for leave to appeal....

* * * *

A short story entitled "Bryson," written by defendant Logsdon, was published by the defendant News America in the March 1991 issue of *Seventeen* magazine as part of a group of stories entitled New Voices in

Fiction. The story, written in the style of a first person narrative, recounts a conflict between the unidentified speaker and her high school classmate, Bryson.

According to the speaker, Bryson, "[a] platinum blond, blue-eye-shadowed, faded-blue-jeaned, black polyester-topped shriek" who lives "on the other side of town" was "after" her. In the course of describing events that led up to an after-school fight between Bryson and the speaker, the speaker discusses an incident that occurred two months earlier.

> About two months ago Bryson was at a bonfire with these two guys that nobody knew. One had a tattoo, and they were all drinking. Lots. Who knows what guys like that made Bryson do. The next day she came into school with a black eye. Beth Harper looked at her too long, and Bryson slammed her up against a glass door and cracked her one clean in the mouth.

> Later that afternoon, as Bryson shouted down the hallways like always, I remembered what a slut she was and forgot about the sorriness I'd been holding onto for her.

The story continues as the speaker describes the fight that ensues between the speaker and Bryson. A footnote at the end of the story identifies the author, Lucy Logsdon, as a "native of southern Illinois."

The plaintiff's second amended complaint, which was dismissed by the trial court, allege[d] that the March 1991 edition of *Seventeen* magazine, including the article entitled "Bryson," was published to the general public. The counts further allege that defamatory language appeared in that magazine "in that the article referred to the [p]laintiff as a 'slut' and implied that the [p]laintiff was an 'unchaste' individual." Each count further alleges that this language and implication were false and that each defendant permitted a false statement to appear through "malice or actual negligence."

Counts I and II, which attempt to state a cause of action for defamation per se against each defendant, allege damage to the plaintiff's reputation and seek appropriate compensatory relief, as well as punitive damages. Counts

III and IV also attempt to state a cause of action for defamation, but allege that the damage to the plaintiff's reputation caused her to suffer pecuniary loss in the form of lost business opportunities and/or lost employment....

* * * *

[W]e [first] consider the allegations in the plaintiff's complaint. A statement is considered defamatory if it tends to cause such harm to the reputation of another that it lowers that person in the eyes of the community or deters third persons from associating with her.... A statement or publication may be defamatory on its face. However, even a statement that is not defamatory on its face may support a cause of action for defamation if the plaintiff has pled extrinsic facts that demonstrate that the statement has a defamatory meaning. *See, e.g., Morrison v. Ritchie & Co.*, 4 Fraser, Sess. Cas., 645, 39 Scot.L.Rep. 432 (1902) (report that plaintiff gave birth to twins considered defamatory, where plaintiff proved, as extrinsic fact, that some readers knew that the plaintiff had been married only one month).

Here, counts I and II of the plaintiff's complaint attempt to state a cause of action for defamation *per se*. Only certain limited categories of defamatory statements are deemed actionable *per se*. If a defamatory statement is actionable *per se*, the plaintiff need not plead or prove actual damage to her reputation to recover.... Rather, statements that fall within these actionable *per se* categories are thought to be so obviously and materially harmful to the plaintiff that injury to her reputation may be presumed.... If a defamatory statement does not fall within one of the limited categories of statements that are actionable *per se*, the plaintiff must plead and prove that she sustained actual damage of a pecuniary nature ("special damages") to recover....

We first consider whether the disputed statements may be considered actionable *per se*. The plaintiff alleges that the article is actionable *per se* because it referred to her as a "slut" and implied that she was an "unchaste" individual.

Under our common law, four categories of statements are considered actionable *per se* and give rise to a cause of action for defamation without a showing of special damages. They are:

> (1) words that impute the commission of a criminal offense;
> (2) words that impute infection with a loathsome communicable disease;

(3) words that impute an inability to perform or want of integrity in the discharge of duties of office or employment; or
(4) words that prejudice a party, or impute lack of ability, in his or her trade, profession, or business....

These common law categories continue to exist except where changed by statute. The Slander and Libel Act [740 ILCS 145/1 *et seq.* (West 1992)] has enlarged the classifications enumerated above by providing that false accusations of fornication and adultery are actionable as a matter of law. Specifically, section 1 of that statute provides:

If any person shall falsely use, utter or publish words, which in their common acceptance, shall amount to charge any person with having been guilty of fornication or adultery, such words so spoken shall be deemed actionable, and he shall be deemed guilty of slander.

The defendants initially claim that this statute has no application here because it applies only to words that are spoken and not in circumstances, such as those here, where the words are written. We reject the defendants' attempt to so limit the statute.

We note initially that the defendants' argument relies upon a distinction between spoken and written defamation (slander and libel) that existed at common law, but was abandoned long ago by our courts. At common law, libel and slander were analyzed under different sets of standards, with libel recognized as the more serious wrong.

Illinois law evolved, however, and rejected this bifurcated approach in favor of a single set of rules for slander and libel. Libel and slander are now treated alike and the same rules apply to a defamatory statement regardless of whether the statement is written or oral.... Given the merger of libel and slander, we reject the defendants' claim that the statute providing for an action where false accusations of fornication are made is not applicable here simply because the alleged defamation was in writing.

Let's pause and address a number of the principles set forth in this case. First, as we noted at the outset and as Chief Justice Bilandic makes clear, defamation is an attack on reputation. But there is a hidden question here: reputation with whom, and adverse effect by whose standards, the victim's or the community's?

Think through this problem for a moment. If the newspaper accuses you of being a murderer, your stature with other criminals might actually rise! But would it be appropriate to permit the newspaper to say it had not defamed you because your reputation had gone up with this limited group? Obviously not.

But let's make the problem more difficult. Suppose the newspaper now misstated someone's religious affiliation. Again, it could be argued that such a misstatement had not defamed because it was not harmful to be called a member of a particular faith. But what if the *Morning Star Times Herald Picayune Tribune News Express* called you a Catholic in its Northern Ireland edition, which was heavily distributed among militants in Belfast? Turn it around. What if the same edition called you a Protestant? Would you have been defamed now?

These hypotheticals force us to focus our attention on what reputation is in the context of defamation. For defamation to have meaning as a doctrine and to not be reduced to a form of petty bickering, the attack must be such as to be expected to produce an adverse effect on a substantial portion of the community. It need not be shown that reputation has been affected *universally*; this would be impossible.

At the opposite end of the spectrum, it clearly cannot be enough to show that the statement would have caused the victim's reputation to have suffered with a tiny group of people, for then the doctrine would become a device to protest every slight or insult.

Defamation Per Se

Now on to the concept of defamation *per se*, and what originally was missing from it.

> ### *Defamation* **per se.** A statement
> ### that is defamatory in and of itself.

At traditional common law, as we see from the opinion, issues of chastity and promiscuity were not included among the categories of defamation *per se.* There are a number of reasons for this, of which two are more important.

The omission reflects the traditionally subordinate status of women in the law,[1] but it also reflects a commercial underpinning for the law of defamation, a common thread in many of the torts we study in this section.

Two of the four common law categories of defamation *per se* set forth by Chief Justice Bilandic directly relate to employment or commerce, and a wrongful statement that someone has committed a crime also has implications in that area. This gloss should not be forgotten in assessing why the law of defamation originally did not encompass wrongful accusations of promiscuity.

But what if the allegedly defamatory statement does not fit within one of the categories for defamation *per se*? Let us skip ahead in the Bryson opinion to follow up on the tantalizing reference to the old Morrison decision from Scotland.

Bryson v. News America Publications, Inc.
174 Ill.2d 77, 672 N.E.2d 1207, 220 Ill. Dec. 1995
Supreme Court of Illinois
1996

CONTINUED

* * * *

We next consider whether the trial court properly dismissed counts III and IV of the plaintiff's complaint, which attempt to state a cause of action for defamation *per quod.* The allegations in counts III and IV of the complaint are identical to those found in counts I and II, except that the plaintiff has alleged that she sustained pecuniary loss ("special damages") as a result of the defendant's publication of the allegedly defamatory statements.

The defendants argue that the trial court properly dismissed these *per quod* counts because they failed to allege any extrinsic facts to show that the statements are defamatory in character. We disagree.

A cause of action for defamation *per quod* may be brought in two circumstances. First, a *per quod* claim is appropriate where the defamatory character of the statement is not apparent on its face, and resort to extrinsic circumstances is necessary to demonstrate its injurious meaning. To pursue a *per quod* action in such circumstances, a plaintiff must plead and prove extrinsic facts to explain the defamatory meaning of the statement....

A *per quod* action is also appropriate, however, where a statement is defamatory on its face, but does not fall within one of the limited categories of statements that are actionable *per se*.... In such *per quod* actions, the plaintiff need not plead extrinsic facts, because the defamatory character of the statement is apparent on its face and resort to additional facts to discern its defamatory meaning is unnecessary. The action is one for defamation *per quod* simply because the statement does not fall into one of the actionable *per se* categories. In other words, the statement is defamatory on its face, but damage to the plaintiff's reputation will not be presumed.... As with any defamation *per quod* action, the plaintiff must plead and prove special damages to recover.

* * * *

In any defamation *per quod* action, the plaintiff must plead and prove actual damage to her reputation and pecuniary loss resulting from the defamatory statement ("special damages") to recover.

Defamation Per Quod

To answer the first and obvious question, the phrase is pronounced "per kwahd." But other questions probably have occurred to you as well.

Defamation per quod. Defamation that is either not apparent but provable, or apparent but not actionable *per se.*

The *Morrison* case[2] referred to in the first excerpt from the *Bryson* opinion is a classic example of what we might think of today as defamation by innuendo. The speaker says something that is apparently bland but has defamatory meaning to the audience.

The reference to the audience is crucial in any *per quod* case, just as we have discussed: the extrinsic circumstances that plaintiff must prove are that the audience would understand the statement to have a defamatory meaning.

But the function of a *per quod* case is not merely to address situations in which there is innuendo. It helps deal with situations where the words have obvious defamatory meaning but do not, for whatever reason, fit within an established category of defamation *per se.*

But what about jokes, satire and ordinary teasing? These, it turns out, are deeper waters than you might imagine because they bring into play not only something called the innocent construction rule, but the First Amendment as well. Let us address the innocent construction rule first by returning to *Bryson.*[3]

Bryson v. News America Publications, Inc.
174 Ill.2d 77, 672 N.E.2d 1207, 220 Ill. Dec. 1995
Supreme Court of Illinois
1996

CONTINUED

* * * *

The defendants ... claim that the assertion that Bryson is a "slut" is not actionable *per se* because the word "slut" may reasonably be innocently construed as describing Bryson as a "bully." "They note that the *American*

Heritage Dictionary includes a number of different definitions for the word "slut," including "a slovenly, dirty woman," "a woman of loose morals," "prostitute," "a bold, brazen girl," or "a female dog." *American Heritage Dictionary* at 1153 (2d Coll. ed. 1985). They argue that, because "a bold, brazen girl" may be considered synonymous with "bully," the court must innocently construe the word "slut."

The defendants apparently believe that the innocent construction rule applies whenever a word has more than one dictionary definition, one of which is not defamatory. The innocent construction rule does not apply, however, simply because allegedly defamatory words are "capable" of an innocent construction.... In applying the innocent construction rule, courts must give the allegedly defamatory words their natural and obvious meaning.... Courts must therefore interpret the allegedly defamatory words as they appeared to have been used and according to the idea they were intended to convey to the reasonable reader.... When a defamatory meaning was clearly intended and conveyed, this court will not strain to interpret allegedly defamatory words in their mildest and most inoffensive sense in order to hold them nonlibellous under the innocent construction rule.

Here, we need not determine whether the word "slut" always implies unchastity or is always defamatory. When we consider the allegedly defamatory language in context, and give the words and implications their natural and obvious meaning, it is evident that the word "slut" was intended to describe Bryson's sexual proclivities. Immediately preceding the sentence in which Bryson is called a "slut," the author describes an incident that occurred two months earlier. The author states that Bryson appeared at a bonfire with "two guys that nobody knew. One had a tattoo, and they were all drinking. Lots. Who knows what guys like that made Bryson do?" The sexual implication underlying the use of "slut" is intensified with the commentary, "Who knows what guys like that made Bryson do." The defendants suggest that this latter statement did not necessarily have sexual undertones, since the author could have been implying that the two men made Bryson engage in conduct of a nonsexual nature, such as shoplifting. The defendants basically ask this court to construe the words used, not in the plain and popular sense in which they are naturally understood, but in their best possible sense.

The innocent construction rule, however, does not require courts to strain to find an unnatural but possibly innocent meaning for words where the defamatory meaning is far more reasonable.... Nor does it require this court to espouse a naiveté unwarranted under the circumstances. Reading the words in the context presented, and giving the words their "natural and obvious" meaning, it is obvious that the word "slut" was used to describe Bryson's sexual proclivities. *See Tonsmeire v. Tonsmeire*, 281 Ala. 102, 106, 199 So.2d 645, 648 (1967) (statement that the plaintiff "had two affairs" could not be innocently construed as referring to platonic associations; statement charged the plaintiff with unchastity and was libelous *per se*); *Jordan v. Lewis*, 20 A.D.2d 773, 774, 247 N.Y.S.2d 650, 653 (1964) (stating that the plaintiff "slept with his secretary" is not susceptible of an innocent construction and, as ordinarily used, charges the plaintiff with sexual promiscuity). Accordingly, we reject the defendant's contention that the defamatory language at issue must be innocently construed as a matter of law.

The defendants finally note that our appellate court has held that it is not defamatory *per se* to call a woman a slut. *Roby v. Murphy*, 27 Ill. App. 394 (1888)....

Roby was decided more than 100 years ago. It is evident that neither the law of defamation nor our use of language has remained stagnant for the last century. Terms that had innocuous or only nondefamatory meanings in 1888 may be considered defamatory today. *See, e.g., Moricoli v. Schwartz*, 46 Ill.App.3d 481, 5 Ill. Dec. 74, 361 N.E.2d 74 (1977) (rejecting the defendant's claim that the term "fag" should be innocently construed, because the dictionary definitions for that term included "cigarette" and "to become weary"; stating that the plaintiff "is a fag" amounted to a charge that the plaintiff was homosexual); *Manale v. City of New Orleans*, 673 F.2d 122 (5th Cir.1982) (referring to the plaintiff, a fellow police officer, as "a little fruit" and "gay" falsely charged the plaintiff with homosexuality and was defamatory *per se*); *Tonsmeire v. Tonsmeire*, 281 Ala. 102, 199 So.2d 645 (1967) ("affair" is commonly understood to mean unchastity rather than a platonic association).

At the time Roby was decided, *Webster's Dictionary* defined the term "slut" as "an untidy woman," "a slattern" or "a female dog," and stated that the term was "the same as 'bitch.'" *Roby*, 27 Ill. App. at 398. Apparently, when *Roby* was decided, none of the dictionary definitions of "slut" implied sexual promiscuity. Moreover, the Roby court found that, even in its "common acceptance," the term "slut" did not amount to a charge of unchastity. *Roby*, 27 Ill. App. at 398.

We cannot simply assume that the term "slut" means the same thing today as it did a century ago. Many modern dictionaries include the definitions of the term "slut" cited in *Roby*, but add new definitions that imply sexual promiscuity. *See, e.g., Webster's New World Dictionary* (2d Coll. ed. 1975) ("a sexually immoral woman"); *American Heritage Dictionary* at 1153 (2d Coll. ed. 1985) ("[a] woman of loose morals," "prostitute"). Moreover, in the present age, the term "slut" is commonly used and understood to refer to sexual promiscuity. *See Smith v. Atkins*, 622 So.2d 795 (La.App.1993) (law professor called a female student a "slut" in class; appellate court

Proof of Damage

The next questions go to proof. How does one prove the extrinsic circumstances or the damage to one's reputation? The next excerpt gives an answer.

Tacket v. General Motors Co.
937 F.2d 1201
United States Court of Appeals
for the Seventh Circuit
1990

Bauer, C.J.:

According to the age-old children's rhyme, "Sticks and stones may break your bones, but names can never hurt you." Plaintiff-Appellee Thomas Tacket and the law of defamation, however, argue otherwise. According to Tacket, another mellifluous rhyme, one that read "TACKET TACKET WHAT A RACKET," when painted on the inside wall of General Motors' Anderson, Indiana, assembly plant and allowed to remain there for seven or eight months, defamed him and irreparably damaged his reputation.

* * * *

The evidence revealed the following. Thomas Tacket was an employee at Delco Remy Division of General Motors ("Delco") in Anderson, Indiana. Tacket was first employed by Delco in 1971 and rose to the level of night superintendent in 1983. In February 1985, Delco's Anderson facility was working on a generator production contract entitled the "9-S1 Project." A problem arose concerning the attainment of wooden shipping crates. Ed Spearman, one of Tacket's subordinates, suggested that "S & T Specialties" provide the needed crates. Tacket received requisition forms for the crates and processed them during off-duty hours. Both he and Spearman signed the forms.

Some time later, the union representing Delco's workers discovered that Delco was buying the crates from an outside supplier and protested the "outsourcing" of work that Delco's own staff could have performed. The union also discovered that Spearman was the "S," and suspected that Tacket was the "T," of "S & T Specialties." (The crates were being constructed in Spearman's garage.)

Delco promptly suspended both Spearman and Tacket, pending an investigation. Delco ultimately fired Spearman, but concluded that it had insufficient evidence to discharge Tacket. He returned to work on April 9, 1985, but his relationship with the workers had soured. Delco thereafter transferred him to a "quality assurance team" with the same rank and salary but with fewer subordinates.

Upon learning of the outsourcing, the workers spread rumors about Spearman and Tacket. At some point, a sign approximately 3' x 30' appeared inside the plant proclaiming the infamous rhyme "TACKET TACKET WHAT A RACKET." This sign stayed up for two to three days during Tacket's suspension. A second, smaller sign, approximately 1'x 4', proclaiming the same message was stenciled on the inside wall of the plant and remained there for at least seven months.

On the issue of damages, Tacket offered the testimony of Frank Connolly, a psychologist, who diagnosed Tacket to have suffered a psychiatric illness know as depressive neurosis. Connolly testified that Tacket was alienated, dysfunctional, and lacked energy. Connolly linked Tacket's condition to the small sign and noted that it affected his job performance. Tacket's job performance before the incident was better than after the incident, as reflected by the poor job performance ratings he received.

At the close of the evidence, the district court instructed the jurors that Tacket could prove damage from the sign in two ways: 1) if the sign were found to impute a crime or to prejudice him in his profession, then injury to his reputation would be established; or 2) if the sign did not impute such things, then the jury was instructed that the plaintiff could recover only if "special damages" were proven. "Special damages" were defined as the loss of something having economic or pecuniary value, or the loss of a benefit that has an indirect financial value to the plaintiff. Special interrogatories were given to the jury to aid their deliberations.

The jury returned a verdict for the plaintiff in the amount of $100,000. The jury indicated on its special verdict form that the sign did not tend to damage the plaintiff's reputation without regard to extrinsic circumstances, but that it did defame the plaintiff when considered with other facts. The jury further found that Delco intentionally and unreasonably failed to remove that sign (thereby "publishing" it), and that plaintiff exercised proper care for the protection of his own interests.

Delco then moved to set aside the verdict, arguing that the jury's finding that the sign did not defame Tacket without consideration of extrinsic facts, coupled with Tacket's alleged failure to plead and prove "special damages" mandated entry of judgment in its favor.

In its Order of July 6, 1989, the district court determined that Indiana libel law allowed recovery of proven psychological injuries as part of special damages and permitted Tacket to amend his pleadings to conform them to the evidence. Thus, based on the amended pleadings and the jury's verdict, the district court found that Tacket had indeed pleaded and proved special damages. The district court denied Delco's motion and allowed the verdict to stand.

* * * *

Though Delco presents several claims on appeal, only one issue concerns us today: whether Tacket.... adequately proved special damages....

The Indiana courts have restated the following general rule on many occasions:

If a communication is defamatory *per se*, then nominal damages
will be presumed by the court and need not be specially pleaded;
however, in the absence of words actionable *per se*, special
damages must be alleged in the complaint.... When we say that
words are actionable only upon proof of "special" damage, we
mean special in the sense that it must be supported by specific
proof, as distinct from the damage assumed to follow in the case of
libel *per se*, or libel *per quod*, which falls into one of the four
special categories.... In other words, special damages must be
proved in the case of slander or libel *per quod* that does not
involve the imputation of a crime, a loathsome disease, unchastity,
or injury to the plaintiff's business, profession, trade or office.

* * * *

Given that special damages are required to be pleaded and proved in Indiana
libel *per quod* cases, we turn to the next question: whether Tacket has done
so in this case. To resolve this issue, we must determine what constitutes
"special damages." As noted above, the district court instructed the jury
that special damages mean that Tacket must show some economic or
pecuniary loss, or the loss of a benefit that places on Tacket an indirect
financial burden. Yet, in its July 6 Order, the district court interpreted
Indiana law "to allow recovery of any damage, pecuniary or otherwise, that
is specially pleaded and proved to be a proximate result of the complained
of circumstances in a defamation case."

The district court determined that, because Tacket showed a specific,
psychiatric injury resulting from the sign, he need not demonstrate any
pecuniary loss.

In *Grzelak v. Calumet Publishing Company*, 543 F.2d 579 (7th Cir.1975),
another case involving Indiana defamation law, we held that a motion to
dismiss properly was granted where the alleged defamatory matter was not
libelous *per se*, even though the plaintiff alleged she had "suffered and
continues to suffer severe mental and emotional pain and agony." *Id.* at
583–84:

Under Indiana law, when allegedly defamatory language is not
libelous *per se*, the plaintiff must plead special damages in order to

state a cause of action.... [Grzelak] has never, in reality, sustained any special damages. Although she claimed to have developed a skin condition as a result of nervousness caused by the publications in question, she also testified that she had neither lost her job nor incurred a decrease in salary nor lost any time from work, as a direct and proximate result of the articles. In this regard, it is well established that mental or emotional distress, even if accompanied by or the cause of a physical illness, is not a legally sufficient claim of special damage.

As the above excerpt reveals, the plaintiff in *Grzelak* allegedly suffered the same kind of injury as Tacket, yet her psychological distress was held insufficient to satisfy the requirement that special damages be pleaded and proved. Tacket's claim must suffer the same fate.

Tacket's burden was to show damages that are "pecuniary in nature" and that "have been actually incurred as a natural and proximate consequence of the wrongful act." *"Stanley v. Kelley*, 422 N.E.2d 663, 668 (Ind. App.1981). *Accord.*, C. McCormick, *Damages* § 114 (1935) ("The 'special damage' required in defamation cases must be some material or pecuniary injury. Injury to reputation without more, humiliation, mental anguish, physical sickness — these do not suffice.").

In the instant case, Tacket presented no evidence of any pecuniary loss. Instead, he demonstrated that he suffered emotional distress and psychological injury. But such maladies, however painful to Tacket, are only general damages—the kind that routinely follow a defamation. Injury to the plaintiff's reputation and standing in the community, personal humiliation, and mental anguish and suffering are the sort of damages that the law presumes to be the natural result of the publication; they are not

This at least answers the questions about damages in a defamation case. The idea of nominal damages in a defamation suit — usually an award of one dollar — may seem strange, but it serves an important purpose: A finding by a jury that a statement was defamatory may help vindicate the plaintiff's reputation. This is what many plaintiffs truly want.

Does it seem fair or make sense to deny plaintiffs the right to put on evidence of bodily or psychological injury as "special damages"? Judge Cudahy, who dissented in *Tacket*, did not think so. He wrote:

> The majority seems to be mired in the jurisdictional conflicts between the ecclesiastical and the common law courts of the sixteenth century. The ecclesiastical courts regarded defamation as a sin and punished it with a penance. For a considerable period, therefore, the common law courts held that, unless "temporal" damage could be proved, defamation was a "spiritual" matter to be left to the Church. *See* Prosser, *The Law of Torts* 772; *see also* Veeder, "The History and Theory of the Law of Defamation," 3 Colum.L.Rev. 546 (1903). Perhaps the majority, too, views a psychological diagnosis as in the "spiritual" realm and thus beyond our competence.
>
> In fact, psychologists may not have really added much to what in another day would have been perceived as a problem of the spirit, best left to ecclesiastical attention. But, given modern postulates and perspectives, I see no reason to equate what purports to be a scientific diagnosis threatening adverse economic consequences (through lowered job performance) with a mere presumption of mental anguish and emotional distress. This is the equation, however, that the majority makes. Despite the scientific trappings of expert testimony, the majority is unwilling to factor these matters of the "spirit" into its calculations.
>
> * * * *
>
> By seeking to interpret Indiana law as congruent with modern concepts of psychology as a science, the district court has hit upon a perfectly acceptable basis for abandoning jurisdictional distinctions of the sixteenth century that have, as far as I can see, no current utility. The majority, on the other hand, adopts a view which might regard proof even of irreversible psychosis as a mere restatement of mental anguish and emotional distress. For a psychosis, too, is a thing of the spirit (albeit an evil one).
>
> I therefore respectfully dissent.

This short dissent (only one paragraph is omitted) demonstrates the way in which law has evolved from different and sometimes surprising roots, and the way in which it will continue to evolve. It also demonstrates the moral and religious connections in the common law, something that should not be entirely forgotten in addressing modern legal questions.

There is one other possible answer to Judge Cudahy's complaint, and it rests upon the *per se* categories of defamation, as well as hard sense. As noted previously, three of the four original categories of defamation *per se* related to a trade or business. Even the idea that someone had a "loathsome disease" had a similar impact, because "good" citizens naturally would stay away from such hideous individuals. In each situation, the damage to a trade, business, or profession could be presumed because it was a natural outgrowth of the statement.

Now consider the psychological side of the issue. People say mean things about each other all the time, many of which hurt deeply, and some of which can have terrible psychological impacts upon the victim. Most do not meet the criteria for defamation *per se*. To open the law of defamation to such slights, as Chief Judge Bauer seems to imply,[4] would create a real risk that the tort would become a vehicle by which courts must resolve "petty" squabbles, disagreements, and quarrels. Admittedly, this kind of a bright line cuts harshly, but it is difficult to find a place to stop short of this harshness. Perhaps the dialogue between majority and dissent in *Tacket* will open a way to resolve this problem.

Defamation With or Without Malice

Now let us address another real-world situation where the law of defamation must go. Suppose you witness what you think is a crime, and you report it. It later turns out that you have identified the wrong person.

Society has an interest in ensuring that crime is reported, but there certainly is no reason to protect those who wrongly report people as criminals out of spite or malice. How shall we resolve this dispute?

Bol v. Cole
561 N.W.2d 143
Supreme Court of Minnesota
1997

Anderson, J.:

Gerald E. Bol commenced a defamation action against Autumn Cole and Range Mental Health Center, Inc. (RMHC) for releasing to a minor patient's mother and her attorney reports of child abuse naming a "Dr. Bol" as the alleged abuser....

Appellant Autumn Cole, Ph.D., is a licensed psychologist employed by appellant RMHC. RMHC is a mental health clinic located in Virginia, Minnesota. Respondent Gerald E. Bol is a Doctor of Chiropractic operating the Eveleth Chiropractic Clinic in Eveleth, Minnesota.

In April 1993, Cole began treating S.P., a five-year-old male, because of an allegation that S.P. had been sexually abused by his father. After treatment began, S.P.'s mother, Sandra Petron, expressed concern that S.P. may have been sexually abused by some of his father's friends. During a therapy session on June 21, 1993, S.P. told Cole that he had been sexually abused by a man he referred to as "Dr. Bol."

Later that same day, June 21, Cole wrote a letter to two social workers with St. Louis County Social Services, informing them that S.P. stated that a "Dr. Bol" had sexually abused him and reporting S.P.'s statements regarding the alleged abuse. Cole subsequently prepared two additional letters, dated September 8 and October 6, in which she reported additional statements S.P. made to her in continuing therapy sessions concerning sexual abuse by S.P.'s father and "Dr. Bol." In these letters, Cole opined that she found S.P. "fairly credible," his story consistent, and his emotional and behavior problems "typical of children who have been sexually abused."

Cole and RMHC released copies of all three letters to Petron and her attorney. Petron showed her copies of the September 8 and October 6 letters to a friend, Kathy Buhr. Petron and Buhr then discussed the contents of the September 8 and October 6 letters in the presence of a third person.

Bol commenced a defamation action against Cole, RMHC, Petron, and Buhr. Bol's claim against Cole alleged that Cole published defamatory statements made by S.P. during therapy sessions and republished the statements by wrongfully giving Petron a copy of the September 8 letter. Bol alleged that the statements published by Cole were "false and untrue" and "imputed the commission of a criminal or indictable offense involving moral turpitude." Bol further alleged that as the result of the publication and republication of the statements, he was injured and damaged personally and professionally. Bol's claim against RMHC alleges that RMHC, as Cole's employer, is vicariously liable for Cole's actions.

* * * *

Cole and RMHC brought a motion for summary judgment. Cole and RMHC asserted that they were entitled to immunity under the Child Abuse Reporting Act, Minn.Stat. § 626.556 (1992), and were protected by a privilege because they released the letters in compliance with the Health Records Act, Minn.Stat. § 144.335 (1992). The district court granted Cole and RMHC's motion for summary judgment, holding that Cole and RMHC were protected by an absolute privilege because the Health Records Act required them to release the letters as health records.

The court of appeals reversed the district court. The court of appeals treated the letters as child abuse reports, determined as a matter of law that child abuse reports are not health records, and held that Cole and RMHC were not immune from suit. Cole and RMHC appeal, claiming ... they are protected by an absolute privilege because the Health Records Act required them to release copies of the letters to Petron; and [that] they are protected by a qualified privilege because they released the letters to Petron in good faith and without malice.

* * *

For a statement to be defamatory, it must be false, it must be communicated to another, and it must tend to harm the plaintiff's reputation.... Bol asserts that S.P.'s statements were false and have become a matter of gossip and rumor, causing harm to his personal and professional reputation.

For the purposes of this appeal, Cole and RMHC do not dispute that S.P.'s statements, recorded in Cole's letters, were defamatory; that Cole and RMHC published the statements by releasing the letters to Petron; or that Petron republished the statements. Rather, Cole and RMHC contend that they are not liable for defamation because they are protected by both immunity and privilege. Based upon the parties' briefs and arguments, we assume that each of Cole's three letters contains defamatory statements, and we decide Cole and RMHC's claims of ... privilege....

* * * *

[W]e must ... decide whether Cole and RMHC are protected by an absolute privilege under the common law. We note that absolute privilege and immunity are often used interchangeably as they were in the pleading and argument of this case; but they are different legal concepts and should not be confused. Perhaps the reason absolute privilege is sometimes referred to as an immunity is because it has the effect of making the publisher of a defamatory statement immune from suit and because the cases in which this court has recognized an absolute privilege often involve defamation suits against government officials....

After a plaintiff establishes a *prima facie* case of the tort of defamation, the defendant may raise the defense of absolute privilege. When an absolute privilege is granted, defamatory statements are not actionable, even if the statements were made with malice.... The *Restatement (Second) of Torts* explains the purpose of granting an absolute privilege:

> These "absolute privileges" are based chiefly upon a recognition of the necessity that certain persons, because of their special position or status, should be as free as possible from fear that their actions in that position might have an adverse effect upon their own personal interests. To accomplish this, it is necessary for them to be protected not only from civil liability but also from the danger of even an unsuccessful civil action. To this end, it is necessary that the propriety of their conduct not be inquired into indirectly by either court or jury in civil proceedings brought against them for misconduct in their position. Therefore, the privilege, or immunity, is absolute and the protection that it affords is complete. *Restatement (Second) of Torts* § 584, at 243 (1977).

Section 592A of the *Restatement (Second) of Torts* provides: "One who is required by law to publish defamatory matter is absolutely privileged to publish it." Section 592A does not require that a publisher of defamatory matter be a government official to be protected by an absolute privilege.

This court cited section 592A with approval in [*Johnson v. Dirkswager,* [315 N.W.2d 215, 223 (Minn.1982)]. In *Dirkswager,* the Commissioner of the Minnesota Department of Public Welfare disclosed defamatory information concerning a dismissed assistant supervisor. This court held that the commissioner was absolutely privileged because he was a high-level government official and because he disclosed the information in performance of his public duties.... Citing section 592A as further support for its decision, this court noted that the commissioner was required to disclose the defamatory information under the Minnesota Government Data Practices Act (MGDPA); thus, the disclosure was absolutely privileged.

* * * *

The public interests implicated by the actions of Cole and RMHC are not as strong as those in *Dirkswager.* Cole recorded S.P.'s statements concerning Bol in S.P.'s patient records. These statements identified and defamed Bol, who was a third party to Cole and S.P.'s psychologist-client relationship. Cole released records containing the defamatory statements to Petron. The public has an interest in encouraging psychologists to record complete and accurate information concerning their patients. Keeping complete and accurate records may sometimes require psychologists to record statements concerning third parties. The public also has an interest in encouraging psychologists to provide full disclosure of health information to their patients without fear of lawsuits by defamed third parties.

But we have held that the doctrine of absolute privilege should be "confined within narrow limits...." For absolute privilege to apply, the public interest served must be one of paramount importance, such that it is entitled to protection even at the expense of failing to compensate harm to the defamed person's reputation. Affording psychologists an absolute privilege with respect to statements contained in patient records concerning third parties would give psychologists less incentive to accurately record such information and would increase the risk of publication to inappropriate persons.

We conclude that the public interest in protecting a psychologist from a lawsuit by a defamed third party is not sufficiently strong to prohibit courts from inquiring into the psychologist's motives in publishing defamatory statements. Accordingly, we hold that an absolute privilege does not apply to Cole and RMHC in this case.

Having declined to recognize an absolute privilege, we must next decide whether Cole and RMHC are entitled to a qualified privilege. One who makes a defamatory statement will not be held liable if the statement is published under circumstances that make it qualifiedly privileged and if the privilege is not abused.... Qualified privilege applies when a court determines that statements made in particular contexts or on certain occasions should be encouraged despite the risk that the statements might be defamatory. For a defamatory statement to be protected by a qualified privilege, the statement must be made in good faith and must be made upon a proper occasion, from a proper motive, and must be based upon reasonable or probable cause....

* * * *

There is a strong public interest in reporting child abuse and protecting children from further abuse. The public has a strong interest in encouraging a psychologist to assess her patients accurately. When a patient is a child, the psychologist has an interest in providing complete and accurate information to the child's parents so that the parents may make well-informed decisions regarding treatment and may act to protect the child. Failure to recognize a privilege when information is properly released would place a heavy burden on psychologists to weigh the necessity of releasing information against the potential civil liability for doing so and would thereby deter psychologists from giving complete and accurate information to parents.

Cole prepared the letters in good faith and released the information upon a proper occasion, with a proper motive, and based upon reasonable or probable cause. We conclude that Cole and RMHC are protected by a qualified privilege.

Because Cole and RMHC are protected by a qualified privilege, Bol, as the plaintiff, has the burden to prove that this privilege was abused because the defamatory statements were made with malice. Malice is generally a question of fact. On review of summary judgment, however, this court determines whether the evidence submitted raises any genuine issues of material fact.

Malice is defined as "actual ill-will or a design causelessly and wantonly to injure plaintiff...." Malice cannot be implied from the statement itself or from the fact that the statement was false. Malice can be shown by extrinsic evidence of personal spite, as well as by intrinsic evidence such as the exaggerated language of the libel, the character of the language used, the mode and extent of publication, and other matters in excess of the privilege....

The language Cole used in her letters does not evince malice. In the letters, Cole related S.P.'s statements, the circumstances in which the statements were made, S.P.'s actions during therapy sessions, S.P.'s fear of discussing the abuse, S.P.'s emotional problems, Cole's opinion of S.P.'s veracity, and the actions Cole took in response to S.P.'s statements. Cole did not use inflammatory language in the letters. The mode of publication also does not evince malice because Cole distributed the letters only to the appropriate government authorities and to Petron and Petron's attorney.... We conclude that all of the evidence in the record, including depositions, affidavits, and exhibits, when viewed in the light most favorable to Bol, is insufficient to create a genuine issue of material fact as to the issue of malice.

We conclude that Cole and RMHC are protected by a qualified privilege. Accordingly, we reverse.

These concepts of absolute and qualified privilege are vital defenses in defamation and other similar torts. But notice that they are defenses. By raising the issue, the defendants permitted the Court to assume that the reports of child abuse were defamatory. This is not to say that raising a claim of privilege prevented the defendants from asserting that the reports were not defamatory or from asserting other defenses (such as truth), but they did have the burden of proof. Failing on a defense such as privilege without a fallback position can be risky indeed.

The most commonly heard statement in any situation involving defamation is "truth is a defense." It is, but the next case may help you understand some nuances that are not apparent from this adage:

Healy v. Suntrust Service Corp.
569 So.2d 458
District Court of Appeal of Florida,
Fifth District
1990

Cobb, J.:

The plaintiff below, Vicki Healy, sued Suntrust Service Corporation, for defamation.... Suntrust provided the data processing and customer account processing services for Sun Bank, where Healy worked until she was discharged on January 15, 1989. The termination was precipitated by the discovery that Healy used the bank's money mover system to transfer the sum of $200 from her father's account to her own. In doing so, she had violated the bank's rule that money could not be moved by this system from one account to another unless the accounts were titled in the same name.

It is undisputed that Healy's father, Jack Haverhill, had agreed to give her the $200. When bank officials learned of the transfer, Healy was called into the office of her supervisor, Mrs. Kovach, where she was advised by several Suntrust officers that she was being discharged for misappropriation of funds. Healy explained that Haverhill gave her permission to transfer the funds, but Suntrust made no effort to verify this information. A police officer was called to the scene by Suntrust, and eventually escorted Healy from the building, but left without making an arrest.

After Healy had gathered her personal belongings and left, Kovach called together approximately 20 to 35 bank employees and told them that Healy had been discharged for "misappropriation of funds." Suntrust asserts that "this was done as standard procedure when an employee was fired to avoid rumor and speculation among bank employees as to what had happened" and to "deter future acts like this by employees."

* * * *

The evidence presented at trial demonstrated that Healy did not misappropriate funds. A reasonable person would equate the term "misappropriation" with theft. Theft is defined by Florida Statutory law as follows:

§ 812.014 Theft

(1) A person is guilty of theft if he knowingly obtains or uses, or endeavors to obtain or use, the property of another with intent to, either temporarily or permanently:
    (a) Deprive the other person of a right to the property or a benefit therefrom.
    (b) Appropriate the property to his own use or to the use of any person not entitled thereto. § 812.014, Fla.Stat. (1989).

Theft is a specific intent crime, requiring actual knowledge on the part of the defendant. Healy did not possess the requisite intent to knowingly deprive Haverhill of his money. She had Haverhill's permission to withdraw funds from his account and to transfer those funds to her own account. Clearly, Healy's failure to comply with Suntrust's transfer procedures alone was not a theft or misappropriation.

Suntrust [also] contended that the funds on deposit did not belong to Haverhill, but that they belonged to Suntrust due to the debtor-creditor relationship existing between a bank and its depositors. The argument that Suntrust, rather than Haverhill, must authorize the transfer of funds is unavailing. If the $200 was owned by the bank before Healy's transfer, then it was also owned by the bank after the transfer because the money remained in Healy's account when she was fired. Hence, the trial court erred in not granting Healy's motion for a directed verdict on the defense of truth.

So, truth is a defense, but it is a defense that is measured against the meaning of what was said *taken in light as to how it would have been understood by the audience.* Here the defendant attempted to equate "misappropriation of funds" with a violation of internal procedures for funds transfer, just as in the *Bryson* case earlier in the chapter, the defendant tried to escape liability by expanding the definition of "slut."

In each case, the defendant attempted to present a position based on "What I really meant...." The law of defamation rests, however, on "What the audience understood...." Always keep this distinction in mind in assessing defamation problems.

Defamation *vis-à-vis* the First Amendment

Finally, we must at least attempt to understand the relationship between the common law of defamation and the constitutional protections for speech and press in the First Amendment of the United States Constitution. This is a complex field with a rich jurisprudence (it also makes for great movies like *Absence of Malice*) that we cannot fully cover in this introductory text. But you should be aware that in defamation matters constitutional issues can arise at any time.

The first prong of this First Amendment test can be explained by returning to the *Bryson* case we have been studying:

Bryson v. News America Publications, Inc.
174 Ill.2d 77, 672 N.E.2d 1207, 220 Ill. Dec. 1995
Supreme Court of Illinois
1996

CONTINUED (AGAIN)

* * * *

Before 1990, this court and others perceived a fundamental distinction between statements of fact and statements of opinion for First Amendment purposes. Statements of opinion were held to be protected by the first amendment and not actionable in a defamation action.... This rule was grounded primarily on dictum contained in *Gertz v. Robert Welch, Inc.*, 418 U.S. 323.... (1974): "Under the First Amendment there is no such thing as a false idea. However pernicious an opinion may seem, we depend for its correction not on the conscience of judges and juries but on the competition of other ideas."

Recently, however, the United States Supreme Court reexamined the law of defamation within the context of the First Amendment and rejected what it called "the creation of an artificial dichotomy between 'opinion' and fact." *Milkovich v. Lorain Journal Co.*, 497 U.S. 1, 19 (1990). The Court

---

explained that the dictum in *Gertz* had been interpreted too broadly and was not intended to create a "wholesale defamation exemption for anything that might be labeled 'opinion.'" *Milkovich*, 497 U.S. at 18.

The Court held that there is no separate First Amendment privilege for statements of opinion and that a false assertion of fact can be libelous even though couched in terms of an opinion. *Milkovich*, 497 U.S. at 18 (simply couching the statement "Jones is a liar" in terms of opinion—"In my opinion, Jones is a liar"—does not dispel the factual implications contained in the statement).

Thus, the test to determine whether a defamatory statement is constitutionally protected is a restrictive one. Under *Milkovich*, a statement is constitutionally protected under the First Amendment only if it cannot be "reasonably interpreted as stating actual facts." *Milkovich*, 497 U.S. at 20, *see, e.g., Hustler Magazine v. Falwell*, 485 U.S. 46, 50 (1988) (parody); *Old Dominion Branch No. 496 v. Austin*, 418 U.S. 264, 284–86 (1974) (hyperbole and imaginative expression); *Greenbelt Cooperative Publishing Ass'n v. Bresler*, 398 U.S. 6, 13–14 (1970) (hyperbole and imaginative expression).

In applying this test we first consider whether a reasonable fact finder could conclude that the allegedly defamatory statement, (i.e., that Bryson was a "slut") was an assertion of fact.... We answer this question in the affirmative. The clear impact of the statement was that Bryson was, in fact, sexually promiscuous. This was not the sort of loose, figurative or hyperbolic language that would negate the impression that the writer was seriously maintaining that the character depicted in the story was unchaste. The assertion is sufficiently factual to be susceptible to being proven true or false. Whether the statement was actually true or false is a question of fact for the jury. We simply hold, as a matter of law, that the allegation of sexual promiscuity in this case contains a provably false factual assertion. Thus, we do not find that the allegedly defamatory statement here was constitutionally protected under the First Amendment.

The defendants argue, however, that the defamatory statement cannot be reasonably interpreted as stating actual facts about the plaintiff because the story was clearly labeled "fiction." The test is not whether the story is or is not characterized as "fiction" or "humor," but whether the charged portions, in context, could be reasonably understood as describing actual facts about the plaintiff or actual events in which she participated....

Journalists and Defamation

Our final stop in this area of defamation and First Amendment is the one that makes movie producers happy: the limitations on defamation claims against journalists. *Absence of Malice* accurately frames the view here, as our final excerpt shows.

Clardy v. Cowles Publishing Co.
81 Wash. App. 53, 912 P.2d 1078
Court of Appeals of Washington
1996

Sweeney, C.J.:

A public figure must prove actual malice to recover for defamation. *New York Times Co. v. Sullivan*, 376 U.S. 254, 279–80 (1964). A public figure is one who has attained special "prominence in the affairs of society." *Gertz v. Robert Welch, Inc.*, 418 U.S. 323, 345 (1974). A person may be a public figure for all purposes or for a limited purpose. *Gertz*, 418 U.S. at 351.

John D. Clardy spearheaded the Mission Springs development, the biggest planned unit development ever proposed for Spokane County. It had an ultimate mortgage value of $45 million. On behalf of Mission Springs Limited Partnership, Mr. Clardy applied for mortgage insurance through the United States Department of Housing and Urban Development (HUD). The development ran into vocal public opposition after it had been approved, but before HUD had committed to insure financing. Mr. Clardy stepped into the hailstorm by attending a meeting with the opposition leader, speaking out in favor of the project, and contacting public officials, all in an attempt to keep the HUD commitment on track. We are asked to decide whether Mr. Clardy became a limited-purpose public figure by his involvement in the Mission Springs project. We conclude that he did and affirm the superior court's summary dismissal of his defamation claim.

FACTS

Two newspaper articles by *The Spokesman Review* reporter Bill Morlin prompted Mr. Clardy's defamation suit. The first, published on July 29, 1993, opened with the headline, "Tax Felon to Get HUD Insurance—Huge

Project under Protest." Mr. Morlin reported that Mr. Clardy had been convicted of federal income tax evasion in 1980. He also reported that on behalf of landlords, Mr. Clardy had attempted to evict 400 families from their rental homes in California in 1972. Reporting on the Mission Springs project, Mr. Morlin told readers that Mr. Clardy had applied for $45 million in federal housing insurance, that neighbors had opposed the project, and that Mr. Clardy had asked the director of the Department of Ecology (DOE) to fire one employee and discipline two others because they opposed the project.

A second article, published on December 14, 1993, was headlined, "Developer's Address Fictitious — Mission Springs Mortgagee Lists Bad Address with HUD." In it, Mr. Morlin reports that paperwork submitted to HUD on the Mission Springs project listed a fictitious address and the same fictitious address was used on Mission Springs "corporation papers." Mr. Morlin reported that corporate papers listed Mr. Clardy as secretary and partner in the Mission Springs project. Finally, he reported that HUD was not concerned about the nonexistent address.

Mr. Clardy sued Cowles Publishing Company, publisher of *The Spokesman Review*, and Mr. Morlin (hereafter, "Cowles") for defamation in January 1994. Following a motion by Cowles, the court summarily dismissed Mr. Clardy's complaint. It concluded that Mr. Clardy was a limited-purpose public figure and therefore had to prove malice by clear and convincing evidence. And he had failed to do so. Mr. Clardy appeals.

* * * *

In *New York Times* [*v. Sullivan*], a plurality of the United States Supreme Court concluded that many traditional common law actions for defamation could interfere with First Amendment rights of free expression. To avoid such interference, it held that a public official could recover damages for defamation only if the official proved that a defamatory statement was made with "actual malice"; that is, with knowledge that the statement was false or with reckless disregard of its truth. *New York Times*, 376 U.S. at 279–80. Actual malice had to be proved with "convincing clarity." *New York Times*, 376 U.S. at 285–86.

Both the standard of fault — actual malice, and the standard of proof — convincing clarity, established in *New York Times* were later extended to public figures who were not public officials. *Curtis Publishing Co. v. Butts*, 388 U.S. 130, 154–55 (1967). *Curtis*, however, gave little guidance on the question of when a private citizen becomes a "public figure."

* * * *

In ... *Gertz* [*v. Welch*, the Supreme Court] set up two categories of public figures: limited-purpose public figures and general-purpose public figures. Limited-purpose public figures are those who voluntarily inject themselves or are drawn into a public controversy and thereby become public figures for a limited range of issues. *Gertz*, 418 U.S. at 351. The threshold question posed in *Gertz* is whether the defamatory statement involves a matter of public concern. The next focuses on the nature and extent of the plaintiff's participation in that public controversy. *Gertz*, 418 U.S. at 352 ("did he engage the public's attention in an attempt to influence its outcome" and did he "thrust himself into the vortex of this public issue"). While an individual could become a public figure through no purposeful action of his own, *Gertz* concluded that instances of truly involuntary public figures "must be exceedingly rare." *Gertz*, 418 U.S. at 345.

Gertz gave greater protection to speech about public figures, than speech about private citizens, because public figures usually have greater media access and hence "a more realistic opportunity to counteract false statements [than] private individuals normally enjoy." *Gertz*, 418 U.S. at 344. Private citizens were also "more deserving of recovery" because they had not assumed the risk of close public scrutiny — a necessary consequence of involvement in public affairs. *Gertz*, 418 U.S. at 344. *See also Wolston v. Reader's Digest Ass'n.*, 443 U.S. 157 (1979).

After *Gertz*, several federal circuits developed tests to determine whether a person was a limited-purpose public figure. In the Fourth Circuit, the test included consideration of whether:

(1) the plaintiff had access to channels of effective communication;

(2) the plaintiff voluntarily assumed a role of special prominence in the public controversy;

(3) the plaintiff sought to influence the resolution or outcome of the controversy;

(4) the controversy existed prior to the publication of the defamatory statement; and

(5) the plaintiff retained public-figure status at the time of the alleged defamation. *Foretich v. Capital Cities/ABC, Inc.*, 37 F.3d 1541, 1553 (4th Cir.1994).

The D.C. Circuit's test requires a three-step analysis:

(1) the controversy at issue must be public in the sense that people are debating it and it has foreseeable and substantial ramifications for nonparticipants;

(2) the plaintiff must have more than a trivial or tangential role in the controversy and must have thrust himself to the forefront of the controversy so as to become a factor in its ultimate resolution; and

(3) the alleged defamation must be germane to the plaintiff's participation in the controversy.

Waldbaum v. Fairchild Publications, Inc., 627 F.2d 1287, 1296–98 (D.C. Cir. 1980); *Tavoulareas v. Piro*, 817 F.2d 762, 771–75 (D.C. Cir. 1987). This three-part test was adopted by the Fifth Circuit in *Trotter v. Jack Anderson Enters, Inc.*, 818 F.2d 431, 433–34 (5th Cir.1987).

* * * *

We believe that balancing the right to report on issues of public interest against the right of private citizens to be free from defamatory comments requires consideration of more than simply whether the plaintiff voluntarily injected himself or herself into the fray. We therefore adopt the five-part test outlined by the court in *Foretich* as a set of nonexclusive considerations for determining whether a plaintiff in a defamation case is a limited-purpose public figure. We then apply those nonexclusive considerations to the facts here.

(1) Access to media. Once the press began to report on the Mission Springs project, it appeared eager to report any comments about the project, including those of Mr. Clardy. Numerous letters to the editor were published. When Mr. Clardy complained about the December 14 story of his fictitious address, the paper ran a correction on December 15.

(2) Voluntariness and nature of role. A person becomes a public figure only if he voluntarily "draw[s] attention to himself" or uses his position in the controversy "as a fulcrum to create public discussion...." *Wolston*, 443 U.S. at 168. He must "thrust himself into the vortex of [the] public issue [and] engage the public's attention in an attempt to influence its outcome." *Gertz v. Robert Welch, Inc.*, 418 U.S. 323, 352 (1974).

Mr. Clardy admits he had a financial stake in the Mission Springs project. And,·at least at some point before the published articles at issue, he was an officer in the corporation. He had also personally owned the option on the land. He signed HUD documents on behalf of the limited partnership to obtain insurance for financing the project and met with HUD officials. All of this would have established Mr. Clardy's role in the development, but without more, would not necessarily have thrust Mr. Clardy into the controversy. These are the acts of many private business people involved in real estate development.

Mr. Clardy voluntarily became more involved in the Mission Springs controversy when he contacted two state legislators, the Governor, the director of DOE, and the head of personnel at Eastern Washington University (EWU). He contacted the latter two agencies to complain about two EWU professors and three DOE employees who had criticized the project. But even here, Mr. Clardy was not trying to influence public opinion so much as move government employees to action.

Mr. Clardy "thrust himself into the vortex of [the] public issue" when he sent letters to residents in the Mission Springs area telling the "new neighbors" about the Mission Springs project and advising them he would be updating them on its progress. These actions were clearly an attempt to influence public sentiment and resolution of the controversy created primarily by the residents to whom the letters were sent. These actions satisfy the *Gertz* requirement that a person voluntarily draw attention to himself or thrust himself to the front of the public controversy.

(3) Statements germane to controversy. The thrust of the July 1993 article was that Mr. Clardy had been convicted of tax evasion and was involved in a project to develop an apartment and townhouse complex with loans guaranteed by HUD. Mr. Morlin also reported that Mr. Clardy had attempted to evict 400 families from rental homes in California in 1972. The article also quoted Mr. Clardy as denying an ownership interest in the

corporation developing the site, Feature Realty. The December 1993 article focuses on what Mr. Morlin had concluded was a false address. These articles focused on basic questions surrounding the project: who, what, and how. By the time these articles were published, controversy surrounded the project.

These articles, while not directly related to events which thrust this project into the limelight — the neighbors' protest — nonetheless answer questions about those involved in the development, their prior experience with government-guaranteed financing and management of residential housing generally. They are therefore germane.

(4) Prior existence of controversy. Public opposition to the City of Spokane's approval of the largest proposed planned unit development in Spokane County existed before publication of Mr. Morlin's articles. Cowles introduced numerous newspaper articles published before the two at issue here which reported the creation of a neighborhood association to oppose the project.

(5) Plaintiff retained public-figure status at the time of the alleged defamation. These articles were printed during the height of the controversy surrounding this project — July and December. Mr. Clardy, as one of the project's principals, retained his public figure status throughout this period.

Mr. Clardy was a limited-purpose public figure with respect to the Mission Springs project....

Affirmed.

As you can see, even this first survey of the constitutional law of defamation reveals a deep, fact-sensitive jurisprudence. Constitutional issues arise in virtually every defamation case; anyone who works in the field must be prepared to recognize them and to understand their nuances as a part of the process by which a defamation case comes to trial.

Key Words and Phrases

actual malice
convincing clarity
defamation *per quod*
defamation *per se*
innocent construction rule
libel
limited-purpose public figure
public figure
slander
special damages

Review Questions

1. Explain the difference in defamation *per se* and defamation *per quod*.

2. In *Tacket* the majority of the court found emotional distress and psychological injury to be general damages. Judge Cudahay dissented. Do you agree with the majority, or do you dissent with Judge Cudahay?

3. Based upon *Bol*, explain the difference in the defense of absolute privilege and the defense of qualified privilege. Why did the court find Cole had one, but not the other?

4. Find a long line at your local supermarket checkout counter and, while waiting in it, review the current tabloid press. Do you find statements that could be a basis for a defamation suit were not the person discussed a public figure?

---

[1] There are dozens of examples. Women could not own property in their own name, inherit real estate, or sue. In Texas, until 1962, a married woman could not sell real estate owned by her alone without first obtaining her husband's signature. Later statutes and court decisions have helped erode these insidious distinctions in the law, but the issue remains a very real one.

[2] You remember the court's summary note about it: "Report that plaintiff gave birth to twins considered defamatory, where plaintiff proved, as extrinsic fact, that some readers knew that the plaintiff had been married only one month."

[3] These excerpts are not reprinted here in the same order that they appeared in the opinion.

[4] "But such maladies, however painful to Tacket, are only general damages—the kind that routinely follow a defamation. Injury to the plaintiff's reputation and standing in the community, personal humiliation, and mental anguish and suffering are the sort of damages that the law presumes to be the natural result of the publication...."

Chapter Twelve

"I WANT TO BE ALONE"
TORTS INVOLVING
PRIVACY AND SECLUSION

"I want to be alone," attributed to the great Hollywood actress Greta Garbo, actually is one of those famous statements that isn't quite accurate. Just as Humphrey Bogart never said, "Play it again, Sam," in *Casablanca*, Garbo never said, "I want to be alone." She said, "I want to be left alone," and in so doing, she unintentionally invoked a legal principle that owes its roots to the work of another of the towering figures in American law.

The Brandeis Legacy Concerning Privacy

Professor of law, inventor of the "Brandeis brief" (in which sociological and economic evidence as well as cold precedent support a position), defender of minimum wage and child labor laws, Associate Justice of the United States Supreme Court, Louis D. Brandeis left a huge legacy both in law and society. But what causes us to focus on Brandeis in this book is another facet of his legacy — an article he wrote with Samuel Warren in 1890. Called "The Right of Privacy,"[1] this bedrock article made the following statement:

> Thus, in the very early times, the law gave a remedy
> only for physical interference with life and property, for
> *trespass vi et armis*. Then the "right to life" served only
> to protect the subject from battery in its various forms;
> liberty meant freedom from actual restraint; and the
> right to property secured to the individual his lands and
> his cattle. Later, there came a recognition of a man's
> spiritual nature, of his feelings and his intellect.
> Gradually the scope of these legal rights broadened; and
> now the right to life has come to mean the right to enjoy

life — the right to be let alone; the right to liberty
secures the exercise of extensive civil privileges; and the
term "property" has grown to comprise every form of
possession — intangible, as well as tangible.[2]

What Garbo took for granted, the right to be left alone, was in reality the
product of a long if quiet struggle to turn protection for the tangible —
goods, property, and bodily injury — into protection for the intangible.
Brandeis most especially was the champion of this quiet revolution.

We should not be surprised at the relatively recent gestation of this tort,
or that the framers of our constitution did not pay any particular
attention to it. After all, in 1787, America had few large cities. Most
Americans could — and did, if they so chose — get all of the privacy
they wanted by farming or by "going west." A small population and
large empty tracts of land made privacy cheap to get and relatively easy
to keep.

Not so, however, by the time of Brandeis' seminal article. Certainly
there were large open spaces still in America, but in a now-industrial
society, large cities were for the first time the home for the majority of
Americans. Telephones, automobiles, corporations and a host of modern
inventions broke down barriers that had helped maintain privacy. The
change was palpable, and it was against the accelerating breakdown of
traditional barriers that Brandeis wrote.

But giving protection to privacy would mean changing and expanding
common law principles, something that traditional notions of *stare
decisis* militated against. Thus, exploring the privacy torts and how they
were adopted gives us a chance to see both the scope of protection
afforded by these torts and the way in which the common law evolves.

Lake v. Wal-Mart Stores, Inc.
582 N.W.2d 231
Supreme Court of Minnesota
1998

Blatz, C.J.:

Elli Lake and Melissa Weber appeal from a dismissal of their complaint for failure to state a claim upon which relief may be granted. The district court and court of appeals held that Lake and Weber's complaint alleging intrusion upon seclusion, appropriation, publication of private facts, and false light publicity could not proceed because Minnesota does not recognize a common law tort action for invasion of privacy. We reverse as to the claims of intrusion upon seclusion, appropriation, and publication of private facts, but affirm as to false light publicity.

Nineteen-year-old Elli Lake and 20-year-old Melissa Weber vacationed in Mexico in March 1995 with Weber's sister. During the vacation, Weber's sister took a photograph of Lake and Weber naked in the shower together. After their vacation, Lake and Weber brought five rolls of film to the Dilworth, Minnesota, Wal-Mart store and photo lab. When they received their developed photographs along with the negatives, an enclosed written notice stated that one or more of the photographs had not been printed because of their "nature."

In July 1995, an acquaintance of Lake and Weber alluded to the photograph and questioned their sexual orientation. Again, in December 1995, another friend told Lake and Weber that a Wal-Mart employee had shown her a copy of the photograph. By February 1996, Lake was informed that one or more copies of the photograph were circulating in the community.

Lake and Weber filed a complaint against Wal-Mart Stores, Inc., and one or more as-yet-unidentified Wal-Mart employees on February 23, 1996, alleging the four traditional invasion of privacy torts — intrusion upon seclusion, appropriation, publication of private facts, and false light publicity. Wal-Mart denied the allegations and made a motion to dismiss the complaint ... for failure to state a claim upon which relief may be granted. The district court granted Wal-Mart's motion to dismiss, explaining that Minnesota has not recognized any of the four invasion of privacy torts. The court of appeals affirmed.

Whether Minnesota should recognize any or all of the invasion of privacy causes of action is a question of first impression in Minnesota. The *Restatement (Second) of Torts* outlines the four causes of action that comprise the tort generally referred to as invasion of privacy.

Intrusion upon seclusion occurs when one "intentionally intrudes, physically or otherwise, upon the solitude or seclusion of another or his private affairs or concerns * * * if the intrusion would be highly offensive to a reasonable person."

Appropriation protects an individual's identity and is committed when one "appropriates to his own use or benefit the name or likeness of another."

Publication of private facts is an invasion of privacy when one "gives publicity to a matter concerning the private life of another * * * if the matter publicized is of a kind that (a) would be highly offensive to a reasonable person, and (b) is not of legitimate concern to the public."

False light publicity occurs when one "gives publicity to a matter concerning another that places the other before the public in a false light * * * if (a) the false light in which the other was placed would be highly offensive to a reasonable person, and (b) the actor had knowledge of or acted in reckless disregard as to the falsity of the publicized matter and the false light in which the other would be placed."

I.

This court has the power to recognize and abolish common law doctrines. The common law is not composed of firmly fixed rules. Rather, as we have long recognized, the common law:

> is the embodiment of broad and comprehensive unwritten principles, inspired by natural reason, an innate sense of justice, adopted by common consent for the regulation and government of the affairs of men. It is the growth of ages, and an examination of many of its principles, as enunciated and discussed in the books, discloses a constant improvement and development in keeping with advancing civilization and new conditions of society. Its guiding star has always been the rule of right and wrong, and in this country its principles demonstrate that there is in fact, as well as in theory, a remedy for all wrongs.

As society changes over time, the common law must also evolve:

> It must be remembered that the common law is the result of growth, and that its development has been determined by the social

needs of the community which it governs. It is the resultant of conflicting social forces, and those forces which are for the time dominant leave their impress upon the law. It is of judicial origin, and seeks to establish doctrines and rules for the determination, protection, and enforcement of legal rights. Manifestly it must change as society changes and new rights are recognized. To be an efficient instrument, and not a mere abstraction, it must gradually adapt itself to changed conditions.

To determine the common law, we look to other states as well as to England.

The tort of invasion of privacy is rooted in a common law right to privacy first described in an 1890 law review article by Samuel Warren and Louis Brandeis. The article posited that the common law has always protected an individual's person and property, with the extent and nature of that protection changing over time. The fundamental right to privacy is both reflected in those protections and grows out of them ....

The first jurisdiction to recognize the common law right to privacy was Georgia. In *Pavesich v. New England Life Ins. Co.*, [122 Ga. 190, 50 S.E. 68 (1905),] the Georgia Supreme Court determined that the "right of privacy has its foundation in the instincts of nature," and is therefore an "immutable" and "absolute" right "derived from natural law." The court emphasized that the right of privacy was not new to Georgia law, as it was encompassed by the well-established right to personal liberty.

Many other jurisdictions followed Georgia in recognizing the tort of invasion of privacy, citing Warren and Brandeis' article and *Pavesich*. Today, the vast majority of jurisdictions now recognize some form of the right to privacy. Only Minnesota, North Dakota, and Wyoming have not yet recognized any of the four privacy torts. Although New York and Nebraska courts have declined to recognize a common law basis for the right to privacy and instead provide statutory protection, we reject the proposition that only the legislature may establish new causes of action. The right to privacy is inherent in the English protections of individual property and contract rights, and the "right to be let alone" is recognized as part of the common law across this country. Thus, it is within the province of the judiciary to establish privacy torts in this jurisdiction.

Today we join the majority of jurisdictions and recognize the tort of invasion of privacy. The right to privacy is an integral part of our humanity; one has a public persona, exposed and active, and a private persona, guarded and preserved. The heart of our liberty is choosing which parts of our lives shall become public and which parts we shall hold close.

Here Lake and Weber allege in their complaint that a photograph of their nude bodies has been publicized. One's naked body is a very private part of one's person and generally known to others only by choice. This is a type of privacy interest worthy of protection. Therefore, without consideration of the merits of Lake and Weber's claims, we recognize the torts of intrusion upon seclusion, appropriation, and publication of private facts. Accordingly, we reverse the court of appeals and the district court and hold that Lake and Weber have stated a claim upon which relief may be granted and their lawsuit may proceed.

And that, as the astronauts would say, is how that is done.

The Protection of Privacy

Are you surprised that Minnesota, often thought of as a progressive state socially and legally, had not protected privacy more vigorously before 1998? There are many reasons for this: some logical, others not. The strongest pressure to avoid change or to proceed in small increments comes from the idea that precedential law, law made as it goes along, should be as predictable as possible.

With only cases to guide the public, supporters of this paradigm assert that change to legal principles should happen as slowly as possible and then only in response to compelling changes in the "real world." Better that everyone should know where they stand than for courts to try to follow every trend or fad. Such deliberateness minimizes uncertainty, even if it leaves some inequitable or obsolete principles on the books.

At its root, however, growth of the common law fundamentally is a matter of right and wrong — not of legal rights, but of the right thing to do. A new situation brought forth in evidence coupled with a feeling in judge or jury that someone has been badly wronged forms the stage on which the law will evolve. A judge who waits, who says "I am going to listen to the evidence before I decide," creates an environment in which this evolution may take place. Here, a pivotal article and the actions of other courts each contributed to the court's decision.

But note also that this process is reactive, at least where the court is concerned. If the two plaintiffs in *Lake* had not filed their lawsuit, the Minnesota Supreme Court would not have been able to act, regardless of its desire to do so. Thus, the common law evolves by an interactive process: Different facts, courageous litigants and counsel, scholarly activities, and judges with a vision are all necessary to change the law.

Judge Harold Leventhal of the D.C. Circuit has properly referred to this process as a dialogue among the ages.[3]

Intrusion upon Seclusion

But what of this Brandeisian legacy? How have the Courts treated the four different but related privacy torts? Let's start with intrusion with seclusion, the first of the four torts described in *Lake*.

Finlay v. Finlay
18 Kan.App.2d 479, 856 P.2d 183
Court of Appeals of Kansas
1993

King, D.J., assigned:

Kenneth and Juanita Finlay (plaintiffs) appeal from an order granting Robert Finlay (defendant) summary judgment on all of their claims and dismissing their cause of action.

The parties are relatives and neighbors. Robert is the nephew of Kenneth and Juanita. A county road separates the properties of the parties by approximately 50 feet. The properties are in rural Osage County.

The farmstead on which Kenneth and Juanita reside was originally occupied by Kenneth's grandfather. They have lived in their present house since 1948 or 1949.

Robert purchased 120 acres directly east of his aunt and uncle's farmstead in 1981. He purchased the property from Harold Widau.

For simplicity and clarity, we will refer to the parties as plaintiffs and defendant. Plaintiffs' claims against the defendant relate to defendant's use of his property, which they contend constitutes a nuisance and an invasion of plaintiffs' privacy....

When defendant purchased his property, it had a holding pen and shed located directly across the road from plaintiffs' house. The previous owner had raised cattle and used the pen for feeding and working his cattle. The cattle were otherwise allowed to roam over a larger pasture area. After defendant acquired the property, he made improvements to the 1.8-acre pen and uses it to feed approximately 50 head of cattle. He keeps his cattle in the pen from November through May.

Plaintiffs contend the smell created by defendant's cattle feeding operation constitutes ... [an] invasion of their privacy [for which t]hey seek ... damages....

* * * *

The facts in this case show that defendant, to an extent, changed the use of the property. Although the previous owners had raised cattle on the property, defendant made improvements to the pen and began conducting a feedlot type operation. The previous owner had allowed his cattle access to additional pasture; defendant confined his cattle to the 1.8-acre pen for substantial periods of time. Therefore ... the record shows that any change in use occurred only on defendant's property and not on the surrounding property.

* * * *

Plaintiffs request damages for invasion of privacy.... The trial court, without specifying the reason for its decision, concluded that "plaintiff does not state a cause of action for invasion of privacy."

Generally, invasion of privacy is actionable where there is: (1) unreasonable intrusion upon the seclusion of another; (2) appropriation of another's name or likeness; (3) unreasonable publicity given to another's private life; or (4) publicity that unreasonably places another in a false light before the public. *Restatement (Second) of Torts* § 652A (1976).

Plaintiffs premise their claim for invasion of privacy upon the defendant's conduct unreasonably intruding upon their seclusion. One who intentionally intrudes, physically or otherwise, upon the solitude or seclusion of another, or his private affairs or concerns, is subject to liability to the other for invasion of his privacy if the intrusion would be highly offensive to a reasonable person. There is no liability for intrusion upon seclusion unless interference with the plaintiffs' seclusion is a substantial one, of a kind that would be highly offensive to the ordinary reasonable person, as the result of conduct to which the reasonable person would strongly object.

The essence of claims for unreasonable intrusion upon seclusion is that an individual's right to be left alone is interfered with by defendant's physical intrusion, or by an intrusion of defendant using his or her sensory faculties. Comment b of the *Restatement (Second) of Torts* § 652B (1976) makes this point:

> The invasion may be by physical intrusion into a place in which the plaintiff has secluded himself, as when the defendant forces his way into the plaintiff's room in a hotel or insists over the plaintiff's objection in entering his home. It may also be by the use of the defendant's senses, with or without mechanical aids, to oversee or overhear the plaintiff's private affairs, as by looking into his upstairs windows with binoculars or tapping his telephone wires. It may be by some other form of investigation or examination into his private concerns, as by opening his private and personal mail, searching his safe or his wallet, examining his private bank account, or compelling him by a forged court order to permit an inspection of his personal documents.

While liability for the intrusion does not require publication of a plaintiff's private affairs, it does require that the defendant place himself physically, or by means of his senses, within plaintiff's zone of privacy. The facts of this case may be distinguished from all other Kansas cases which have considered claims for intrusion upon seclusion. In this case, there is no physical intrusion by the defendant, nor by defendant's senses.

The requirement that the intrusion be a substantial one, while somewhat flexible, is designed to serve the same end. All kinds of small irritations go on at home and in the office on a daily basis, but making them a tort serves no purpose except to make the courts a vehicle for resolution of spats and quarrels.

The final protection against the small insult and petulant plaintiff is the requirement that the intrusion be offensive to an ordinary person, at least as conceived by a jury. The easily offended should not find refuge in this tort.

Appropriation of a Likeness or Image

Appropriation of a likeness or image, the next subset of privacy torts, might also be thought of as a celebrity tort, since it is celebrities who most often are targets of this kind of wrongdoing. It is they who most often fight back, as our next excerpt demonstrates.

Eastwood v. Superior Court for the County of Los Angeles
149 Cal.App.3d 409, 198 Cal. Rptr. 342
1983

Thompson, J.:

[Clint] Eastwood, a well-known motion picture actor, filed a complaint containing two causes of action against the *Enquirer*. The gist of the first cause of action is for false light invasion of privacy. The second cause of action is for invasion of privacy through the commercial appropriation of name, photograph and likeness under both the common law and Civil Code section 3344.

The following pertinent facts emerge from the allegations of the first cause of action. The *Enquirer* publishes a weekly newspaper known as the *National Enquirer*, which enjoys wide circulation and is read by a great number of people. In its April 13, 1982, edition of the *National Enquirer*, the *Enquirer* published a 600-word article about Eastwood's romantic involvement with two other celebrities, singer Tanya Tucker and actress Sondra Locke. On the cover of this edition appeared the pictures of Eastwood and Tucker above the caption "Clint Eastwood in Love Triangle with Tanya Tucker."

The article is headlined "Clint Eastwood in Love Triangle" and appears on page 48 of this edition. Eastwood alleges the article is false.

Eastwood further asserts that *Enquirer* "published the offending article maliciously, willfully and wrongfully, with the intent to injure and disgrace Eastwood, either knowing that the statements therein contained were false or with reckless disregard of ... their ... falsity." *Enquirer* used Eastwood's name and photograph without his consent or permission. As a consequence thereof, Eastwood alleges that he has suffered mental anguish and emotional distress and seeks both compensatory and punitive damages.

The second cause of action of the complaint incorporates all the allegations of the first cause of action concerning the status of *Enquirer* and the falsity of the article. It does not, however, incorporate the allegation that the article was published with knowledge or in reckless disregard of its falsity.

Additionally, Eastwood alleges that the *Enquirer* made a telecast advertisement in which it featured Eastwood's name and photograph and mentioned prominently the subject article. Moreover, Eastwood alleges that the telecast advertisements, as well as the cover of the April 13 publication, were calculated to promote the sales of the *Enquirer*. Eastwood asserts that the unauthorized use of his name and photograph has damaged him in his right to control the commercial exploitation of his name, photograph and likeness, in addition to injuring his feelings and privacy. Eastwood seeks damages.

California has long recognized a common law right of privacy ... which provides protection against four distinct categories of invasion. These four distinct torts identified by Dean Prosser and grouped under the privacy rubric are: (1) intrusion upon the plaintiff's seclusion or solitude, or into his private affairs; (2) public disclosure of embarrassing private facts about the plaintiff; 3) publicity which places the plaintiff in a false light in the public eye; and (4) appropriation, for the defendant's advantage, of the plaintiff's name or likeness. [Citations omitted.]

* * * *

Eastwood has framed his complaint against *Enquirer* on the third and fourth branches of the right of privacy. His first cause of action, which is not at issue here, rests on the theory that the subject publication placed him in a false light in the public eye. The focus of this tort is the falsity of the published article. His second cause of action ... is at issue here....

A common law cause of action for appropriation of name or likeness may be pleaded by alleging (1) the defendant's use of the plaintiff's identity; (2) the appropriation of plaintiff's name or likeness to defendant's advantage, commercially or otherwise; (3) lack of consent; and (4) resulting injury.

Here, Eastwood has alleged that the *Enquirer* employed his name, photograph and likeness on the front page of the subject publication and in related telecast advertisements, without his prior consent, for the purpose of promoting the sales of the *Enquirer*. Therefore, Eastwood states an actionable claim in his second cause of action under ... the common law ... if two conditions are satisfied: (1) *Enquirer*'s use of Eastwood's name, photograph and likeness constitutes an appropriation for commercial purposes, and (2) *Enquirer*'s conduct constitutes an impermissible infringement of Eastwood's right of publicity.

Enquirer argues that the failure of Eastwood to allege the appearance of an "endorsement" of the *Enquirer* is fatal to stating a cause of action for commercial appropriation.

California law has not imposed any requirement that the unauthorized use or publication of a person's name or picture be suggestive of an endorsement or association with the injured person.... [Prior] decisions merely hold that the exploitation of another's personality for commercial purposes constitutes an invasion of privacy. They did not purport to limit the scope of this tort. The exploitation in [one case] took the form of advertising, which suggested a false endorsement by plaintiff. In [another], the court found exploitation where a professor's lecture notes were sold without his permission. The case at bench involves a different situation. This fact does not necessarily preclude a right of action here.

Further, *Enquirer* contends that ... an appropriation of name and likeness for commercial purposes can only be shown by Eastwood, if their use has impressed the *Enquirer* with a secondary meaning.... [The California Supreme Court] recognized that the right of publicity includes not only the power to control the exploitation of one's personality through licensing agreements, but also the right to obtain relief, both injunctive and/or for damages, when a third party appropriates one's name and likeness for commercial purposes without permission.

The first step toward selling a product or service is to attract the consumers' attention. Because of a celebrity's audience appeal, people respond almost automatically to a celebrity's name or picture. Here, the *Enquirer* used Eastwood's personality and fame on the cover of the subject publication and in related telecast advertisements. To the extent their use attracted the readers' attention, the *Enquirer* gained a commercial advantage. Furthermore, the *Enquirer* used Eastwood's personality in the context of an alleged news account, entitled "Clint Eastwood in Love Triangle with Tanya Tucker" to generate maximum curiosity and the necessary motivation to purchase the newspaper.

Moreover, the use of Eastwood's personality in the context of a news account, allegedly false but presented as true, provided the *Enquirer* with a ready-made "scoop" —a commercial advantage over its competitors which it would otherwise not have.... We therefore conclude that Eastwood has sufficiently alleged that the *Enquirer* has commercially exploited his name, photograph, and likeness under ... the common law....

This seems to be rather a large concept to digest, but at its heart, it reduces to a simple concept, one that has underpinnings in copyright and similar concepts of intellectual property. Each of us, as this opinion points out, has the right to control the exploitation of our personality through licensing agreements, as well as the right to obtain relief, both injunctive and for damages, when a third party appropriates our name and likeness for commercial purposes without permission. This is just about the same thing as saying that we own a copyright, which is protection for the fruits of our literary or artistic endeavors, or a patent, which protects the fruits of our technological endeavors.

Thus, this tort is not so much a "right of privacy" as a right of publicity, or at least the right to control what is said about us by others. As you can guess from saying this, there are substantial constitutional issues associated with this tort, principally because publication almost always involves the media. Thus, the rights conferred in this tort are subject to First Amendment considerations. Is the publicity newsworthy and true? If so, no cause of action will lie. If fictional — that is, if the celebrity's name is added to fictional events portrayed as true — was there malice or recklessness? Would the author or publisher have published the account anyway with awareness of the truth, the definition of "recklessness" in this context?

Remember, as the court in *Eastwood* noted, "Normally, in a commercial appropriation case involving the right of publicity, the only question is who gets to do the publishing, since the celebrity is primarily concerned with whether he gets the commercial benefit of such publication." That this is so is the hallmark of this special — and limited — cause of action.

Wrongful Public Disclosure of Private Facts

But what about noncelebrities? Don't they have some right to have their private lives kept private? Protection of this interest is the purpose of the third privacy tort, wrongful public disclosure of private facts. As the next excerpt shows, these cases can involve difficult and extremely sensitive issues.

Robert C. Ozer, P.C. v. Bourquez
940 P.2d 371
Supreme Court of Colorado, *En Banc*
1997

Vollack, C.J.:

In June of 1990, Borquez began working as an associate attorney for Ozer & Mullen, P.C. (the Ozer law firm). During his employment with the Ozer law firm, Borquez received three merit raises, the last of which was awarded on February 15, 1992, eleven days prior to his termination.

On February 19, 1992, Borquez, who is homosexual, learned that his partner was diagnosed with Acquired Immune Deficiency Syndrome (AIDS). Borquez' physician advised him that he should be tested for the human immunodeficiency virus (HIV) immediately. Borquez was anxious about his health and determined that he could not effectively represent a client in a deposition that afternoon and an arbitration hearing the following day. Borquez subsequently telephoned his secretary and attempted to arrange for a colleague to fill in for him at the deposition and hearing. Borquez' secretary and another staff member told the president and shareholder of the law firm, Robert Ozer (Ozer), about Borquez' telephone call. Ozer then directed Borquez' secretary to transfer to him any further telephone calls from Borquez.

Borquez and Ozer subsequently spoke twice on the telephone. During the second conversation, Borquez decided that he would disclose his situation to Ozer. Borquez asked Ozer to keep the information he was about to disclose confidential, but Ozer made no reply. Borquez then told Ozer that he was homosexual, that his partner had been diagnosed with AIDS, and that he needed to be tested for HIV. Ozer responded by stating that he would handle the deposition and arbitration hearing and that Borquez should "do what [he needed] to do."

After speaking with Borquez, Ozer telephoned his wife, Renee Ozer, and told her of Borquez' disclosure. Additionally, Ozer informed the law firm's office manager about Borquez' situation and discussed Borquez' disclosure with two of the law firm's secretaries. On February 21, 1992, Borquez returned to the office and became upset when he learned that everyone in the law firm knew about his situation. Later that afternoon, Ozer met with Borquez and told him that Ozer had not agreed to keep Borquez' disclosure confidential.

On February 26, 1992, one week after Borquez made his disclosure to Ozer, Borquez was fired. The Ozer law firm asserted that Borquez was terminated due to the law firm's poor financial circumstances. Borquez filed suit against the Ozer law firm and against Ozer as an individual, claiming ... invasion of privacy.... Borquez further asserted that Ozer violated his right to privacy by disseminating private facts which Borquez had revealed and requested remain confidential. In addition to compensatory damages, Borquez sought exemplary damages ... for the violation of his right to privacy.

On July 12, 1993, a five-day trial commenced in this case.... The jury found in favor of Borquez and awarded him damages totaling ... $20,000 for the invasion of privacy claim, and awarded exemplary damages in the sum of $40,000.

In accordance with most jurisdictions, we now recognize in Colorado a tort claim for invasion of privacy in the nature of unreasonable publicity given to one's private life. In order to prevail on such a claim, we hold that the following requirements must be met: (1) the fact or facts disclosed must be private in nature; (2) the disclosure must be made to the public; (3) the disclosure must be one which would be highly offensive to a reasonable person; (4) the fact or facts disclosed cannot be of legitimate concern to the public; and (5) the defendant acted with reckless disregard of the private nature of the fact or facts disclosed.

The first requirement of a tort claim for invasion of privacy in the nature of unreasonable publicity given to one's private life is that the facts disclosed be private in nature.... The disclosure of facts that are already public will not support a claim for invasion of privacy. [Citations omitted.] In contrast, facts related to an individual's sexual relations, or "unpleasant or disgraceful" illnesses, are considered private in nature and the disclosure of such facts constitutes an invasion of the individual's right of privacy. *Restatement (Second) of Torts* § 652D cmt. b (1976).

The second requirement of a tort claim for invasion of privacy based on unreasonable publicity given to one's private life is that the disclosure be made to the public.... The requirement of public disclosure connotes publicity, which requires communication to the public in general or to a large number of persons, as distinguished from one individual or a few. [P]ublic disclosure may occur where the defendant merely initiates the process whereby the information is eventually disclosed to a large number of persons.... Although the disclosure must be made to the general public or to a large number of persons, there is no threshold number which constitutes "a large number" of persons. Rather, the facts and circumstances of a particular case must be taken into consideration in determining whether the disclosure was sufficiently public so as to support a claim for invasion of privacy.

The third requirement of a tort claim for invasion of privacy in the nature of unreasonable publicity given to one's private life is that the disclosure be one which would be highly offensive to a reasonable person. [Citations omitted.] The term "highly offensive" has been construed to mean that the disclosure would cause emotional distress or embarrassment to a reasonable person. The determination of whether a disclosure is highly offensive to the reasonable person is a question of fact and depends on the circumstances of a particular case.

The fourth requirement of a tort claim for invasion of privacy in the nature of unreasonable publicity given to one's private life is that the facts disclosed are not of legitimate concern to the public. The right of privacy may potentially clash with the rights of free speech and free press guaranteed by the United States and Colorado Constitutions. The rights of free speech and free press protect the public's access to information on matters of legitimate public concern.... As such, the right of the individual to keep information private must be balanced against the right to disseminate newsworthy information to the public. As the Tenth Circuit Court of Appeals [has] stated, "[T]o properly balance freedom of the press against the right of privacy, every private fact disclosed in an otherwise truthful, newsworthy publication must have some substantial relevance to a matter of legitimate public interest."

The term "newsworthy" is defined as "[a]ny information disseminated 'or purposes of education, amusement or enlightenment, when the public may reasonably be expected to have a legitimate interest in what is published.'" *Restatement (Second) of Torts* § 652D cmt. j (1976). In determining whether a subject is of legitimate public interest, "[t]he line is to be drawn when the publicity ceases to be the giving of information to which the public is entitled, and becomes a morbid and sensational prying into private lives for its own sake." *Restatement (Second) of Torts* § 652D cmt. h (1976).

The newsworthiness test properly restricts liability for public disclosure of private facts to the extreme case, thereby providing the breathing space needed by the press. As such, the requirement that the facts disclosed must not be of legitimate concern to the public protects the rights of free speech and free press guaranteed by the United States and Colorado Constitutions.

The final requirement of a tort claim for invasion of privacy in the nature of unreasonable publicity given to one's private life is that the defendant acted with reckless disregard of the private nature of the fact or facts disclosed. A person acts with reckless disregard if, at the time of the publicity, the person knew or should have known that the fact or facts disclosed were private in nature.

As with the tort of appropriation, notice the limits on this kind of invasion of privacy. The matter must be private, not only in the sense of not having previously a matter of disclosure or public record but also one that does not meet the requirements of "newsworthiness" or legitimate public interest that would erect a constitutional shield around disclosure.

The idea of newsworthiness is amorphous, but as with the tort of wrongful appropriation, its presence is an essential limitation on both the tort of publication of private facts and on the media. Newsworthiness is the concept by which we divide public and private affairs. It takes in the person involved, the extent to which that person seeks publicity. In *Bourquez*, for example the plaintiff did not seek publicity or disclosure of his sad news, while in *Eastwood*, the plaintiff clearly wanted some publicity, just not what he got — and the event or facts involved.

As celebrity status goes up, the right to poke and pry into what otherwise would be private also rises, *but not indefinitely*. Everyone has the right to some citadel of privacy, even those who seek publicity with what others might call reckless abandon. Drawing the line remains the function of the jury.

False Light Invasion of Privacy

Finally we come to false light invasion of privacy, a cause of action that has proven to be quite controversial, so controversial, in fact, that Texas, Minnesota, and several other states have refused to adopt it. But before we criticize it, let us first see what it is.

Frye v. IBP, Inc.
15 F. Supp. 2d 1032
United States District Court for the District of Kansas
1998

Vratil, J.:

* * * *

IBP, Inc., operates a beef processing facility in Emporia, Kansas, where plaintiff began work on August 16, 1982. On April 8, 1996, IBP promoted plaintiff to lead mechanic on the third shift (10:00 p.m. until 6:30 a.m.). As lead mechanic, plaintiff reported to two slaughter maintenance supervisors who shared responsibility for third shift operations. One of the supervisors was Robert Brown; Carl Cannon held the other position until early 1996, when Ed Rohling assumed it. Mike Fiehler was IBP's Emporia Complex Manager.

At all relevant times, IBP posted a Drug/Alcohol Policy at the Emporia Plant. According to Fiehler, IBP conducted drug testing only pursuant to this policy. IBP expected employees to comply with the policy, and employees expected IBP to comply with it.

In April 1996, IBP employees Robert Judd and Paul White contacted Steve Rumbo, a plant security officer. They told Rumbo that White had seen plaintiff and Brown smoking something and, at the same time, smelled marijuana. They also told Rumbo that White had discovered marijuana in the engine room and lift station. Judd reported that while he had not seen plaintiff and Brown smoking, he had observed them in the same area as the marijuana odor at least five times.

Security officers told Fiehler that they had received information that Brown and "the lead man on third shift" (plaintiff) were smoking marijuana on the job. They undertook surveillance in an effort to observe the reported drug use, but they saw nothing.

IBP asked plaintiff to provide a urine sample for drug testing purposes. He did so, and the sample was negative. Shortly thereafter, however, IBP managers received information implying that plaintiff had obtained a sample from another person. IBP asked plaintiff to provide another sample.

When plaintiff refused to do so, IBP fired him.

Plaintiff filed a claim for unemployment compensation, which he received after a hearing on appeal. IBP's position at the hearing was that it had given plaintiff a drug test on September 5, 1996, because it suspected him of smoking marijuana at work; that it fired plaintiff for refusing to provide a second sample; and that a second sample was appropriate because IBP suspected plaintiff of tampering with the first. Plaintiff is not aware that IBP communicated information about his termination, or the alleged falsification of his drug test, to anyone outside of IBP. No one contacted IBP about a job reference for plaintiff and in any event, IBP's policy is to provide only hire dates, termination dates and sometimes wages.

On written job applications, plaintiff stated that he had left IBP due to "wrongful discharge," without describing the circumstances. Plaintiff claims that IBP compelled him to disclose further information in job interviews, but he participated in only three interviews. One of those employers offered him a job, which he started on December 2, 1996. Plaintiff withdrew his application from the second employer, and the third did not call him back.

* * * *

[Plaintiff asserts a claim for invasion of privacy by placing him in a false light.] In order to prevail on a claim for false light invasion of privacy, plaintiff must establish (1) publication to a third party; (2) that the publication falsely represents plaintiff, and (3) that the representation would be highly offensive to a reasonable person. Plaintiff claims that defendant "depicted plaintiff at proceedings before the unemployment referee, as having violated company policy, which was not true," and that he was then "compelled to indicate to prospective employers that he was discharged from his job for refusal to take a drug test, which was false."

Without conceding the second and third elements, defendant argues that plaintiff cannot meet the first element because there was no "publication" as required for proof of this claim.

Courts generally treat false light invasion of privacy claims in the same way that they treat defamation claims.... The difference between defamation and false light claims lies in the expanded publicity requirement. To support a claim for defamation, communication of the allegedly false information to a single third person is sufficient publication.

In the context of a false light invasion of privacy claim, however, publication means that "the matter is made public, by communicating it to the public at large, or to so many persons that the matter must be regarded as substantially certain to become one of public knowledge...." *Restatement (Second) of Torts* § 652D, comment a ... Plaintiff must prove such widespread disclosure of private matters as to constitute publicizing. Thus it is not an invasion of the right of privacy ... to communicate a fact concerning the plaintiff's private life to a single person or even to a small group of persons. "Publicizing" information, even if private, to employees with a legitimate need to know the information does not constitute widespread disclosure within the meaning of a false light invasion of privacy claim.

Plaintiff's false light claim, as it relates to communications at the unemployment hearing, fails to meet the publicity requirement due to lack of widespread disclosure. The hearing was attended only by plaintiff, his lawyer, the administrative hearing officer and IBP management representatives. As a matter of law, statements in the unemployment hearing were not "widely publicized."

Plaintiff's other false light claim — that IBP compelled him to tell prospective employers that he had been fired for refusing a drug test — also fails the publicity requirement. Plaintiff stated on his written job applications that the reason for leaving IBP was "wrongful discharge," but he provided no details. Even assuming that IBP wrongfully discharged plaintiff, this coerced publication did not place plaintiff in a false light, or even in a negative light; on the contrary, it placed IBP in a negative light. It was only in job interviews — three in number — that plaintiff described the circumstances of his discharge. As a matter of law, communication to only three prospective employers is not "publicity" which is sufficient to sustain a false light claim.

Nor are we persuaded by plaintiff's argument that IBP "clearly" conveyed information "well beyond those who ha[d] a need to know." Without evidence of publication to more than a few individuals, plaintiff cannot demonstrate that IBP communicated false information "to so many persons that the matter must be regarded as substantially certain to become one of public knowledge."

Accordingly, we conclude that IBP is entitled to judgment as a matter of law on plaintiff's claims for publicity placing person in a false light.

Notice how the court in *Frye* treated defamation and false light invasion of privacy as closely related torts. It is the closeness of that relationship that has caused the controversy. Let us return to the first opinion we read in this chapter to learn about the ongoing debate:

Lake v. Wal-Mart Stores, Inc.
582 N.W.2d 231
Supreme Court of Minnesota
1998

We decline to recognize the tort of false light publicity at this time. We are concerned that claims under false light are similar to claims of defamation, and to the extent that false light is more expansive than defamation, tension between this tort and the First Amendment is increased.

False light is the most widely criticized of the four privacy torts and has been rejected by several jurisdictions. Most recently, the Texas Supreme Court refused to recognize the tort of false light invasion of privacy because defamation encompasses most false light claims and false light "lacks many of the procedural limitations that accompany actions for defamation, thus unacceptably increasing the tension that already exists between free speech constitutional guarantees and tort law." Citing "numerous procedural and substantive hurdles" under Texas statutory and common law that limit defamation actions, such as privileges for public meetings, good faith, and important public interest and mitigation factors, the court concluded that these restrictions "serve to safeguard the freedom of speech." Thus to allow recovery under false light invasion of privacy, without such safeguards, would "unacceptably derogate constitutional free speech."

The court rejected the solution of some jurisdictions — application of the defamation restrictions to false light — finding instead that any benefit to protecting nondefamatory false speech was outweighed by the chilling effect on free speech.

Additionally, unlike the tort of defamation, which over the years has become subject to numerous restrictions to protect the interest in a free press and discourage trivial litigation, the tort of false light is not so restricted. Although many jurisdictions have imposed restrictions on false light actions identical to those for defamation, we are not persuaded that a new cause of action should be recognized if little additional protection is afforded plaintiffs.

Generalizing, are these concerns legitimate? Do we really gain from all of this debate over the privacy torts, especially when we remember that they only work after the fact? Did the award of money damages that might come at the end of the cases we've just read make up for disclosure that someone is HIV-positive? Or of those pictures in the shower in *Lake*?

These are difficult questions, made even less easy by our efforts to balance constitutional concerns for free and full expression with individuals' rights to be left alone. The lack of a prospective remedy — something like an injunction that can be used to prevent problems before they happen[4] — also aggravates the situation.

The continuing and clearly expressed desire of the public for some kind of protection from intrusions of this kind more than justifies the ongoing efforts to create privacy torts. They will increasingly be a part of our interconnected world as the years go by.

Key Words and Phrases

appropriation of a likeness or image
celebrity
false light publicity
intrusion upon seclusion
invasion of privacy
newsworthiness
privacy
publication of private facts

right of free speech
seclusion

Review Questions

1. Of the four privacy torts — intrusion upon seclusion, appropriation, publication of private facts, and false light publicity — which might most deeply affect you as a student? Why?

2. Of the four privacy torts, which might most deeply affect you when you are a fully employed legal professional working on client matters? Why?

3. Of the four privacy torts, which might most deeply affect a person who had been nominated for a responsible position in the federal government? Why?

4. Of the four privacy torts, which might most deeply affect a celebrity in show business? Why?

5. There is a competition funded by the University of Hawaii Journalism Department's Carol Burnett Fund for Responsible Journalism, established in 1981 with an endowment from actress Carol Burnett. Perform factual research to find out why this actress would particularly value responsible journalism and where she got the money that originally funded the endowment. (If you were reading papers in 1981, you may remember the matter.)

   The Burnett matter is described in an interesting article, "Tabloid Law," from the August 1999 issue of *The Atlantic Monthly*. As this textbook went to press, the article was available on the Internet at www.theatlantic.com/issues/99aug/9908tabloids.htm.

---

[1] Warren & Brandeis, "The Right of Privacy," 4 Harv. L. Rev. 193 (1890).

[2] *Id.* at 193

[3] *United States v. Brawner,* 471 F.2d 969 (D.C. Cir. 1972, *en banc*).

[4] This is because of First Amendment concerns. Preventing speech before it happens, a situation known as prior restraint, is particularly disfavored because it constitutes real censorship.

Chapter Thirteen

COURT TORTS: MALICIOUS PROSECUTION, ABUSE OF PROCESS, AND FALSE ARREST

Given the kinds of misconduct that we have studied in previous chapters, it will probably not surprise you to learn that people occasionally misuse some part of the legal system. Sometimes that misuse is deliberate, and the perpetrator intends to cause harm to another's reputation or finances. In other cases, however, the misuse may be the product of a mistake or some genuine misunderstanding. The question is to determine under what circumstances misuse of the legal system can give rise to liability in tort.

Complicating our analysis are two basic principles. First, we *want* people to use and rely on the courts as a vehicle for resolving disputes. We would much rather have controversy resolved in the courtroom, where the rules are clear (well, more or less) and the proceedings involve a theoretically rational search for a correct and fair result, than we would trials by combat or similarly violent or absurd procedures. Because of this, we do not want to threaten people who take genuine, if somewhat weak, disputes to court.

The second principle is just as important. For the court system to be effective, people must know that a dispute taken to court will be resolved at some point. This principle, called **finality**, is important in many ways. It is obvious that people generally will not use a system for resolving disputes that does not function, just as they would not use a can opener that did not open cans! At a deeper level, it is not just about users and their feelings about what is most convenient or easiest to use. The concept of finality serves a societal role as well because it requires disputants to actually *resolve* their disputes. Moreover, for those convicted of a crime or subject to injunction or penalty, the moment of finality is the moment when the "music must be faced" — a point of considerable import for the person being punished and society.[1]

This finality onion has a third layer! If, at the end of a case, the parties could go right back to court to conduct a case about the prior case, there is nothing to stop them from going back when that case is done to conduct a case about the case about the case. And if that is true, what is to prevent later cases about cases about cases about cases, and so on in an infinite downward cycle, a perpetual *Bleak House*? The answer is nothing except exhaustion and lack of resources, and even these have not stopped some litigants. The point is that it is better to raise the drawbridge early than late, and the law has strongly favored such an approach, even against the potentially staggering costs of litigation. In the long run, the costs associated with infinite cycles of litigation are much higher.

With these thoughts in mind, let us turn to the "court torts," malicious prosecution, false arrest or imprisonment, and abuse of process. As its name implies, malicious prosecution involves the wrongful prosecution of a criminal or civil case. False arrest and imprisonment also give an idea of what they involve: the improper detention of another, usually, though by no means always, as a part of a legal arrest. Abuse of process involves the improper use of a court summons, citation, or subpoena. We begin with malicious prosecution.

Malicious Prosecution

Richey v. Brookshire Grocery Co.
952 S.W.2d 515
Supreme Court of Texas
1997

Spector, J.:

The issue in this malicious prosecution case is whether Brookshire Grocery Store lacked probable cause to initiate criminal proceedings against Kelley Richey. The jury found, along with the other elements of malicious

---

prosecution, that Brookshire lacked probable cause to file a criminal prosecution against Richey and awarded him damages. The court of appeals reversed, holding that there was no evidence to support the jury's finding on the probable cause issue.... We agree with the court of appeals and therefore affirm.

I.

On December 11, 1989, at approximately 2:30 a.m., Richey entered a Brookshire Super 1 Food Store. Brookshire night manager Russell Farris saw Kelley Richey enter the store and place a pack of cigarettes in his shopping cart. Farris then observed Richey "twiddle" the cigarettes in his hand and later put them in his coat pocket. As night manager, Farris was required to be alert to potential shoplifting, cigarettes topping the list of items commonly taken. As Richey checked out, he wrote a check for $51.75 for some groceries and began to bag them. He did not pay for the cigarettes in his pocket. Before walking out of the store, Richey pulled a food carton from one of the bags and read the label. Then Richey proceeded toward the door, stopping near a bin in which customers could place items to be donated to charity. He got a sack, went back to the food aisles and filled the sack with baby food, and paid $8.89 in cash. He still did not pay for the cigarettes. Richey then placed the baby food in the charity bin and left the store.

In the parking lot, Farris and another employee asked Richey if he had forgotten to pay for anything. Richey said that he had not. When Farris mentioned the cigarettes in Richey's pocket, Richey stated that he had inadvertently put them there and offered to pay for them. Following company policy, Farris refused to accept payment for the cigarettes. When the police arrived, Richey asked the police officer to mention in his report that Richey had contributed to the charity bin. Richey was interrogated, given a citation, and released. On his way out of the store, Richey removed the baby food from the charity bin and took it to his car. Farris later signed a sworn complaint charging Richey with theft of the cigarettes.

At the criminal trial, the jury found Richey not guilty after deliberating only a few minutes. Richey then filed this suit for ... malicious prosecution. The jury in the civil trial returned a verdict ... in his favor on the malicious prosecution claim, awarding him $18,400 in actual damages and $18,400 in exemplary damages. The court of appeals, with one justice dissenting, reversed and rendered judgment in favor of Brookshire, holding that there was no evidence to support the jury's finding that Brookshire lacked probable cause to prosecute Richey.

II.

A plaintiff in a malicious criminal prosecution claim must establish

   (1) the commencement of a criminal prosecution against the plaintiff;
   (2) causation (initiation or procurement) of the action by the defendant;
   (3) termination of the prosecution in the plaintiff's favor;
   (4) the plaintiff's innocence;
   (5) the absence of probable cause for the proceedings;
   (6) malice in filing the charge; and
   (7) damage to the plaintiff.

[Citations omitted.] At issue in this appeal is whether Brookshire had probable cause to initiate criminal proceedings against Richey.

We have long defined probable cause as the existence of such facts and circumstances as would excite belief in a reasonable mind, acting on the facts within the knowledge of the prosecutor [complainant], that the person charged was guilty of the crime for which he was prosecuted. The probable-cause determination asks whether a reasonable person would believe that a crime had been committed given the facts as the complainant honestly and reasonably believed them to be before the criminal proceedings were instituted.

Malicious prosecution actions involve a delicate balance between society's interest in the efficient enforcement of the criminal law and the individual's interest in freedom from unjustifiable and oppressive criminal prosecution. Accordingly, there is an initial presumption in malicious prosecution actions that the defendant acted reasonably and in good faith and had probable cause to initiate the proceedings. That presumption disappears once a plaintiff produces evidence that the motives, grounds, beliefs, and other evidence upon which the defendant acted did not constitute probable cause. The burden then shifts to the defendant to offer proof of probable cause.

Whether probable cause is a question of law or a mixed question of law and fact depends on whether the parties dispute the underlying facts. When the facts underlying the defendant's decision to prosecute are disputed, the trier of fact must weigh evidence and resolve conflicts to determine if probable cause exists, as a mixed question of law and fact. It has long been true, however, that "[w]hen the facts are not contested, and there is no conflict in the evidence directed to that issue, the question of probable cause is a question of law which is to be decided by the court." [Citations omitted.] Probable cause in this case, in which the facts and events leading up to Richey's arrest are undisputed, is therefore a question of law for the court and not the trier of fact.

III.

Because lack of probable cause in this case is a question of law, the issue for the Court is whether the undisputed facts underlying the decision to prosecute support a reasonable belief that Richey was guilty of theft. Because Richey concealed merchandise, retained the merchandise in his possession, and passed through the check-out line without paying for the merchandise, the only probable-cause issue is the reasonableness of Brookshire's belief as to Richey's state of mind at the time of the appropriation.

In a malicious prosecution case based on a criminal complaint, the complainant's failure to make a further investigation into the suspect's state of mind does not constitute lack of probable cause if all objective elements of a crime reasonably appear to have been completed.... In this case, in which the store manager observed Richey leave the store without paying for an item in his concealed possession, the store employees had no duty to inquire into Richey's state of mind before prosecuting. See *Delchamps, Inc. v. Morgan*, 601 So.2d 442, 445 (Ala.1992) ("Because Morgan undisputedly had a visible pack of cigarettes in her pocket, [the store employee] could have entertained 'an honest and strong suspicion' that she had concealed store property. Therefore, the malicious prosecution count should not have been submitted to the jury."); *Melia v. Dillon Cos., Inc.*, 18 Kan.App.2d 5, 846 P.2d 257, 261 (1993) ("Here, it is uncontested that Melia concealed and failed to pay for merchandise belonging to the store. Consequently, the existence of probable cause in this case is not a jury question.") As one court of appeals has noted, "A private citizen has no duty to inquire of the suspect whether he has some alibi or explanation before filing charges."

Marathon Oil Co. v. Salazar, 682 S.W.2d 624, 627 (Tex.App.-Houston [1st Dist.] 1984, writ ref'd n.r.e.); *see also* 52 Am.Jur. 2d, Malicious Prosecution § 54 (1970).

Even if Richey's intent to shoplift could not be presumed under these circumstances, the undisputed facts of this case dictate that it was not unreasonable for Brookshire's employees to believe that Richey intended to steal the cigarettes. Richey admitted that he placed the cigarettes in his pocket and did not pay for them. At trial, he testified that his behavior could lead someone to believe that he was shoplifting:

> Q: I know you had no intent but yet from your actions it looks like somebody was actually shoplifting by picking up those cigarettes and concealing them, isn't that right?
> A: That's right.

> * * * *

> Q: And the reason why it was a mistake is because somebody could look at that and think you were in fact shoplifting based on what they observed about your conduct.
> A: That's right.

Richey thus admitted that it was reasonable to believe that he had committed theft. Neither Richey's charity contribution nor his offer to pay after passing through the checkout line with the cigarettes negates Farris's reasonable belief that Richey intended to deprive Brookshire of the cigarettes. It was therefore reasonable for Brookshire's employees to believe that Richey intended to steal the cigarettes.

Richey argues that Brookshire's failure to fully and fairly disclose all relevant facts to the police constitutes a lack of probable cause. It has been stated that the malicious-prosecution defendant lacks probable cause if he or she makes a material misrepresentation or does not disclose all known material facts in good faith to law enforcement officials.... [W]e have held that knowingly providing false information to a public official satisfies the causation element, rather than the lack-of-probable-cause element, of a malicious prosecution claim.

We similarly conclude today that failing to fully and fairly disclose all material information and knowingly providing false information to the prosecutor are relevant to the malice and causation elements of a malicious prosecution claim but have no bearing on probable cause.... The probable cause inquiry asks only whether the complainant reasonably believed that the elements of a crime had been committed based on the information available to the complainant before criminal proceedings began. When a complainant reasonably believes a crime has occurred, the reasonableness of that belief is not negated by the failure to fully disclose all relevant facts to the officer. Thus, the extent of the disclosure to the prosecutor is not probative of lack of probable cause, but rather indicates whether the complainant may have acted with malice or may have, by knowingly providing false information, caused the prosecution.... Whether Brookshire's employee failed to fully disclose all relevant information to the officer is therefore immaterial to the probable-cause inquiry currently before us. As a matter of law, then, we hold that Brookshire had probable cause to initiate criminal proceedings against Richey.

IV.

Actions for malicious prosecution create a tension between the societal interest in punishing crimes and the individual interest in protection from unjustifiable criminal prosecution. We are not called upon today to pass on the wisdom of Brookshire's policy of prosecuting customers who reasonably appear to have taken merchandise from the store without paying—regardless of the value of the merchandise taken. In this case, Brookshire should not and cannot be punished for prosecuting Richey when Brookshire's employees saw Richey conceal merchandise, retain the merchandise in his possession, and pass through the checkout line without paying for the merchandise.

Affirmed.

Here the Texas Supreme Court sets out in a single paragraph the elements of malicious prosecution as they pertain to a criminal case:

- the commencement of a criminal prosecution against the plaintiff

- causation (initiation or procurement) of the action by the defendant
- termination of the prosecution in the plaintiff's favor
- the plaintiff's innocence
- the absence of probable cause for the proceedings
- malice in filing the charge
- damage to the plaintiff.

The elements of malicious prosecution in a civil action are essentially the same, except that the defendant must have instituted or continued a civil lawsuit without probable cause and with malice. Many states also omit a separate requirement that the plaintiff be innocent of the charge brought, holding that the termination of proceedings in the plaintiff's favor is sufficient to protect these interests.

Note the extensive discussion of the probable cause element. In a civil case, probable cause amounts to the same thing: knowledge of facts and circumstances as would justify a reasonable person in filing the lawsuit or claim that forms the basis for the action. In civil cases, the defense of advice of counsel arises more frequently for the obvious reason that the defendant usually goes to a lawyer before filing a lawsuit. The general rule is that advice of counsel is a defense to a claim of malicious prosecution — defense meaning that the defendant has the burden of proof — if he or she provided full and complete information to the attorney. But there's a catch: by asserting that he or she relied upon the advice of counsel, the plaintiff may waive any right to rely upon the attorney-client privilege to shield his discussions with an attorney.[2]

Finally, consider the lengths to which the Texas Supreme Court went in discussing the distinction between lack of probable cause and malice. There are a number of reasons for this, the most important of which are old cases holding that malice can be inferred from a lack of probable cause. In one way this is understandable; a person who acts without probable cause under the definition used by the Texas Supreme Court (and indeed adopted about everywhere) has acted unreasonably. Acting unreasonably — whether defined as without regard for others or by pushing forward without caring at all — is something of a demonstration of one's intent.

But try looking at the problem from the other direction. Suppose Montague thoroughly despises Capulet. Does that necessarily mean that Capulet lacks probable cause if he sees Montague rob a bank? While a good lawyer might try to show that malice clouded Capulet's judgment, the plain fact is that gloating over another's misfortune — even hoping for the opportunity to inflict it — does not turn an otherwise appropriate prosecution into a tort. As we noted before, the law still desires even the worst of enemies to come to court rather than to engage in duels, feuds, or vendettas. Ultimately, this is why courts go to such lengths to distinguish lack of probable cause and malice.

False Arrest or Imprisonment

What if one person simply detains or restrains another without calling authorities in the first place? This leads to the next concept for this chapter: false arrest or false imprisonment.

Garza v. Clarion Hotel, Inc.
119 Ohio App.3d 478, 695 N.E.2d 811
Court of Appeals of Ohio
1997

Bettman, J.:

This case arose out of an allegedly unpaid bar tab at the Top of the Crown restaurant at the Clarion Hotel (the "Clarion"). The plaintiffs in this case, Roger Garza and Joseph Simon, were exhibitors at a firefighters' convention in Cincinnati. Both men sold hydraulic rescue equipment used to rescue trapped accident victims. Firefighters were major customers of this product.

Garza and Simon were guests at the Clarion. On the evening of April 7, 1990, spilling over to the early morning of April 8, Garza and Simon were having drinks at the Top of the Crown. They were in a group of six or seven men. They had been invited for drinks by Donald Harrison, a business associate in a similar line of work. Harrison was also a guest at the Clarion.

For the second night in a row, Harrison asked the bartender, defendant Sandy Beach, to run a tab for a group having drinks. The first night he paid

---

the tab with his American Express credit card. On April 8, however, Beach testified that Harrison did not provide a key, room number, or credit card, and she did not know where to charge the bar bill.

On the night of April 8, the entire group of men, including Simon and Garza, decided to leave the Top of the Crown and go to Caddy's, another local bar. The entire group left together. No one paid the bill. Beach called down to inform the front desk of this unpaid bill and was able to describe Simon and Garza.

A hotel security guard followed the group down the street to Caddy's. Garza and Simon were identified there by the guard, handcuffed by the Cincinnati police and brought back to the Clarion. The two men explained that Harrison had agreed to pay the bill, and they assumed that he had. Simon attempted at that point to sign the bar tab to Harrison's room. However, the Clarion, through its night manager, did not accept Simon's offer but instead insisted that theft charges be pressed against Garza and Simon. When Harrison later learned that Simon and Garza had been arrested, he went to the front desk to see if the bar tab had been added to his room charges. Harrison's bill reflected that the bar tab had been added to his room charges. Harrison paid the bar tab with the rest of his charges when he checked out of the hotel.

Garza and Simon were tried for theft and were acquitted. Thereafter, they filed a civil action against the Clarion, Beach, and two individuals named Richard Heinlein and Robert Terrell, allegedly employed by the Clarion, but never otherwise identified. The complaint stated two claims for relief, one for malicious prosecution with attendant punitive damages, and one for false imprisonment. The trial court granted summary judgment to all defendants on the malicious-prosecution claim, but allowed the false-imprisonment claim to proceed to trial.

A jury trial was held. The trial court directed a verdict in favor of Terrell and Heinlein, but permitted the case to go to the jury against Beach and the Clarion. The jury found for Simon and Garza and against the Clarion, awarding $12,000 to each plaintiff. Beach was not found liable. Judgment was entered on the jury's verdict, and both sides appealed.

In case No. C-960316, Simon and Garza challenge the granting of summary judgment on their malicious-prosecution claim. In case No. C-960342, the

Clarion challenges the failure of the trial court to direct a verdict in its favor on the false-imprisonment claim. We sustain elements of both appeals. We regret that this is required, because two sets of fact-finders, a panel of arbitrators and a jury, have evaluated this conduct, and both awarded the same amount of money to Simon and Garza. Nonetheless, the case should have gone to the jury on the malicious-prosecution claim and not on the false-imprisonment claim.

* * * *

Much has been written about the difference between malicious prosecution and false arrest or false imprisonment.... The elements of the tort of malicious prosecution are ... (1) malice in instituting or continuing the prosecution, (2) lack of probable cause, and (3) termination of the prosecution in favor of the accused.

Examining each of these elements in the case at bar, we hold that there is no question that the third element was met. Garza and Simon were acquitted of theft. We must determine whether there was a genuine issue of material fact on the other two elements of malicious prosecution.

In a claim for malicious prosecution, malice has been defined as an improper purpose, or any purpose other than the legitimate interest of bringing an offender to justice. Malice may be inferred from the absence of probable cause.... As to the element of lack of probable cause, which is the gist of the action for malicious prosecution, the defendant's conduct must be weighed in view of the facts and circumstances that the defendant knew or should have known at the time of the instigation of the criminal proceedings.

The determinative issue is not whether a particular crime was actually committed, but whether there was a reasonable ground of suspicion, supported by circumstances sufficiently strong in themselves to warrant a cautious man in the belief that the person accused was guilty of the offense with which he was charged.... Although this issue may be determined as a matter of law when reasonable minds could come to only one conclusion based on the evidence presented, it is ordinarily a question of fact to be resolved at trial.

* * * *

False imprisonment involves the unlawful restraint by one person of the physical liberty of another. The essence of the tort is depriving the plaintiff of his or her liberty without lawful justification. In a false imprisonment, the detention is purely a matter between private persons for a private end.... In this case, there was simply no evidence that any of the employees of the Clarion unlawfully restrained the liberty of Simon or Garza. [The false imprisonment claim therefore should not have been allowed.]

"[T]he detention is purely a matter between private persons...." Indeed this is the key distinction between false arrest or false imprisonment and malicious prosecution, and one that renders the two separate.

If you search through cases on false arrest or imprisonment, you will see that the great majority arise from the detention of suspected shoplifters by merchants. As you might expect, and as the *Richey* case implies, a store owner's efforts to protect its goods from thievery creates a natural point of conflict with those who feel that they have been detained unjustly. To assist store owners, virtually every state has passed legislation immunizing detentions of reasonable length and purpose from suit. This statutory defense has done much to make false arrest/false imprisonment into something of a backwater in tort law.

Abuse of Process

Finally, there is the third "court tort," abuse of process. As you will see, it too is a bit different from the other kinds of torts we have studied. Even so, it still has a role to play.

Volk v. Wisconsin Mortgage Insurance Co.
474 N.W.2d 40
Supreme Court of North Dakota
1991

Erickstad, J.:

* * * *

On November 23, 1983, Volk granted SMI a real estate mortgage in exchange for a loan under the North Dakota First-Time Home Buyers' Program. The $63,300 in loan proceeds were used to purchase a home in Dickinson. The mortgage was subject to the provisions of the Short-Term Mortgage Redemption Act, Chapter 32-19.1, N.D.C.C. Pursuant to § 32-19.1-07, N.D.C.C., a mortgagee is not entitled to a deficiency judgment upon foreclosure of a mortgage subject to the provisions of the Act.... Through various assignments, NDHFA obtained an interest in the mortgage while SMI continued to service the mortgage.

Pursuant to the First-Time Home Buyers' Program, Volk was required to pay premiums that were used for the purchase of mortgage insurance from Mortgage Guaranty Insurance Corporation, now known as WMAC, guaranteeing Volk's payment to SMI or its assignee, NDHFA.

Volk defaulted in October 1986. In February 1987 SMI sent Volk a "Legal Notice Pursuant to Mortgage Default" which stated in part that "We (as 'Lender') have the right to pursue a deficiency judgement (*sic*) against you if the sale of this property fails to satisfy the full debt." Volk offered to give NDHFA a quitclaim deed to the property in lieu of a foreclosure action "so that I wouldn't have to go through the embarrasment (*sic*) and suffer the damage which a foreclosure action would cause to me."

NDHFA, pursuant to the terms and conditions of the mortgage insurance contract, requested approval from WMAC to accept the deed in lieu of foreclosure. WMAC refused, but entered into negotiations with Volk and inquired about Volk's financial circumstances. WMAC decided to approve a deed in lieu of foreclosure if Volk would agree to pay $9,200, payable at the rate of $2,000 down plus $300 per month for 24 months to help contribute to the anticipated loss caused by Volk's default. Volk refused to contribute the money to avoid the foreclosure action and NDHFA thereafter commenced foreclosure proceedings against Volk. NDHFA did not seek a deficiency judgment in its foreclosure complaint.

According to Volk, after foreclosure proceedings had begun, he contacted a representative of WMAC:

to find out if they ha[d] agreed to accept the deed, but she advised that she had not yet seen the further financial information she had requested from me which I sent to her on September 2nd. During this conversation she advised me that it was clear to her that I was not sufficiently destitute to qualify to give a deed in lieu, and that such deed would therefore not be accepted unless I would pay a portion of the loss which [NDHFA] would suffer from this loan.

Volk refused to pay the money, and a judgment of foreclosure was entered in February 1989 granting all right, title, and interest in the property to NDHFA.

Volk brought this action for damages in February 1990 alleging that NDHFA, SMI, and WMAC had committed abuse of process.... The trial court granted ... summary judgment against Volk dismissing the actions against each defendant. Volk appealed.

* * * *

The tort of abuse of process is described in *Restatement (Second) of the Law of Torts* § 682 (1976): "One who uses a legal process, whether criminal or civil, against another primarily to accomplish a purpose for which it is not designed, is subject to liability to the other for harm caused by the abuse of process." The essential elements of the tort are discussed in Prosser and Keeton, *The Law of Torts* § 121, at p. 898 (5th ed. 1984):

The essential elements of abuse of process, as the tort has developed, have been stated to be: first, an ulterior purpose, and second, a willful act in the use of the process not proper in the regular conduct of the proceeding. Some definite act or threat not authorized by the process, or aimed at an objective not legitimate in the use of the process, is required; and there is no liability where the defendant has done nothing more than carry out the process to its authorized conclusion, even though with bad intentions. The improper purpose usually takes the form of coercion to obtain a collateral advantage, not properly involved in the proceeding itself, such as the surrender of property or the payment of money, by the use of the process as a threat or a club. There is, in other words, a form of extortion, and it is what is done in the course of negotiation, rather than the issuance or any formal use of the process itself, which constitutes the tort....

In other words, the gist of the tort of abuse of process is the misuse or misapplication of legal process to accomplish an end other than that which the process was designed to accomplish.... It is the purpose behind the use of the legal process that is controlling....

The evidence, viewed in the light most favorable to Volk, reflects that the defendants refused to accept a deed in lieu of foreclosure unless Volk paid $9,200 to absorb a part of the loss caused by Volk's default. Volk characterizes this request for payment as an attempt to coerce or extort a deficiency judgment from him, which is not recoverable under the North Dakota Short-Term Mortgage Redemption Act. Indeed, we have said that a deficiency judgment is one of the least favored creatures of the law and we have often recognized the Legislature's avowed public policy against deficiency judgments in real estate litigation....

The defendants characterize the proposal that Volk pay the $9,200 as merely an attempt during negotiations to receive consideration for accepting the deed in lieu of foreclosure. The trial court apparently agreed, determining that "Superior was neither threatening nor abusive in offering to negotiate away its right to foreclose in exchange for monetary consideration." The defendants assert that once the negotiations for Volk's contribution to the loss broke down, the foreclosure proceeding was the only proper remedy available to them.

The defendants are correct in their assertion that a mortgagee is ordinarily not required to accept a deed in lieu of a foreclosure proceeding.... However, whether the defendants were legally entitled to use the foreclosure proceeding as a remedy after Volk defaulted is not the dispositive inquiry; rather, the issue is whether the defendants attempted to use the foreclosure proceeding as a vehicle to coerce Volk into paying $9,200 which he was not otherwise required to pay under North Dakota law.... We believe the evidence in this case raises a reasonable inference that the defendants attempted to use the foreclosure action as a means of coercing Volk into paying a deficiency judgment which is not allowed under North Dakota law. It is for the trier of fact to determine whether the foreclosure action was brought to coerce Volk into paying a deficiency judgment or whether the action was brought to accomplish the lawful purpose for which it was designed.

NDHFA asserts that summary judgment was nevertheless proper because no action was taken to seek payment after the foreclosure proceeding was initiated. We disagree for two reasons. First, Volk's affidavit indicates that after foreclosure proceedings had begun, payment was demanded in order to qualify for acceptance of a deed in lieu of foreclosure. Second, we have expressly rejected the view that an improper act must occur after process has issued in order to maintain an action for abuse of process.

* * * *

The defendants also assert that Volk has failed to show that he suffered any damages because he did not pay the $9,200 requested for acceptance of the deed in lieu of foreclosure. However, an action for abuse of process is recognized where no property is taken at all and where the attempted extortion was wholly unsuccessful.... Thus, Volk's refusal to pay the $9,200 for acceptance of the deed in lieu of foreclosure is not fatal to his action for abuse of process.

The defendants assert that summary judgment was proper because the injuries he alleges to have suffered, (i.e., damage to his personal reputation, credit rating, financial reputation, unfavorable publicity, embarrassment, humiliation, and ridicule caused by the foreclosure action) would have occurred from any foreclosure action. We disagree. The matter of damages is a question of fact.... We believe that whether Volk has suffered harm, if any, from the defendants' alleged improper conduct is a question to be determined by the trier of fact....

Because there exist genuine issues of material fact, we conclude that the trial court erred in granting summary judgment dismissing Volk's abuse of process action against the three defendants.

Notice that abuse of process does not depend upon the validity of the lawsuit per se; here the suit itself was valid as far is it went. Abuse of process is, as Dean Prosser has noted, a form of extortion. "Give me something I'm not entitled to, or I will sue you for something I am legally entitled to have." The threat or abuse may work because the victim cannot afford a lawyer or because the victim fears the litigation process for some reason. It may work simply because the intended victim does not know any better. But no matter what the perpetrator's malice, simply filing a lawsuit and using process — summons or other court papers — to bring the defendant into court for a proper purpose is never abuse of process.

The "court torts" do not occur as frequently as those involving allegedly defective products or negligence, but they have an important place in the law of torts. They represent the legal system's first efforts to prevent misuse of litigation or court proceedings. As such, they remain an important check upon improper litigation and the foundation for many of the modern rules and statutes prohibiting "Rambo litigation" and frivolous or abusive lawsuits.

Key Words and Phrases

finalty
malice
"Rambo litigation"

Review Questions

1. In legal journals or in your local newspaper, seek current, real-life examples of the principle of "finality." As an illustration, recall the seven-month saga in late 1999 and 2000 of the young Cuban boy, Elian Gonzales. Various parties, including members of Congress, inserted themselves into the situation. Parties continually appealed to federal and state courts and questioned the authority of federal agencies. Be prepared to explain to your classmates the elements of one case you find.

2. Explain the distinctions drawn in opinions between "lack of probable cause" and "malice."

3. A death penalty case has a finality all its own. Depending on how much time you have left in the semester (and the inclination of you, your classmates, and your instructor), consider a debate on the death penalty. Have any of these matters involved malicious prosecution, abuse of process, or false arrest? (This is a weighty matter; don't get into it if you have little time!)

---

[1] The other part of this process that must be accounted for is the reliability of the system; that is, how accurate are the decisions at the point when they become final. Clearly, finality does little good if at the point we reach it, a court decision is very likely to be inaccurate. The late Judge Henry Friendly wrote extensively on this topic, which is of considerable concern, though beyond the scope of this book.

[2] This makes perfect sense. After all, it would be inappropriate to deny to the plaintiff the information he or she needs to cross-examine or cast doubt on the advice of counsel claim.

Chapter Fourteen

RISKY BUSINESS:
FRAUD, MISREPRESENTATION, AND
TORTIOUS INTERFERENCE
WITH CONTRACTS

In Chapter One of this book, we discussed the differences between tort and contract, the differing duties that form the bases for these fields of law, and the distinctions that exist between them.

As we have progressed, we have noted that there might be overlaps between the remedies afforded by tort and contract for certain kinds of misconduct. Implied warranty and strict liability for defective products each address the same issues, and provide an area of overlap between tort remedies and contract rights. In this chapter, we address another area of overlap composed of fraud, misrepresentation, and interference with business relationships.

Much of what we are about to discuss can be viewed as growing out of something that looks a lot like this: You decide that you want to buy a house. Seeing one that you like, you contact the owner, who tells you, "It's been a great place to live. Hate to leave it, but I've been transferred to the East Podunk division. The roof? Put a new roof on three years ago. Air? The air conditioner is two years old. Works great. Termites? Shoot. They'd get indigestion trying to eat this house." And so, being reassured, you buy the place. (If this were a property book, we would call this property Blackacre.)

Six months later, the roof has leaked all over your bedroom ceiling. The air conditioner compressor has turned out to be one of the five ever to bear the "Edsel" brand name. Termites come from seven states to feast on your beams and joists. What do you do?

After fuming over what you were told, you might say to yourself, "I was induced by those lies to enter into the contract to buy this house. I wouldn't have done it if I'd known the truth. I want the contract to be nullified." This you can do under the law of contracts, through a claim for **rescission** of the contract, a cause of action by which the contract is nullified and the parties are restored to the positions they held before executing the contract. This means giving up the house and any other benefits you got.

Or, you might say, "He lied to me. I'm going to sue to get what I paid for." This is the common sense hallmark of a claim in tort for fraud. There is no need to give up the house, but you have to keep making the payments. Your remedy may be limited to the difference between what you thought you were getting and what you actually got.

As you can see, the claim in contract for rescission and the claim in tort for fraud are very much alike. If you compare the elements of causes of action for the two, you will see that they are virtually identical. The difference, and it is a relatively small one, is in the remedy, the proper measure of damages. But since this is a book on torts, we can leave comparisons for another day[1] and focus on the elements of a tort claim for fraud or misrepresentation:

Foiles v. Midwest Street Rod Association of Omaha, Inc.
254 Neb. 552, 578 N.W.2d 418
Supreme Court of Nebraska
1998

Wright, J.:

Larry Foiles sued Midwest Street Rod Association of Omaha, Inc. (Midwest), and Championship Auto Shows, Inc. (Championship Auto), for damages he incurred when his trailer was stolen from a trailer parking lot at the 39th Annual World of Wheels exhibition in April 1994....

Foiles was in Omaha, Nebraska, in April 1994 for the 39th Annual World of Wheels exhibition held at the Civic Auditorium. Foiles attempted to park his pickup and trailer along the curb adjacent to the Civic Auditorium;

however, representatives of Midwest and Championship Auto told Foiles that he could not park at that location.... Before leaving for the lot, Foiles inquired whether the lot was secure. He was told by agents of Midwest and Championship Auto that the lot had 24-hour security.

Foiles parked his pickup and trailer at the trailer parking lot.... While at the lot, Foiles again testified that he asked about its security and was told that "[w]e have 24-hour security. You have nothing to worry about."

Foiles attended the car show, and while inside the auditorium, he observed uniformed security officers patrolling the arena. On the morning of April 9, 1994, Foiles went to the trailer parking lot and discovered that his trailer and the supplies he had left in the trailer had been stolen.

Foiles sued Midwest and Championship Auto to recover the damages he incurred as a result of the loss of his trailer.... Foiles alleged [a cause of action based on] fraudulent misrepresentation.... In order to maintain an action for fraudulent misrepresentation, a plaintiff must allege and prove the following elements: (1) that a representation was made; (2) that the representation was false; (3) that when made, the representation was known to be false or made recklessly without knowledge of its truth and as a positive assertion; (4) that it was made with the intention that the plaintiff should rely upon it; (5) that the plaintiff reasonably did so rely; and (6) that the plaintiff suffered damage as a result....

Foiles established that, after depositing his equipment in the Civic Auditorium, an agent of Midwest and Championship Auto directed him to the trailer parking lot and informed him that the lot had 24-hour security. At the lot, another agent of Midwest and Championship Auto told Foiles that the lot was secure and would be patrolled by security 24 hours per day. The district court was not clearly wrong in finding that agents of Midwest and Championship Auto made a representation to Foiles.

Midwest and Championship Auto admitted at trial that security was not provided for the trailer parking lot and that their agents' statements were either false or recklessly made. This evidence satisfies the second and third elements of fraudulent misrepresentation—that the representation was false and that, when made, was known to be false or made recklessly without knowledge of its truth as a positive assertion. Intent to deceive is not an indispensable element of a cause of action for fraud based on misrepresentation. A party may be liable for misrepresentation when a representation was false when made and the party knew that it was false or made it recklessly and without knowledge of its truth or falsity. The final three elements are that the representation was made with an intention that the plaintiff should rely upon it, that the plaintiff did reasonably so rely, and that the plaintiff suffered damage as a result.

A person is justified in relying upon a representation made to him as a positive statement of fact, when an investigation would be required to ascertain its falsity.... Foiles testified that he observed security guards on patrol inside the Civic Auditorium and that two persons dressed in white T-shirts and wearing Midwest name tags and insignias specifically told him that the trailer parking lot had 24-hour security. In order to determine if the representation made to him was false, Foiles would have had to investigate these statements.

Midwest and Championship Auto also argue that there is no evidence that they intended the information provided by their agents to influence Foiles. We disagree. Foiles testified that when an agent informed him about the trailer parking lot and pointed him toward the lot, he expressed concerns that the lot was dark and that he was not certain that his trailer would be safe. Foiles stated that the agent "just kind of waved ... off [my concerns,] saying, 'It's safe. We have 24-hour security. You don't need to worry.'" Another agent of Midwest and Championship Auto also told Foiles that the lot had 24-hour security and that he should not worry about it.

In viewing the evidence and making every reasonable inference deducible from the evidence in favor of Foiles, we conclude that the district court was not clearly wrong in finding that Midwest and Championship Auto had knowingly or recklessly made false representations with the intent that Foiles rely upon those representations and that Foiles did in fact rely upon the representations to his detriment....

Let's pause here and work through these elements, because they contain some limitations on the idea of fraud that may not be apparent at a first glance.

The first element universally required to sustain a claim of fraud is that a **representation** was made. But a representation of *what*? The law is clear that fraud lies only for *representations of fact*. Opinions, prognostications, sales pitches, puffing, hype, guessing, predictions, and similar statements generally may not be the basis for a claim of fraud.

This rule is not etched in stone. There are statements of opinion or sales pitches than can figure in a claim for fraud,[2] but you can see the reason for a distinction here. Clearly, if any statement of opinion, any guess, any prediction, any hype can be the basis of a claim for fraud, no one will talk in a commercial or business context to anyone else. There must be room for parties to engage in haggling, banter or discussions without those *per se* forming the basis for a cause of action.

Suppression of the Truth

In practice, however, the problem is less with where to draw this line than to handle a "half truth," a representation that is true as far as it goes, but which is incomplete. The missing piece would change the victim's mind, if known. Sometimes called suppression of the truth or fraudulent suppression, this area has been difficult, as our next excerpt shows.

The Alabama Supreme Court well expressed this problem in a 1998 case, *State Farm Fire and Casualty Co. v. Owen*, 729 So.2d 830, (Ala. 1998):

> It is well established that a party's mere silence as to a material fact does not constitute fraud unless that party is under a duty to disclose that fact.... Any analysis of a fraudulent-suppression claim must begin by asking the fundamental question whether the parties, given the situation, should be required to speak. In answering this question, we must examine what the parties actually did, as well as judge what they ought to have done. That process requires both legal analysis and factual inquiry....
>
> The leading treatise on tort law states the question of duty: "[W]hether, upon the facts in evidence, such a

relation exists between the parties that the community
will impose a legal obligation upon one for the benefit
of the other—or, more simply, whether the interest of
the plaintiff which has suffered invasion was entitled to
legal protection at the hands of the defendant. This is
entirely a question of law, to be determined by reference
to the body of statutes, rules, principles, and precedents
which make up the law; and it must be determined only
by the court. It is no part of the province of a jury to
decide...." W. Page Keeton *et al.*, *Prosser and Keeton on
Torts* § 37, at 236 (5th ed.1984)

In evaluating the question whether [the defendant] had a
duty to speak, we must consider a number of factors: (1)
the relationship of the parties; (2) the relative knowledge
of the parties; (3) the value of the particular fact; (4) the
plaintiff's opportunity to ascertain the fact; (5) the
customs of the trade; and (6) other relevant
circumstances.

As you can see, the idea of a half-truth is difficult at many levels. The
main point of the prior opinion is a simple one, however. In the absence
of a **fiduciary relationship** or some special duty to disclose, mere
silence cannot be the basis for fraud.

Fiduciary relationship. A relationship in which one
person has a duty to act in the best interest of another.

What are some of these relationships? A trustee owes a fiduciary
relationship and therefore must disclose. Doctors often fall in the
"special circumstances" category and must disclose on that basis.
Lawyers have the obligation to disclose, but only to clients. There is no
implicit obligation to disclose to opponents, however, except as may be
required by court rules and ethical principles.

Because of this inconsistency in who must disclose what, many states have enacted legislation requiring disclosures in certain circumstances. The most common statute requires the seller of a home or real property to disclose its condition accurately. Other consumer protection legislation also may contain duties of disclosure. These statutes clearly are efforts to "level the playing field" and make it possible for full disclosures to be obtained in many common consumer transactions.

Recklessness   .

The next criterion of fraud is that the statement, when made, was known to be false or made **recklessly without knowledge of its truth** and as a positive assertion. This rarely provides much in the way of legal excitement, but it often can provide interesting problems at trial, because only rarely will a person alleged to have committed fraud admit the untruth. Much more often, the party claiming fraud must piece the defendant's intent together from circumstantial evidence. This can be the most difficult part of a fraud case in the courtroom.

A note about recklessness in this context. Many states would change the phrasing of this basic standard slightly to make it reckless *disregard* of a statement's truth or falsity. By phrasing it this way, you can see that it can be equated to a simple question: Would the defendant have said it anyway even knowing it to be untrue? That is recklessness.

Scienter

The next two elements of fraud — that the statement was made with the intention that the plaintiff should rely upon it and that the plaintiff reasonably did so rely — take us into the slightly murky world of *scienter* (Latin for **"guilty knowledge"**).

Fraud is among the most interactive of torts in that it requires not just action, but reaction. Clearly the statement, "I am an outer space alien from the planet Neptune," is false, and presumably it would be known by its speaker to be so. Yet, it most likely never could be the basis for a claim of fraud because it would be unreasonable for anyone to rely upon it. This action-reaction element of fraud is a very important limitation on its scope.

Damages

Finally we come to the question of damages. Our next excerpt gives you the proper measure of damages in a case of fraud.

Little v. Morris
967 S.W.2d 685
Missouri Court of Appeals, Southern District
1998

Montgomery, C.J.:

Defendants Morgan and Lottie Morris (Sellers) appeal the trial court's judgment finding for Plaintiff Janice Little (Buyer) on ... her petition alleging fraudulent misrepresentation. By its amended judgment, the trial court awarded Buyer damages of $11,000 on Count I. We affirm the judgment except for the damage award. That portion of the judgment is reversed, and the cause is remanded for retrial on the issue of damages.

In the summer of 1992, the parties agreed that Sellers would build a "Wick Home" for Buyer. Buyer took possession of the home in October 1992, and the parties closed on the sale of the home on January 16, 1993. The sale price was $66,769.16.

Buyer filed her petition against Sellers on September 9, 1993. Count I alleged a theory of fraudulent misrepresentation. Specifically, Buyer alleged that Sellers represented they would construct a "Wick Home" for her but failed to do so.

At the nonjury trial, Buyer introduced evidence of various construction defects in her home. Buyer testified she spent $3,154 in improvements and $1,364.53 for repairs on the home. In January 1997, Buyer sold the home for $65,000.

Sellers' sole point relied on alleges the trial court erred in awarding damages of $11,000 because no substantial evidence supports the award.

Specifically, Sellers assert that Buyer failed to introduce evidence "of what the residence would have been worth had it been a Wick Home or of the residence's actual worth on the date of purchase."

In Missouri, a victim of fraud has two options—he can return what he purchased and get his money back (rescission), or keep what he purchased and sue for damages measured as the difference between its value as represented and its true value as of the date of purchase (benefit of the bargain).... Thus, the measure of damages in a fraud case where the defrauded party retains the property — and in the absence of special damages — is the benefit of the bargain. Clearly, the damages are measured at the time of the transaction. Finally, a defrauded party may recover special damages necessarily incurred solely by reason of the fraud.

Application of these principles to the instant case makes it clear that Buyer's damage award is not supported by substantial evidence. Buyer failed to offer evidence on the value of her home as it was represented to be and its true value as of the date of purchase. Buyer only testified as to the purchase price of her home and as to the sale price four years later. Although the purchase price may have been some evidence of the home's value as represented (Buyer apparently believed it was a Wick Home at closing), the record is devoid of any evidence concerning the actual value of the property at closing.

We agree with Buyer's contention that under certain circumstances, a defrauded party may recover special damages in addition to any loss under the benefit of the bargain rule. However, even if we assume that some, if not all, of Buyer's expenditures on the home were special damages incurred solely by reason of the fraud, the damage award far exceeded the amount Buyer expended for "repairs" and "improvements."

Again you can see the overlap with contractual theories and damages here. The buyer can rescind the transaction, a contract remedy, or keep the property and get the difference in value. This approach sometimes is known as the **"benefit of the bargain" rule**. Special damages here are not like those in a defamation case; they are instead "ordinary" special damages, actual out-of-pocket costs, and even emotional distress and other similar damages. Punitive damages also are available, given the nature of the tort and the requirement of malicious intent or recklessness.

As we have just seen, fraud is an intentional tort; that is, it requires recklessness or an intent to defraud. This is more than the simple lack of care necessary to sustain a case for negligence. But what if the party making the statement is merely negligent? Can the plaintiff properly file a lawsuit for negligent misrepresentation?[3]

Answering this question requires us to examine Justice Cardozo's second great contribution to the law of torts, *Ultramares Corp. v. Touche*, 255 N.Y. 170, 174 N.E. 441 (N.Y. 1931). There an accounting firm negligently audited the corporate records of an importing firm. A creditor of the firm asked for and received a copy of the auditor's report and relied on it in extending credit to the importer. The importer went bankrupt within a month after the loans were made.

Turning to the opinion itself, notice how Justice Cardozo sets up the issues.

We think the evidence supports a finding that the audit was negligently made, though in so saying we put aside for the moment the question whether negligence, even if it existed, was a wrong to the plaintiff....

We are brought to the question of duty, its origin and measure.

The defendants owed to their employer a duty imposed by law to make their certificate without fraud, and a duty growing out of contract to make it with the care and caution proper to their calling. Fraud includes the pretense of knowledge when knowledge there is none. To creditors and investors to whom the employer exhibited the certificate, the defendants owed a like duty to make it without fraud, since there was notice in the circumstances of its making that the employer did not intend to keep it to himself.... A different question develops when we ask whether they owed a duty to these to make it without negligence. If liability for negligence exists, a thoughtless slip or blunder, the failure to detect a theft or forgery beneath the cover of deceptive entries, may expose accountants to a liability in an indeterminate amount for an indeterminate time to an indeterminate class.

The hazards of a business conducted on these terms are so extreme as to enkindle doubt whether a flaw may not exist in the implication of a duty that exposes to these consequences.

We put aside for the moment any statement in the certificate which involves the representation of a fact as true to the knowledge of the auditors. If such a statement was made, whether believed to be true or not, the defendants are liable for deceit in the event that it was false. The plaintiff does not need the invention of novel doctrine to help it out in such conditions. The case was submitted to the jury, and the verdict was returned upon the theory that, even in the absence of a misstatement of a fact, there is a liability also for erroneous opinion.

The expression of an opinion is to be subject to a warranty implied by law. What, then, is the warranty, as yet unformulated, to be? Is it merely that the opinion is honestly conceived and that the preliminary inquiry has been honestly pursued, that a halt has not been made without a genuine belief that the search has been reasonably adequate to bring disclosure of the truth? Or does it go farther and involve the assumption of a liability for any blunder or inattention that could fairly be spoken of as negligence if the controversy were one between accountant and employer for breach of a contract to render services for pay?

The assault upon the citadel of privity is proceeding in these days apace. How far the inroads shall extend is now a favorite subject of juridical discussion.... Even in that field, however, the remedy is narrower where the beneficiaries of the promise are indeterminate or general. Something more must then appear than an intention that the promise shall redound to the benefit of the public or to that of a class of indefinite extension. The promise must be such as to bespeak the assumption of a duty to make reparation directly to the individual members of the public if the benefit is lost.

* * * *

We have said that the duty to refrain from negligent representation would become coincident or nearly so with the duty to refrain from fraud if this action could be maintained. A representation, even though knowingly false, does not constitute ground for an action of deceit unless made with the intent to be communicated to the persons or class of persons who act upon it to their prejudice.

Liability for negligence if adjudged in this case will extend to many callings other than an auditor's. Lawyers who certify their opinion as to the validity of municipal or corporate bonds, with knowledge that the opinion will be brought to the notice of the public, will become liable to the investors, if they have overlooked a statute or a decision, to the same extent as if the controversy were one between client and adviser. Title companies insuring titles to a tract of land, with knowledge that at an approaching auction the fact that they have insured will be stated to the bidders, will become liable to purchasers who may wish the benefit of a policy without payment of a premium. These illustrations may seem to be extreme, but they go little, if any, farther than we are invited to go now.

Negligence, moreover, will have one standard when viewed in relation to the employer, and another and at times a stricter standard when viewed in relation to the public. Explanations that might seem plausible, omissions that might be reasonable, if the duty is confined to the employer, conducting a business that presumably at least is not a fraud upon his creditors, might wear another aspect if an independent duty to be suspicious even of one's principal is owing to investors. Everyone making a promise having the quality of a contract will be under a duty to the promisee by virtue of the promise, but under another duty, apart from contract, to an indefinite number of potential beneficiaries when performance has begun. The assumption of one relation will mean the involuntary assumption of a series of new relations, inescapably hooked together. The law does not spread its protection so far.

Our holding does not emancipate accountants from the consequences of fraud. It does not relieve them if their audit has been so negligent as to justify a finding that they had no genuine belief in its adequacy, for this again is fraud. It does no more than say that, if less than this is proved, if there has been neither reckless misstatement nor insincere profession of an opinion, but only honest blunder, the ensuing liability for negligence is one that is bounded by the contract, and is to be enforced between the parties by whom the contract has been made. We doubt whether the average business man receiving a certificate without paying for it, and receiving it merely as one among a multitude of possible investors, would look for anything more....

Utramares is tough ground. It is a "negating" or "limiting" opinion, written not so much to advance a new proposition or theory of law, but to prevent the expansion of a theory or line of cases thought to have dangerous consequences.

The second problem with *Ultramares* is that it is somewhat counterintuitive. The idea of a "public" representation like those described in the opinion—a statement made on behalf of a business by an accountant, lawyer or title company, to use the examples in the opinion—is an important part of the public's confidence that it can transact its affairs without nasty surprises. The lawyers, accountants, and others who make such statements often know in advance the purposes for which they will be used. They can protect themselves by qualifying their opinions—that is, by putting in appropriate language as to the assumptions they have made and what they have not done. It does not seem entirely fair to limit exposure in such circumstances to the person or entity that hired the speaker.

Additionally, many, and perhaps most, misrepresentations do not take place in an employment relationship such as existed between the rubber company and its accountant in *Ultramares*. For that reason, it is difficult to limit negligent misrepresentation in the way proposed in Justice Cardozo's opinion.

Nonetheless, Justice Cardozo's writing in *Ultramares* remains the benchmark in this area, precisely because it attempts to set limits and standards for a tort that otherwise could become dangerously overused. These efforts to create limits still have an impact today, as our next excerpt explains.

M-L Lee Acquisition Fund L.P. v. Deloitte & Touche
320 S.C. 143, 463 S.E.2d 618
South Carolina Court of Appeals
1996

Howell, C.J.:

In this negligent misrepresentation case, ML-Lee Acquisition Fund, L.P. (ML-Lee) appeals the trial court's grant of summary judgment in favor of Deloitte & Touche (Deloitte)....

To state a claim for negligent misrepresentation, the plaintiff must allege that (1) the defendant made a false representation to the plaintiff; (2) the defendant had a pecuniary interest in making the statement; (3) the defendant owed a duty of care to see that he communicated truthful information to the plaintiff; (4) the defendant breached that duty by failing to exercise due care; (5) the plaintiff justifiably relied on the representation; and (6) the plaintiff suffered a pecuniary loss as the proximate result of his reliance on the representation. Because the trial court decided the case in Deloitte's favor on the issues of duty and reliance only, we likewise address only those elements of ML-Lee's negligent misrepresentation claim.

* * * *

[T]hree main approaches have developed. The most restrictive approach, requiring strict contractual privity before liability could be imposed, was first enunciated by Chief Judge Cardozo of the New York Court of Appeals in *Ultramares Corp. v. Touche, Niven & Co.*... The *Ultramares* strict privity standard was relaxed to extend recovery to third parties enjoying a relationship to the accountant that "sufficiently approaches privity." Thus, under New York's "near privity" approach, accountants may be liable to third parties only if: (1) the accountants actually know their reports will be used for a particular purpose; (2) the accountants know that a nonclient is expected to rely on the reports in furtherance of a particular purpose; and (3) there has been some conduct on the part of the accountants linking them to that party or parties, which evinces the accountant's understanding of that party's or parties' reliance. Several states follow New York's "near privity" approach.

The second approach, which ML-Lee wishes this Court to adopt, is the foreseeability approach, which extends an accountant's liability to all persons who the accountant should reasonably foresee might obtain and rely on the accountant's work. This approach, which subjects accountants to liability on the same basis as other tortfeasors, has been adopted in few jurisdictions....

The majority view is set forth in the *Restatement (Second) of Torts* § 552 (1977), which provides, in pertinent part:

(1) One who, in the course of his business, profession or employment, or in any other transaction in which he has a pecuniary interest, supplies false information for the guidance of others in their business transactions, is subject to liability for pecuniary loss caused to them by their justifiable reliance upon the information, if he fails to exercise reasonable care or competence in obtaining or communicating the information.

(2) ... [T]he liability stated in Subsection (1) is limited to loss suffered

(a) by the person or one of a limited group of persons for whose benefit and guidance he intends to supply the information or knows that the recipient intends to supply it; and

(b) through reliance upon it in a transaction that he intends the information to influence or knows that the recipient so intends or in a substantially similar transaction.

Thus, under the *Restatement*, an accountant's duty is limited to the client and third parties whom the accountant or client intends the information to benefit. The *Restatement* approach recognizes that an accountant's duty should extend beyond those in privity or near-privity with the accountant, but is not so expansive as to impose liability where the accountant knows only of the possibility of distribution to anyone, and their subsequent reliance.

* * * *

[W]e conclude the *Restatement* approach represents the soundest method of determining the scope of an accountant's duty to third persons for negligent misrepresentation. [W]e conclude that the *Restatement* approach balances the need to hold accountants to a standard that accounts for their contemporary role in the financial world with the need to protect them from liability that unreasonably exceeds the bounds of their real undertaking.

And so it goes. Justice Cardozo's *Ultramares* opinion remains a check
on the overextension of negligent misrepresentation, but the tort grows
and has a recognized place in the law, particularly in business
transactions.

Tortious Interference with Contract

Standing alone in this area of business torts is **tortious interference
with contract** or business expectancy.

The name gives a strong hint as to the concept behind the cause of
action. What if someone induces you to breach a contract with a third
party. You may be liable for the breach. Should the person who made
you do it also be liable?

Della Penna v. Toyota Motor Sales, USA, Inc.
11 Cal.4th 376, 902 P.2d 740, 45 Cal.Rptr.2d 436
Supreme Court of California
1995

Arabian, J.:

* * * *

John Della Penna, an automobile wholesaler doing business as Pacific
Motors, brought this action for damages against Toyota Motor Sales,
U.S.A., Inc., and its Lexus division, alleging that certain business conduct
of defendants ... constituted an intentional interference with his economic
relations. The impetus for Della Penna's suit arose out of the introduction of
Toyota's Lexus automobile.

Fearing that auto wholesalers in the United States might re-export Lexus
models back to Japan for resale, and concerned that, with production and
the availability of Lexus models in the American market limited, re-exports
would jeopardize its fledgling network of American Lexus dealers, Toyota
inserted in its dealership agreements a "no export" clause, providing that the
dealer was authorized to sell Lexus cars only to customers located in the
United States.

* * * *

During the years 1989 and 1990, plaintiff Della Penna did a profitable
business as an auto wholesaler purchasing Lexus automobiles, chiefly from

the Lexus of Stevens Creek retail outlet, at near retail price and exporting them to Japan for resale. By late 1990, however, plaintiff's sources began to dry up, primarily as a result of the "offenders list." Stevens Creek ceased selling models to plaintiff; gradually other sources declined to sell to him as well.

In February 1991, plaintiff filed this lawsuit against Toyota Motors, U.S.A., Inc., alleging ... and interference with his economic relationship with Lexus retail dealers.... The tort cause-of action went to the jury, however, under instructions requiring plaintiff to prove that defendant's alleged interfering conduct was "wrongful."

Although legal historians have traced the origins of the so-called "interference torts" as far back as the Roman law, the proximate historical impetus for their modern development lay in mid-19th century English common law.... The opinion of the Queen's Bench in *Lumley v. Gye* (1853) 2 El. & Bl. 216, a case that has become a standard in torts casebooks, is widely cited as the origin of the two torts — interference with contract and its sibling, interference with prospective economic relations — in the form in which they have come down to us. The plaintiff owned the Queen's Theatre, at which operas were presented. He contracted for the services of a soprano, Johanna Wagner, to perform in various entertainments between April 15 and July 15, with the stipulation that Miss Wagner would not perform elsewhere during that time without his permission.

In an action on the case, the theater owner alleged that Gye, the owner of a rival theater, knowing of the Wagner-Lumley agreement, "maliciously" interfered with the contract by "enticing" Wagner to abandon her agreement with Lumley and appear at Gye's theater. Gye's demurrer to the complaint was overruled by the trial court, a ruling that was affirmed by the justices of the Queen's Bench on the then somewhat novel grounds that (1) "enticing" someone to leave his or her employment was not limited to disrupting the relationship between master and servant but applied to a "dramatic artiste" such as Miss Wagner, and (2) "wrongfully and maliciously, or, which is the same thing, with notice, interrupt[ing]" a personal service contract, regardless of the means the defendant employed, was an actionable wrong.

As a number of courts and commentators have observed, the keystone of the liability imposed in Lumley and other English cases, to judge from the opinions of the justices, appears to have been the "malicious" intent of a defendant in enticing an employee to breach her contract with the plaintiff, and damaging the business of one who refused to cooperate with the union in achieving its bargaining aims. While some have doubted whether the use of the word "malicious" amounted to anything more than an intent to commit an act, knowing it would harm the plaintiff, Dean Keeton, assessing the state of the tort as late as 1984, remarked that "[w]ith intent to interfere as the usual basis of the action, the cases have turned almost entirely upon the defendant's motive or purpose and the means by which he has sought to accomplish it. As in the cases of interference with contract, any manner of intentional invasion of the plaintiff's interests may be sufficient if the purpose is not a proper one." *Prosser and Keeton on Torts* (5th ed. 1984) (Interference with Prospective Advantage, § 130, p. 1009)....

These and related features of the economic relations tort and the requirements surrounding its proof and defense led, however, to calls for a reexamination and reform as early as the 1920's. A new *Restatement* provision, section 766B, required that the defendant's conduct be "improper," and adopted a multifactor "balancing" approach, identifying seven factors for the trier of fact to weigh in determining a defendant's liability.

The *Restatement (Second) of Torts*, however, declined to take a position on the issue of which of the parties bore the burden of proof, relying on the "considerable disagreement on who has the burden of pleading and proving certain matters" and the observation that "the law in this area has not fully congealed but is still in a formative stage."

In the meantime, however, an increasing number of state high courts had traveled well beyond the Second *Restatement*'s reforms by redefining and otherwise recasting the elements of the economic relations tort and the burdens surrounding its proof and defenses.... Over the past decade or so, close to a majority of the high courts of American jurisdictions have explicitly approv[ed] a rule that requires the plaintiff in such a suit to plead and prove the alleged interference was either "wrongful," "improper," "illegal," "independently tortious" or some variant on these formulations....

* * * *

The courts provide a damage remedy against third party conduct intended to disrupt an existing contract precisely because the exchange of promises resulting in such a formally cemented economic relationship is deemed worthy of protection from interference by a stranger to the agreement. Economic relationships short of contractual, however, should stand on a different legal footing as far as the potential for tort liability is reckoned. Because ours is a culture firmly wedded to the social rewards of commercial contests, the law usually takes care to draw lines of legal liability in a way that maximizes areas of competition free of legal penalties.

A doctrine that blurs the analytical line between interference with an existing business contract and interference with commercial relations less than contractual is one that invites both uncertainty in conduct and unpredictability of its legal effect. The notion that inducing the breach of an existing contract is simply a subevent of the "more inclusive" class of acts that interfere with economic relations, while perhaps theoretically unobjectionable, has been mischievous as a practical matter. Our courts should, in short, firmly distinguish the two kinds of business contexts, bringing a greater solicitude to those relationships that have ripened into agreements, while recognizing that relationships short of that subsist in a zone where the rewards and risks of competition are dominant.

Beyond that, we need not tread today. It is sufficient to dispose of the issue before us in this case by holding that a plaintiff seeking to recover for alleged interference with prospective economic relations has the burden of pleading and proving that the defendant's interference was wrongful by some measure beyond the fact of the interference itself.

Again, tough going, this time because of the philosophical problems inherent in this area of the law. The opinion makes it clear that there is a tension between protecting contractual rights and permitting free competition. This is not particularly difficult to understand, and it certainly accounts for the lower level of protection given prospective relations than to existing contracts. The winner gets more protection.

Responsibility

Why such a "to do" about who should be responsible for proving that the purported interference was wrongful?

Everyone agrees on most of the elements of the tort:

- existence of a contract or relationship
- defendant's knowledge of the contract relationship
- intentional acts on the part of the defendant designed to disrupt the relationship
- actual disruption of the relationship
- damages to the plaintiff proximately caused by the acts of the defendant.

Is there *really* any practical difference between making plaintiff prove that defendant's conduct was wrong and making a defendant prove that the conduct was justified, privileged, or otherwise immune from scrutiny? Having tried several of these cases, the author believes that this is a distinction without a difference. It is the rare defendant indeed that lacks any reason for "interfering" with someone else's business relationships, and rarer still is the defendant who is unwilling to explain it. The choice is the jury's, and usually it weighs the propriety of the parties' positions, regardless of who has the burden of proof.

A thorough understanding of these business torts requires weighing many factors ranging from consumer protection legislation, which supplements and expands common law concepts of fraud and contract, to economic realities or government securities regulation. Torts have a real role in regulating business and protecting consumers and will continue to be active for many years to come.

Key Words and Phrases

"benefit of the bargain" rule
disclosure
fiduciary relationship
fraudulent suppression
guilty knowledge
recklessly without knowledge of truth
representation of fact
rescission

scienter
suppression of the truth
tortious interference with contract

Review Questions

1. Justice Cardozo's *Ultramares* decision, which sets a standard of strict privity before liability can be imposed, attempts to set limits and standards on the tort of negligent misrepresentation so that the tort is not "dangerously overused." Can you see examples in today's society of overuse of this tort in lawsuits?

2. Do you feel Justice Cardozo's "strict privity" standard in *Ultramares* or the "near privity" standard in *Credit Alliance* is most appropriate? Why?

---

[1] We also leave for another day issues relating to securities fraud, that is, fraud in the purchase and sale of stocks, bonds and other similar investments. There is a great deal of overlap between the principles in these two areas, but because securities fraud involves state and federal statutes and regulations, we leave those issues for a more focused treatment in the context of corporate law.

[2] For example, you might receive a geologist's prediction that a certain area was likely to produce oil or gas. Such a prediction might in the context of a larger presentation be sufficient to constitute a misrepresentation, particularly if it was made without having done anything to try to see if the area was a good prospect for oil exploration.

[3] Note the word "properly" there. You may be asked: "Can they sue?" The literal answer is "Yes, they can!" Anyone can file a lawsuit for anything, even ridiculous claims against nonexistent or noncorporeal entities. What you're really being asked is "Will they win?"

Chapter Fifteen

WEIRD SCIENCE?
THE DEVELOPING LAW
OF TOXIC TORTS

No area of tort law — and perhaps no area of civil law — can hold a candle to toxic torts when it comes to grabbing headlines. Here is where you are most likely to find nationwide class actions and huge settlements. Here is where the scientific establishment meets the mavericks. Here is where you hear the names with the ugly reputations: asbestos, Agent Orange, tobacco, dioxin, lead, radium, x-rays, DES, silicone, PCBs, TCE, DPT, Bendectin, chlordane, and others.

It's a veritable alphabet soup of exotic and possibly dangerous substances. *A Civil Action*, a big-budget movie about a toxic tort matter, was a hit at the box office. This certainly is the glamour field of tort law.

Now the surprise: there is no such thing as a **toxic tort**! If you were to read the complaints in a case involving any of these substances, you would see claims like negligence, strict liability, and breach of warranty. You might see trespass or nuisance, even fraud — but not the term "toxic tort."

That's because toxic tort law really is about **causation** and **injury**, not whether there should be redress for certain kinds of wrong.

Pinpointing Causation

The problem we study in this chapter arises from a situation you may have experienced in your own life. Assume that you and some friends go out for pizza. A couple of days later, one friend has a sick stomach, another one diarrhea, a third has a fever, and you just don't feel very well. As you talk to each other and find out about these illnesses, you and your friends each begin to think and say to each other, "It must have been the pizza." Or was it? It seems plausible enough. After all, you all were healthy before you went to dinner together. Your symptoms all *seem* to be the kind that could be from eating tainted food. There's nothing else you can think of that can explain why all of you got sick at about the same time.

But what you and your friends may really be suffering from is something that has been called "**pizza syndrome.**"[1] Your shared experience could be the cause of your shared problems. So could lots of other things, and their appearance could be coincidence.

Additionally, you could all be the victims of "self-selection," a process somewhat like the well-documented "**placebo effect.**"[2] As you talk and share your complaints, they reinforce each other. Some studies have shown that this process can result in both a strengthening and spreading of these "symptoms." Something you would have lived with (and probably ignored) becomes a symptom because another person has given it credence.

The real problem in toxic tort cases—or eating pizza with friends—is determining which of these hypotheses is correct. Are your symptoms a product of bad pizza, or something else? Have the plaintiffs been injured by exposure to a toxic substance? Have they been injured at all?

In whatever legal "pigeonhole" we try to place the claim, these issues of causation are the heart and soul of toxic tort law.

Burden of Proof

As you probably have also guessed by now (and perhaps recall from earlier parts of this book), toxic tort law, almost more than any other, is a field of experts and **expert testimony**. And here we come to a second problem, one that we have not addressed to any extent earlier in this book, the **burden of proof**.

In a civil case, the party with the burden of proof generally can succeed if it proves its case by a **preponderance of the evidence**. You probably have heard about this concept in terms of the scales of justice. If the plaintiff's evidence is even the slightest bit heavier than the defendant's, the plaintiff has proven its case by a preponderance of the evidence.

In most situations, questions about a preponderance of the evidence just don't come up. The judge gives a form instruction on the subject, and the jury does the weighing. Appellate courts are reluctant to interfere with that process so long as each side has put on some evidence.

Now make it harder. Medical and other scientific opinion evidence generally is admissible if the witness testifies with a reasonable degree of professional certainty. This does not mean that the witness has to be entirely certain, but somewhere between "more probable than not" and "entirely certain." Yet many witnesses who testify in toxic tort cases aren't, and indeed can't be, entirely certain that long-term exposure to X causes Y.

That lack of certainty, inevitable with even the best of witnesses in many situations, has a real impact on the jury's weighing of evidence in these matters. Add to it the "mumbo jumbo" often inherent in these cases, stir in the probability that there will be dozens of lawyers, troops of doctors, and humongous piles of documents, and the problem becomes almost intractable.

This then is our task in this chapter: a brief sketch of the unique issues that go into modern toxic tort law. A thorough study of this expanding field and of the class actions that increasingly form its backbone is far beyond what we can do. But we can begin to look at and understand how courts have attempted to cope with the legal and scientific challenge presented in this area. Let us use one trial judge's efforts to do so.

In re Breast Implant Litigation
11 F. Supp. 2d 1217
United States District Court for the District of Colorado
1998

Sparr, J.:

Currently pending in this court are numerous silicone breast implant cases brought against various breast implant manufacturers. Plaintiffs seek damages for injuries they allege to have suffered from their silicone breast implants. Making claims under Colorado law for strict liability, negligence, and breach of warranty, Plaintiffs allege that their silicone breast prostheses have caused "auto-immune diseases" and have injured the Plaintiffs "in and about their body and extremities."

* * * *

Plaintiffs assert tort claims for negligence and strict liability, as well as claims for breach of express and implied warranty. In Colorado, "[i]n order to prevail on a tort claim, a plaintiff must prove by a preponderance of the evidence that a defendant committed an act which caused an injury to that plaintiff." ... Plaintiffs premise many of their alleged injuries on the existence of various kinds of "atypical connective tissue disease" ("ACTD"). This "disease" allegedly manifests itself through a "constellation" of symptoms and is allegedly caused by an autoimmune response to silicone from breast implants. Plaintiffs' claims implicate several areas of scientific study, including rheumatology, neurology, and epidemiology.

Causation in toxic tort cases is discussed in terms of general and specific causation.... General causation is whether a substance is capable of causing a particular injury or condition in the general population, while specific causation is whether a substance caused a particular individual's injury.

In order to establish their claims, Plaintiffs "must show both general and specific causation — that is, that breast implants are capable of causing" the conditions complained of, and that "breast implants were the cause-in-fact" of the specific conditions.

The diseases and symptoms allegedly associated with breast implants occur in non-implanted women as well as implanted women. Many of the conditions that Plaintiffs attribute to breast implants appear in the general population. Without a controlled study, there is no way to determine if these symptoms are more common in women with silicone breast implants than women without implants.

The most important evidence relied upon by scientists to determine whether an agent (such as breast implants) causes disease is controlled epidemiologic studies. Epidemiology can be viewed as the study of the causes of diseases in humans. Therefore, epidemiological studies are necessary to determine the cause and effect between breast implants and allegedly associated diseases. A valid epidemiologic study requires that study subjects, cases, and controls are chosen by an unbiased sampling method from a definable population. Epidemiology is the best evidence of causation in the mass torts context. Linda A. Bailey, *et al.*, *Reference Guide on Epidemiology, Reference Manual On Scientific Evidence* at 126 (1994) ("In the absence of an understanding of the biological and pathological mechanisms by which disease develops, epidemiological evidence is the most valid type of scientific evidence of toxic causation")....

[T]he Ninth Circuit [has] focused on [a] crucial issue referenced by [earlier cases]: whether expert witness opinion evidence is admissible when the available epidemiology does not demonstrate that the plaintiff's alleged injury was "more likely than not" caused by the defendant. The Ninth Circuit defined the plaintiff's burden as follows:

> [Plaintiffs] must establish not just that their mothers' ingestion of Bendectin increased somewhat the likelihood of birth defects, but that it more than doubled it — only then can it be said that Bendectin is more likely than not the source of their injury.

In short, [ruling cases] instruct that if the available body of epidemiology demonstrates that breast implants do not double the risk of any known disease, then plaintiffs' causation evidence is inadmissible.

There exists in the context of breast implanted women a "background rate" of injury; that is, the injuries of which the breast implant plaintiffs complain are not unique, but occur frequently in women without breast implants. Because the injuries of which Plaintiffs complain occur commonly in women without breast implants, Plaintiffs must present expert testimony demonstrating that exposure to breast implants more than doubled the risk of their alleged injuries. If exposure to breast implants does not at least double the risk of injury, then more than half of the population suffering from the injuries allegedly caused by breast implants would be injured anyway (the background rate of injury), thereby disproving legal causation.

* * * *

The difference between groups is often expressed as the ratio between the incidence of the disease in the exposed group and the incidence in the unexposed group. Marcia Angell, M.D., *Science on Trial* (1996) at 164. The relative risk simply indicates how high above the background level the risk is. The threshold for concluding that an agent was more likely the cause of a disease than not is a relative risk greater than 2.0. Recall that a relative risk of 1.0 means that the agent has no effect on the incidence of disease. When the relative risk reaches 2.0, the agent is responsible for an equal number of cases of disease as all other background causes. Thus, a relative risk of 2.0 implies a 50% likelihood that an exposed individual's disease was caused by the agent.

* * * *

To prove causation, Plaintiffs Zelinger and Roberts offer the testimony of rheumatologist Dr. Kassan, neurologist Dr. Klapper, neuropsychiatrist Dr. Hoffman, and biomaterials scientists Dr. Guidoin and Dr. Blais.

No Plaintiffs' expert witness report states an opinion on general causation; the physician witnesses offer only specific causation opinions and the non-physician witnesses purportedly do not offer opinions about causation. The reports submitted by Plaintiffs' experts fail to present a single peer-reviewed, controlled epidemiologic study that support their causation theories.

This is not to say that epidemiological studies are required in this type of tort action. Epidemiological studies are not the magical cure for legal disputes. In many instances, epidemiological data may be unavailable. A lack of epidemiology should not end the inquiry, but rather begin the inquiry into what other types of evidence a plaintiff can present to satisfy the burden of proof. There is a range of scientific methods for investigating questions of causation, for example, toxicology and animal studies, clinical research, and epidemiology, all of which have distinct advantages and disadvantages. The court's inquiry is whether reliable scientific evidence, based on sound methodology, has been presented. What is significant in this case is that the substantial body of epidemiological evidence demonstrates that silicone breast implants do not double the risk of any known disease.

* * * *

Plaintiffs seek to introduce expert testimony from clinicians (i.e., treating physicians) who claim to be able to diagnose a patient with a disease caused by breast implants through the process of differential diagnosis. Drs. Klapper and Kassan have provided written opinions which state that they, as treating physicians of the Plaintiffs, have used the medical procedure of differential diagnosis and have determined to "a reasonable degree of medical certainty" that the illnesses and symptoms from which the Plaintiffs suffer are caused by the silicone from their silicone gel breast implants.

Such testimony is not scientifically reliable in the cases before the court because it confuses two distinct burdens. Plaintiffs must demonstrate two types of causation: general causation and specific causation. By using differential diagnosis, a clinician can identify possible diseases the patient may have and, through a process of elimination, rule out diseases until a disease or symptom is left as the diagnosis. Differential diagnosis is not a scientific method by which a physician can determine whether silicone breast implants can cause disease in humans.... As a practical matter, the cause of many diseases remains unknown; therefore, a clinician who suspects that a substance causes a disease in some patients very well might conclude that the substance caused the disease in the plaintiff simply because the clinician has no other explanation. *See* Margaret A. Berger, "Evidentiary Framework," *Reference Manual On Scientific Evidence* at 81 (1994).

The kind of causation testimony offered by Plaintiffs' experts was summarized and rejected by Judge Prado:

[T]he witness admits that if the Plaintiff did not have breast implants but had the exact same symptoms and blood chemistry, then his diagnosis would have been non-implant-caused Sjogren's Syndrome. Essentially, this is a bit like saying that if a person has a scratchy throat, runny nose, and a nasty cough, that person has a cold; if, on the other hand, that person has a scratchy throat, runny

> nose, nasty cough, and wears a watch, they have a watch-induced
> cold. Such reasoning is extremely suspect, which has prompted
> other courts to reject it as unscientific in the absence of convincing
> epidemiology evidence.

The single most important thought in Judge Sparr's opinion is not so
much its scholarly analysis of legal principle, which is superb, but the
following statement: "In the absence of an understanding of the
biological and pathological mechanisms by which disease develops,
epidemiological evidence is the most valid type of scientific evidence of
toxic causation."

This statement, almost thrown away in a parenthetical, forms the real
basis for most of toxic tort law. If we know the exact causal mechanism
by which a particular disease or condition begins, none of this debate is
necessary. We simply look to see if it exists with respect to a particular
plaintiff, and that's that.

Causal Mechanism

The sad fact is that we don't understand the causal mechanism by which
many diseases develop. To name just one, the biological or pathological
mechanism by which "cancer" — really not a single disease, but an
array of them — and a host of other conditions come about simply is
beyond the understanding of science at this time. We have clues,
correlations, opinions, intuition, strong ideas, even the beginnings of
general theory, but not a reliable explanation of cause-and-effect:
ingesting so much of substance X causes Y to happen, producing disease
Z.

Epidemiology steps into this gap in our knowledge by looking
macroscopically at the cause and effect relationship, attempting to
isolate "vectors" by which disease can develop.

General Causation

Now all of what we have done goes to general causation, to the question of whether a given substance can have the effect on the plaintiffs seen in the particular case. To prove causation in toxic tort matters, the plaintiff must prove (and the defendant must disprove):

- that the plaintiff in fact ingested the substance
- that the amount of exposure was sufficient to cause the harm alleged
- that in this particular plaintiff's case, something else didn't cause the problem.

Proving That the Substance Was Ingested

Ingestion of a substance is fact-intensive, and it can be tricky.[3] In many toxic tort cases, there is eyewitness evidence of exposure and ingestion. Sometimes the allegedly toxic entity remains in the body. Silicone gel breast implants and other medical devices are examples. The plaintiffs may be in a dust-filled room or mine or constantly dip their hands in a tank of chlorinated solvents. But in many cases such proof does not exist, so the only way to proceed is circumstantially.

For example, in one case on which the author worked, plaintiffs attempted to show that they were exposed to pesticide residue on carpets in their apartments. They had a laboratory analyze samples of the carpet for the pesticide in order to show that such exposure could take place.

Proving the Amount of Exposure to a Substance

However, this was not enough. Did the plaintiffs wear shoes or socks in their apartments? How much could get in if the only area of contact was the soles of their feet? How much pesticide could be absorbed through the skin in a given period of time? Tough questions!

This leads to one of the most difficult decisions facing any plaintiff in a toxic tort case: must I test myself to see if any of the substance or its metabolic products remains in me? Plaintiffs have to show that they have ingested enough of a substance to have had an effect on them. Thus, the plaintiff who would not even consider performing such a test faces a difficult time when it comes to proving his or her case.

By the same token, the test may be painful, highly invasive, or even dangerous. In some cases, the substance is metabolized quickly and does not remain in significant amounts in the body for long periods. Even doing the test can be of little value. For example, in the author's pesticide case, the plaintiffs alleged exposure to a substance that had been used throughout the United States for many years. It was highly likely that the plaintiffs had absorbed some of it on other occasions. How would we know whether any pesticide in their system was from the exposure they were suing over?

Proving the Substance Caused the Exhibited Symptoms

The final battle in this area is over whether the symptoms being exhibited are actually caused by the substance to which the plaintiffs claim exposure. This is particularly important when the plaintiffs only can point to "low level" symptoms as evidence of their ingestion. This means a detailed examination of prior medical histories to see if other diseases can account for what plaintiffs now claim "ails 'em."

This medical detective work can be difficult, but it has to be done. As an example, in another case in which the author was involved, a rural family claimed to have developed porphyria, a liver disease, from exposure to paraquat, a herbicide. They also claimed damage to their herd of cattle. The family's medical records revealed that the person who allegedly had been most seriously affected had for many years before the incident taken a medication that could produce the kinds of abnormality in liver tests that allegedly were caused by the paraquat. As for the cows, a consultation with a veterinarian revealed that a common fungus that grew on feed grass could produce the symptoms being observed in the cows. A test of the grass in the allegedly affected pasture revealed large amounts of this fungus. Voila!

While defendants most often benefit from this kind of detective work, it is usually because the plaintiff's team hasn't been thorough enough in its investigation. Success in toxic tort work comes about in the same way that success in other cases does, by hard investigation and an understanding of facts and their implications.

Elements in General Causation

There are several ongoing battlegrounds in this area. The first of these is **consistency**. Are the harmful effects of a substance consistent from person to person? Think about it. When you go to the doctor, he or she often performs tests on you. Measurements of your temperature, blood count, liver enzymes and a gazillion other functions generally fall within a range that is roughly similar to everyone else. Your body operates pretty much the same way, using the same processes, as everyone else. Thus, it is reasonable to hypothesize that if a substance has an adverse effect, it will repeat itself and be consistent over a large enough population.

For example, we know that workers exposed to asbestos fibers for long periods consistently develop mesothelioma. Not every worker gets it, but virtually no unexposed person does. Consistent effects are a hallmark of general causation.

The second battle often is over something called **the dose response curve**. Paracelcus, a medieval physician considered the founder of toxicology, stated it this way: "The dose makes the poison." This means the effect on a human system increases as the exposure and intake of a substance increases. Think of acetaminophen, the common "nonaspirin" pain reliever doctors prefer. Two tablets can stop your headache. Taking an entire bottle will cause your liver to fail. This is an example of the dose-response curve at work.[4]

Establishing a dose-response curve is another essential step in establishing causation, both general and specific. At the general causation level, a consistent dose-response curve is a strong indicator of what a substance can do. This, of course, is the hallmark of general causation. Knowing how much exposure to a particular substance is necessary to produce a given response also helps establish or disprove specific causation for any specific plaintiff.

The third reason that this issue is important is that many plaintiffs can only show ingestion of a low dose of a particular material. Our assumptions about many substances rest upon high-dose testing, a method that has come under increasingly critical scrutiny.[5] Additionally, for many substances, there is a level of ingestion that can be dealt with by the body without ill effects. Acetaminophen, which definitely has toxic effects in large doses (as we have seen above) generally is quite harmless if you take it as directed. Understanding what, if anything, happens at low-dose levels therefore can be very important.

The final battleground in toxic causation (and the regulation of substances generally) is one that we hear about from time to time even in the general media: **animal studies**. Animal studies divide into several categories: tests in which large groups of animals ingest relatively high doses of a substance to see what happens, generally called *in vivo* **studies**, and tests using animal tissue, called *in vitro* **studies**.

Whichever kind of study is involved, however, there are serious conceptual difficulties with relying too heavily on animals to show toxicity in humans.[6] Two of the most important are:

- *Dose size*. In most studies, the animals receive a dose of the substance being tested that is much higher than what they would receive under normal conditions. This is done for legitimate reasons, but it creates a very real risk that the dangerous effects of a substance are exaggerated. Almost anything can cause problems if given in large enough doses.
- *Differences in metabolism*. There are many similarities between the animals used in these studies and humans, but they are not complete. Thus, there can be surprising differences in how humans and animals react to the same drugs.[7]

Even with these problems, animal studies do have a role in this area. They often are all we have to judge by, and there often are correlations between animal data and human problems. Scientists and regulators rely on the studies, so a legal professional should be aware of what they are and how they are used.

Recognizing that this area contains many difficult issues tends to mask another issue that has proven very difficult: Are courts really equipped to handle this kind of dispute, which involves subjects most of us barely know how to pronounce, let alone understand? At one level, the answer is that it doesn't matter. Courts must be open so that aggrieved parties can resolve their disputes; if that means judges learning epidemiology, so be it. Few judges seemed to have complained about that part of the process. However, there are legitimate issues here about how judges should evaluate the quality of this scientific evidence. It is an area where an extensive jurisprudence has developed, as Judge Sparr (our "guinea pig" in this chapter) has noted.

In re Breast Implant Litigation
11 F. Supp. 2d 1217
United States District Court for the
District of Colorado
1998

CONTINUED

The Federal Rules of Evidence govern the admission of expert scientific testimony in a federal trial. *Daubert v. Merrell Dow Pharmaceuticals, Inc.*, 509 U.S. 579, 113 S.Ct. 2786, 125 L.Ed.2d 469 (1993). Fed.R.Civ.P. 702, governing expert testimony, provides:

If scientific, technical, or other specialized knowledge will assist the trier of fact to understand the evidence or to determine a fact in issue, a witness qualified as an expert by knowledge, skill, experience, training, or education, may testify thereto in the form of an opinion or otherwise.

Under the Rules, federal trial judges must ensure that any and all scientific testimony or evidence admitted is not only relevant but also reliable. The Plaintiffs have the burden of proving that the testimony of their expert witnesses is admissible pursuant to Fed.R.Evid. 702 and the standards set forth in it.

Under the first prong of the *Daubert* test for admissibility of expert testimony, "[t]he adjective 'scientific' implies a grounding in the methods and procedures of science. Similarly, the word 'knowledge' connotes more than subjective belief or unsupported speculation." *Daubert*, 509 U.S. at 590, 113 S.Ct. 2786. The trial court's obligation under Rule 702 and *Daubert* is to determine evidentiary reliability, that is, trustworthiness. 509 U.S. at 590 n. 9, 113 S.Ct. 2786. "In a case involving scientific evidence, evidentiary reliability will be based on scientific validity." *Daubert*, 509 U.S. at 590 n. 9, 113 S.Ct. 2786. "[I]n order to qualify as 'scientific knowledge,' an inference or assertion must be derived by the scientific method. Proposed testimony must be supported by appropriate validation— i.e., 'good grounds,' based on what is known. In short, the requirement that an expert's testimony pertain to 'scientific knowledge' establishes a standard of evidentiary reliability." *Daubert*, 509 U.S. at 590, 113 S.Ct. 2786; *accord. Summers v. Missouri Pacific Railroad System*, 132 F.3d 599, 603 (10th Cir.1997).

[T]here are important differences between the quest for truth in the courtroom and the quest for truth in the laboratory. Scientific conclusions are subject to perpetual revision. Law, on the other hand, must resolve disputes finally and quickly. The scientific project is advanced by broad and wide-ranging consideration of a multitude of hypotheses, for those that are incorrect will eventually be shown to be so, and that in itself is an advance. Conjectures that are probably wrong are of little use, however, in the project of reaching a quick, final, and binding legal judgment—often of great consequence—about a particular set of events in the past. We recognize that, in practice, a gatekeeping role for the judge, no matter how flexible, inevitably on occasion will prevent the jury from learning of authentic insights and innovations. That, nevertheless, is the balance that is struck by Rules of Evidence designed not for the exhaustive search for cosmic understanding but for the particularized resolution of legal disputes. *Daubert*, 509 U.S. at 596–97, 113 S.Ct. 2786.

The Supreme Court has provided some guidance for the task of determining scientific validity. *Daubert* sets forth several non-exhaustive factors to assist trial courts in determining whether a theory or technique constitutes "scientific knowledge" within the meaning of Rule 702, including whether the methodology, principles and reasoning underlying the proposed experts' opinions: (1) can be and have been empirically tested; (2) have been subjected to peer review and publication; (3) have a known or potential rate of error; and (4) have gained general acceptance in the relevant scientific community.

Rule 702's second prong concerns relevancy, or "fit." "The scientific knowledge must be connected to the question at issue." The trial court must ensure that the proposed expert testimony is "relevant to the task at hand, that it logically advances a material aspect of the proposing party's case." ... Scientific expert testimony introduces special dangers to the fact-finding process because it can be both powerful and quite misleading because of the difficulty in evaluating it. Therefore, federal judges must exclude proffered scientific evidence under Rule 702 unless they are convinced that it speaks clearly and directly to an issue in dispute in the case, and that it will not mislead the jury. *Daubert*, 43 F.3d at 1321.

Daubert, the focus of this part of Judge Sparr's scholarly opinion, hit town like a tornado, and its effects have not yet fully revealed themselves.[8] Judges suddenly found themselves having to keep gates that they didn't know had existed. It hasn't been easy.

What happens in real life when a *Daubert* challenge exists? In most courts, the objecting party files a written objection to an expert's proposed testimony some time before trial. The court then convenes a hearing in which the proponent of the expert opinion has to put on evidence sufficient to satisfy the three *Daubert* criteria.

The expert must show the **empirical support** for his or her theory. In other words, the expert must show what kinds of properly controlled experiments have been done to support his or her position. This may take the form of the expert's own work, or it may rest upon studies done by others.

Next, the proponent must show that the substance of his findings were **"peer reviewed,"** examined by others in the same field who critiqued the method and results for error. Usually, peer review occurs when a scientist submits a paper to a scientific journal, but it may also occur in the context of applying for a research grant or an academic position.[9]

It is at the error stage that many theories fail the *Daubert* test. In many cases, the sample is so small that rates of error cannot reliably be charted. In others, the possible rate of error is so large as to invalidate the result. This is a tough passage even for results that may someday prove themselves to be correct.

The final *Daubert* criterion is **general acceptance**, which is something of an enigma and a problem. General acceptance of a result or position usually comes after other scientists have repeated the first experiment and gotten the same or similar results. Sometimes corroboration of the proposed mechanism must come from another source as well.

These three areas — repeatability, consistency, and independent corroboration by other means — form the foundation on which general acceptance rests.

As a real world exercise, *Daubert* also involves one implicit criterion of considerable importance: which side has the better teacher? It will be the rare judge who has independent substantive knowledge in a scientific field. Thus, putting the information necessary to support a "go-no go" *Daubert* ruling before the court in a form that it can understand and digest is essential. The party that explains its position more clearly usually "wins."

To get another perspective on the impact of *Daubert*, let us pause briefly to examine the standard it replaced in another case involving injuries allegedly caused by the drug Bendectin:

Blum v. Merrell Dow Pharmaceuticals, Inc.
705 A.2d 1314
Superior Court of Pennsylvania
1997

Beck, J.:

This is a pharmaceutical products liability action. Plaintiffs-appellees are Jeffrey Blum, a minor, and his parents and natural guardians, Joan and Fred Blum. Jeffrey Blum was born with clubfeet. The Blums filed this action against defendant-appellant Merrell Dow Pharmaceuticals, Inc. ("Merrell Dow"), the manufacturer of the drug Bendectin. While pregnant with Jeffrey, Joan Blum took Bendectin, which was prescribed by her doctor to relieve pregnancy-related nausea. After trial in 1986, the jury returned a verdict in favor of the Blums, finding specifically that his mother's ingestion of Bendectin during pregnancy caused Jeffrey Blum's clubfeet....

In an effort to answer the critical causation question, the Blums proffered scientific expert testimony from several witnesses. Alan K. Done, M.D., and Adrian Gross, D.V.M., testified at the first trial, and their testimony was read to the jury during the second trial. In the second trial, Stuart Newman, Ph.D., testified via videotaped deposition. These witnesses offered their opinions that Bendectin is a human "teratogen," while conceding that birth defects occur even in the absence of Bendectin exposure. Done, Gross and Newman all testified as to general causation, that is, the teratogenic potential of Bendectin. Only Dr. Done opined more specifically that Bendectin caused Jeffrey Blum's clubfeet.

An expert witness is qualified to offer an opinion if he or she has sufficient skill, knowledge, or experience in a field or calling as to make it appear that his or her opinion or inference will probably aid the trier in its search for truth.

In the words of an old country lawyer, the difference between the *Daubert* standard and the older, "generally accepted" *Frye* test is like the difference between lightning and lightning bugs. In theory, the *Frye* test could form the basis for exclusion of expert testimony, but it was the rare judge indeed who used it that way. In practice, most judges simply listened passively as experts from A to Z opined that their method was indeed generally accepted and deduced from a well-accepted scientific theory. As a result, virtually any scientific position that had some support somewhere in the literature found its way into the courtroom. It was from this *laissez-faire* attitude that *Daubert* ultimately sprang.

Does *Daubert* make it impossible for plaintiffs to put on a toxic tort case? No. There remain many cases in which experts offered by plaintiffs pass *Daubert* muster, and the case goes forward.

What *Daubert* does do is take courts and juries out of the business of peer review, that is, of being the first to hear new, radical, or fringe medical or scientific theories. Whether the fence should be drawn here is something about which reasonable minds may differ, but the fact that there now is a fence has undeniably changed the field.

Key Words and Phrases

burden of proof
causal mechanism
causation
confidence interval
consistency
Daubert criteria
dose response curve
empirical support
epidemiology
expert testimony
general acceptance
general causation
in vitro animal studies
in vivo animal studies
injury
peer review
"pizza syndrome"
"placebo effect"
preponderance of the evidence

specific causation
toxic tort

Review Questions

1. What did the Supreme Court rule in *Kumho Tire Co., Ltd. v. Carmichael*, 526 U.S. 137 (1999)?

2. Review news of the past month and note how many articles you find that involve "toxic torts." Consider current litigation, allegations from activists, warnings from government agencies, and other newsworthy items. Choose one to share with your colleagues in class. What formal claims, such as negligence or trespass, are involved?

---

[1] So far as the author is aware, this term and hypothetical that goes with it are the brainchild of Dr. John Kasik of the University of Iowa Medical School, who uses them to explain some of the problems that can exist in toxic tort cases.

[2] A placebo is an inactive dose of medicine usually given with the suggestion that taking it will help the recipient get better. In a significant number of cases, people who take placebos *do* report an improvement in their symptoms. The suggestion thus plays a role in helping the patient improve or change his or her condition.

[3] For example, a common method of testing for long-term lead ingestion is analysis of a ground-up tooth. To test for chlorinated solvents or pesticides, doctors analyze a sample of body fat. Neither process is particularly simple.

[4] The curve isn't quite that simple when it comes to carcinogenic substances (cancer causing agents) or teratogens (agents that cause genes to mutate). It is possible in theory for a single infinitesimal exposure to one of these agents to change or mutate the cell so that it becomes the start of a cancerous growth or the source of a transmitted mutation. This is called the "one hit" theory. Although it is largely rejected today, it remains a concept that you will hear about in many toxic tort cases.

[5] *See, e.g.*, Ames and Gold, "The Prevention of Cancer," 30(2) Drug Metabolism Reviews 201 (1998).

[6] For those interested, Gold, Slone and Ames, "What Do Animal Cancer Tests Tell Us About Human Cancer Risk?: Overview of Analyses of the Carcinogenicity Potency Database," 30(2) Drug Metabolism Reviews 359 (1998), presents a very comprehensive and generally rather readable account of some of the difficulties associated with animal testing and the use of animal test results in humans.

[7] Cortisone presents a surprising but real example. Several animal studies of this substance found that it causes severe cleft palate birth defects in several animal species, but it does not cause this effect in humans. Injections of cortisone will precipitate labor in pregnant sheep, cows, goats, rabbits, and rats; this does not occur in humans. There are many other examples.

[8] As this book is written, the Supreme Court has before it a case that would make the *Daubert* process applicable to experts in the "soft sciences" like economics. *See Kumho Tire Co., Ltd. v. Carmichael*, 526 U.S. 137 (1999).

[9] At its best, as the author has learned in the past when he has submitted works to peer-reviewed journals, which is a difficult but enlightening process. Things the author thought certain, or at least unexceptionable, may not seem so obvious when examined by someone else. This testing helps strengthen the paper, and the thinking that underlies it.

Chapter Sixteen

THE ROLE OF INSURANCE IN THE LAW OF TORTS

There is an old trick that helps explain the concept of insurance. If you go into a room with thirty people in it, the chances are virtually 100% that at least two will have the same birthday.[1] We cannot say *which* of the two people it will be, but it is very likely that at least two will share the same birthday. This simple exercise — which admittedly doesn't have too much to do with insurance — nonetheless illustrates the first important characteristic of the field: the statistical sharing of an event or characteristic.

Take that same group of people, and stay in touch with them over time. When all have passed away, you will have knowledge of their average life expectancies. With enough people, you might be able to compute life expectancy by sex, weight, height, or any of a dozen other factors. When coupled with an understanding of the distribution of the population by age, these life expectancy tables (which have been done, by the way) enable us to make a rather precise statistical assessment of both the possible number and distribution of deaths in the population over any given period.[2]

It's Called "Insurance"

Now we have something that begins to look familiar, perhaps like a life insurance ad on TV. In fact, this *is* the basis for life insurance. Each member of our group shares a statistical risk of dying over some discrete period of time. We do not know which of the group, if anyone, will become the statistic, but we know that each faces a particular probability of death at any point. We can therefore calculate the likely number of deaths within the group in a similar period.

Now we have two of the essential aspects of insurance: **sharing of an event** (life expectancy) that carries a **risk** with it.

Now onto the third part of insurance. If you were to continue your analysis, you would see that the burial costs and funeral expenses were a certain sum of money. The members of our group could agree among themselves to **share those expenses** by making contributions to a fund sufficient to pay off the total amount of expenses that the group is likely to incur in a given year.

For example, if three people in a group of 100 are likely to pass away in a given year and the average expenses for each are $5,000, the group could agree to make payments into a fund of $15,000, the amount our statistics say is necessary to pay these costs. This would mean each member would have to pay $150 that year. In return for this contribution, group members would have the security of knowing that they or their estate could recover funeral expenses from this fund.

The contribution is not a savings account, but the **sharing of a common risk by a group**. Each member puts in his or her money, knowing that he or she might not need to make a claim on the fund in a given year. The payment is both a right to participate in the fund — to share with others — and part of the fund's assets.

This fund for sharing the possible risks associated with burial *is* insurance because it involves the sharing of specified risks among a group of people. Add a person or entity to hold the money and administer claims, and you have the transfer of risk to an insurance company.

Before we go onto the idea of liability insurance, let us pause to see if our homely analysis is at all accurate.

Barberton Rescue Mission Inc. v. Insurance Division
of the Iowa Department of Commerce
586 N.W.2d 352
1998

Larson, J.:

* * * *

Barberton Rescue Mission of Barberton, Ohio, is a nonprofit corporation operating as a Christian ministry. In 1982 it began distributing a publication called "The Christian Brotherhood Newsletter." Of approximately 33,000 worldwide subscribers to the newsletter, 116 are in Iowa. Barberton designed a system for its subscribers to share health care costs based on a Biblical passage urging Christians to "bear ye one another's burdens." Gal. 6:2. Under this system, subscribers help with each other's qualifying medical and health care expenses up to $100,000 per person, per incident. The newsletter also operates a separate program called "Brothers Keeper" to help with bills over $100,000. Disputed claims are resolved by a rotating panel of members selected at random.

Under the basic newsletter program, claims are subject to a $200 deductible floor, and the program excludes physical examinations and certain routine tests, such as mammograms. Each subscriber is to refrain from using alcohol, tobacco, and illegal drugs. Subscribers must also furnish a certificate from a minister stating the member is in good standing in a Christian church.

Subscribers seeking financial assistance submit their medical bills to the newsletter. If the newsletter staff determines the expenses qualify for assistance, the newsletter publishes the name and address of the claimant. In the same publication, the newsletter assigns enough other subscribers to cover the medical expenses of the claimant. The designated subscribers mail a check for the amount they have agreed to pay each month (currently $50 for an individual, $100 for a couple, and $150 for a family) directly to the subscriber to whom they have been assigned. Once a year, subscribers make their monthly payments directly to the newsletter to pay administrative costs.

The application for membership states:

> I understand that the Christian Brotherhood Newsletter is a
> publication and not an insurance company. Any help I may receive
> will come directly from other subscribers and not the publisher. I
> understand the publisher will not be responsible to send me any

money and will have no obligation to me, other than to publish medical needs members have chosen to share, for certain members of my family. I understand that the Christian Brotherhood program does not provide, in any way, a contract for indemnification of my medical expenses, death benefit or any other loss. No subscriber is personally responsible to send gifts to the need recommended to them in the newsletter. I am not guaranteed payment for any need of mine that is published in the newsletter. I participate voluntarily to practice Christian principles as the Bible teaches and to contribute to others' needs. I agree that I have no legal recourse against any subscriber or the publisher, even if I do not receive any money for needs of mine submitted for publication in the newsletter. I understand that no contract for indemnification involving the Christian Brotherhood Newsletter, staff, employees or subscribers exists.

If a subscriber does not mail a check as assigned and has received three reminder letters from the newsletter without fulfilling the payment obligation, the subscriber is dropped from the main list, and a new subscriber is assigned to contribute. Any subscriber who is dropped from membership may elect to become a member of the "O" or optional group whose needs may be met by other members on a purely voluntary basis.

In May 1992 the Insurance Division of the Department of Commerce charged Barberton with selling insurance without a license. It requested the imposition of civil penalties and insurance premium taxes. The Insurance Division, in its final decision, ruled that Barberton was in fact selling insurance and was subject to supervision.

* * * *

The initial question is whether this program is "insurance" under our law. Our statutes do not define insurance, but we have said that

> [a] contract is one of insurance if it meets the following test: one party, for compensation, assumes the risk of another; the party who assumes the risk agrees to pay a certain sum of money on a specified contingency; and the payment is made to the other party or the party's nominee.

> In deciding whether a plan is insurance, its wording is not controlling ...:
>
> [W]e must look through the form of the transaction to determine whether the relationship of insurer and insured exists. Whether the contract is one of insurance must be determined from its purpose, effect, content, terminology, and conduct of the parties, and not from its designation therein, since a contract which is fundamentally one of insurance cannot be altered by the use or absence of words in the contract itself. The court must look also to the intention of the parties in making this determination.

It looks as if our "model" is reasonably accurate. For a relationship to be insurance, the participants must agree to share and transfer the risk of a particular event to a third party, which must agree to make a payment upon the happening on presentation of a claim involving the risk being shared.[3]

What Insurance Covers

Now that we have defined what insurance is, it should be apparent that many different kinds of risks can be insured. We all have heard of the movie stars who have insured their most prominent or notorious features against loss; the owner of a communications satellite can insure it against everything from failure at launch to collision with another space object. There is insurance on ships[4] and their cargoes, cars, paintings, and just about every other object under the sun. You can purchase insurance against the risk of fire, wind, flood, hail, kidnapping, theft, revolution, earthquake, and a gazillion other risks.

And, of course, the same basic concepts allow people to share the risks that their conduct will somehow cause harm to others. We can make reasonably accurate assessments of how many car crashes there are likely to be in a given period and we can estimate the average cost of injury and property for each accident. At that point, of course, the analysis looks quite like what we used for life insurance. On this basis, liability insurance can exist.[5]

Provisions for Insurance

As the Genie said in *Aladdin*, "There are just a few ifs, buts, whereases and provisos." The first is something we will only brush at in this book; it is called "**insurable interest**." In common sense terms, a person has an insurable interest if he or she has some interest or stake in the person or thing being insured such that he or she ordinarily would not want the harm being insured against to happen.

An illustration may help this rather complicated definition fall into place and show you why it is needed. If I can buy insurance on a stranger's house — that is, if I can buy the right to be paid if that stranger's house catches on fire — do you suppose that I might just possibly be a teensy bit tempted to, how shall we say it, make the risk come true? Now, we all know that I personally would *never* have such evil thoughts, but obviously there might be others less honorable. This is one reason why the law requires insurable interests; *objectively,* people with an interest in the life or property being insured are more likely to want it to stay around in an unhurt condition.

There is a second reason. Without an insurable interest, the person who buys an insurance policy is nothing other than a gambler, spending money [premiums] on the possibility that a tragedy will happen in regard to the insured property. The common law does not permit gambling contracts to begin with, and gambling on other people's misfortunes or losses is particularly abhorrent. Hence the requirement of an insurable interest.

Anyone who has seen *Double Indemnity*[6] knows that having an insurable interest does not prevent every kind of insurance-related problem, and fraudulent claims are a recurring problem. However, this is not a book about insurance (or criminal law, because insurance fraud also is a crime), so we will return to the very basic idea that *is* important to our understanding, and one that our speculation on the author's criminal motives embodies.

Consider again the idea of being able to "make the risk come true." If you or I know that a loss or risk covered by insurance has occurred or is about to occur, we have, in essence, cheated if we are allowed to buy an insurance policy covering that very risk.

The classic statement of the principle is in *Bartholomew v. Appalachian Ins. Co.*, 655 F.2d 27 (1st Cir. 1981), "It is too late to purchase insurance against a flood when water is already in the living room." It is a central, if unspoken, premise, but one that insurance relies upon centrally to survive, that the risk being insured against is outside of our control. Another word for this concept is that the risk is **external**. All of these issues we lump together under the heading "fortuity." Our next case introduces this vital concept.

Two Pesos, Inc. v. Gulf Insurance Co.
901 S.W.2d 495
Court of Appeals of Texas, Houston (14th Dist.).
1995

Lee, J.:

* * * *

Two Pesos operated a chain of fast-food restaurants serving Mexican food. In 1987, Taco Cabana, Inc. ("Taco Cabana"), another Mexican food restaurant, sued Two Pesos in the United States District Court for the Southern District of Texas, Houston Division, alleging in part that the "trade dress and appearance" of Two Pesos' restaurants was confusingly similar to those of Taco Cabana and that Two Pesos used trade secrets belonging to Taco Cabana. (The "trade dress" of a product is essentially its total image and overall appearance.)

After a jury trial, the federal court entered a judgment dated December 30, 1988, against Two Pesos awarding over $2 million in damages to Taco Cabana for intentional and deliberate infringement of its trade dress and misappropriation of trade secrets. In the judgment, the federal court also issued a permanent injunction ordering Two Pesos to change the appearance

---

of its restaurants. Two Pesos then appealed to the Fifth Circuit Court of Appeals and the United States Supreme Court, and both courts affirmed the judgment.

On August 6, 1991, while these appeals were pending, Taco Cabana filed a motion in federal district court asking the court to award "supplemental" damages it suffered after the entry of the original judgment. Taco Cabana sought these damages because it alleged Two Pesos "has not changed its conduct or its trade dress during the pendency of its appeal and Taco Cabana has been damaged as a result of Two Pesos' continuing violation of its rights." In its motion, Taco Cabana claimed that "supplemental damages" were proper "since trade dress infringement is a continuing tort."

Two Pesos obtained the general liability policy at issue from Gulf after the judgment was rendered and under appeal, but Two Pesos disclosed the litigation on its application. The policy covered the period of March 1, 1990, through March 1, 1991. Two Pesos notified Gulf of the supplemental damages claim and sought coverage under the Gulf policy's advertising injury liability provisions. By letter dated February 27, 1992, Gulf denied coverage. Gulf then filed this action in state court seeking a declaration of non-liability regarding its duty to defend and duty to indemnify Two Pesos in the Taco Cabana suit....

Gulf moved for summary judgment, claiming that its policy did not afford coverage because ... Taco Cabana's "supplemental damages" claim did not arise from a "fortuitous" loss against which liability insurance is intended to cover, but was instead a "known loss" or "loss in progress...."

* * * *

Gulf alleges that the claim is not covered because it is not a fortuitous loss. Generally, fortuity is an inherent requirement of all risk insurance policies.... The concept of insurance is that the parties, in effect, wager against the occurrence or nonoccurrence of a specified event; the carrier insures against a risk, not a certainty.

Two Pesos contends that because the "advertising injury" liability coverage does not contain any requirement for an "occurrence," or accident, there is no fortuitous loss requirement under that section of the policy. While the Gulf policy makes coverage for "bodily injury" contingent upon the conduct being an "accident," the policy makes no such contingency for "advertising injuries." The policy specifically covers intentional conduct such as misappropriation of advertising ideas or style of doing business, and infringement of copyright, title or slogan.

The Gulf policy makes no attempt to exclude such intentional conduct from its coverage, in spite of the fact that it does exclude intentionally false oral or written publication of material, and willful violations of penal statutes and ordinances. Thus, Two Pesos maintains that the policy does not exclude, by means of either a fortuity requirement or any specific exclusion, Taco Cabana's claim for supplemental damages from continued trade dress infringement.

We disagree. The fortuity doctrine not only concerns whether the offending conduct is accidental or intentional, but also incorporates the "known loss" and "loss in progress" principles. These aspects of the fortuity doctrine focus on the proposition that insurance coverage is precluded where the insured is, or should be, aware of an ongoing progressive loss or known loss at the time the policy is purchased. The "loss in progress" principle is recognized as part of standard insurance law. An insured cannot insure against something that has already begun and which is known to have begun.

Texas has long recognized that it is contrary to public policy for an insurance company knowingly to assume a loss occurring prior to its contract.

* * * *

Even though not precisely on point, we find the reasoning in *Appalachian Ins. Co. v. Liberty Mutual Ins. Co.*, 676 F.2d 56, 61–63 (3rd Cir.1982) instructive. There, the court determined that the injurious effects of the insured's discriminatory employment policies began immediately upon their adoption. Although these effects continued into the insurer's policy period, the occurrence required to trigger coverage took place when the injuries first manifested themselves, which occurred before the inception of the insurance policy. *Id.* at 62. Therefore, there was no personal injury liability coverage for the sexual discrimination claims. The court further recognized that any other result "would contravene the rule that an insured cannot insure against something which has already begun," because "the purpose of insurance is to protect insureds against unknown risks." *Id.* at 63, citing *Bartholomew*, 655 F.2d at 29.

We conclude that Taco Cabana's motion did not allege an offense occurring during Gulf's policy period, and that coverage for Two Pesos' continued trade dress infringement is precluded because the claim constitutes a known loss or loss in progress. Here, as in *Appalachian*, the risk of liability was no longer unknown because injuries resulted when Two Pesos first copied Taco Cabana's trade dress. *See Appalachian Ins. Co.*, 676 F.2d at 63.

The risk of injury from continued infringement was readily apparent, or should have been. Moreover, affording coverage to Two Pesos would violate public policy by allowing protection for a known loss and permitting an insured to benefit from its wrongdoing. *See Grumman Sys. Support Corp. v. Travelers Indem. Co.*, 828 F.Supp. 11, 13 (E.D.N.Y. 1993) (indemnification was precluded where continued use of proprietary software was an intentional act, done in violation of an injunction, that defendant knew would cause injury).

We hold that Taco Cabana did not allege a claim potentially within Gulf's policy coverage. Therefore, the trial court did not err in finding Gulf owed no duty to defend Two Pesos....

As you can see, **fortuity** takes in two concepts. The first is the idea of a **"loss in progress,"** the idea of not being able to buy insurance against a flood when the water is already in the house. But the other part of fortuity goes to our ability to control risks consciously. Fortuity assumes that we will act without a conscious intent to cause an insured peril to happen. The person who says, "I was trying to be careful, but I just didn't see the light turn red," is an example of this idea in action. The result here was accidental and fortuitous.[7] Our next excerpt takes in the other kind of behavior.

Weedo v. Stone-E-Brick, Inc.
81 N.J. 233, 405 A.2d 788
Supreme Court of New Jersey
1979

Clifford, J.:

* * * *

Pennsylvania National Mutual Insurance Company (hereinafter
Pennsylvania National) issued a general automobile liability policy to
Stone-E-Brick, Inc., a corporation engaged in masonry contracting. As part
of the policy, there was included Comprehensive General Liability
Coverage (hereinafter CGL).

During the term of the policy, Calvin and Janice Weedo contracted with
Stone-E-Brick to pour a concrete flooring on a verandah and to apply stucco
masonry to the exterior of their home. The completed job revealed cracks in
the stucco and other signs of faulty workmanship, such that the Weedos had
to remove the stucco and replace it with a proper material. Thereupon the
Weedos instituted suit against Stone-E-Brick and its principal, defendant
Romano, alleging in pertinent part that

> (a)s a result of the defective and unworkmanlike manner in which
> the defendants applied the said stucco, plaintiffs were compelled to
> and did cause the defects existing therein to be remedied, where
> possible, and the omissions to be supplied, and, in general, were
> compelled to and did furnish all the work, labor, services and
> materials necessary to complete the application of the said stucco
> in accordance with the contract and were compelled to and did
> expend large sums of money for that purpose in excess of the price
> which plaintiffs agreed to pay defendants for the application of said
> stucco, all of which was to plaintiffs' damage. (Emphasis
> supplied.)

While the same CGL policy was in effect, Stone-E-Brick performed roofing
and gutter work on a house being constructed for plaintiffs Gellas, under a
sub-contract agreement with the general contractor, defendant Vivino. After
completion of the home, the Gellases brought suit against Vivino based on
breach of contract due to defects in workmanship and seeking recovery of
costs "in connection with the repair and/or replacement of material
necessary to correct the ... defects in construction." Vivino in turn sought
indemnification from Stone-E-Brick by way of third-party complaint,
contending that plaintiffs' damages were the result of Stone-E-Brick's
"faulty workmanship, materials or construction...."

Thereafter Stone-E-Brick requested that Pennsylvania National take over the defense and indemnify it in regard to both complaints. The carrier refused, asserting that the policy of insurance did not furnish coverage for the claims made or, in the alternative, that exclusionary clauses specifically precluded coverage. By way of third-party complaint in the Weedo case and fourth-party complaint in the Gellas suit, Stone-E-Brick demanded judgment against Pennsylvania National for all sums found due as against the insured and in favor of the respective plaintiffs....

II.

Under the CGL provisions of the policy in question, Pennsylvania National agreed to pay "on behalf of the insured all sums which the insured shall become legally obligated to pay as damages because of ... bodily injury ... or Property damage to which this insurance applies, caused by an occurrence...." This is the standard language found in the great majority of CGLs written in this country. These provisions, developed by casualty rating bureaus over a period of nearly fifty years, have become an established norm of underwriting policy....

We set forth these basic principles simply to emphasize that, semantical rules of construction aside, contracts of insurance do contain relevant language frequently developed, as here, over the years after experience with different terms of expression which serves to define the risks underwritten. In the present instance Pennsylvania National's policy undertook to furnish certain coverage to Stone-E-Brick as a concern engaged in masonry contracting. In order to determine whether the claims of plaintiffs fall within the coverage provided, we start with an examination of the insured's business relationships with its customers.

In the usual course of its business Stone-E-Brick negotiates with homeowners to provide masonry work. As part of the bargaining process the insured may extend an express warranty that its stone, concrete and stucco products and services will be provided in a reasonably workmanlike fashion. Regardless of the existence of express warranties, the insured's provision of stucco and stone generally carries with it an implied warranty of merchantability and often an implied warranty of fitness for a particular purpose. These warranties arise by operation of law and recognize that, under common circumstances, the insured-contractor holds himself out as having the capacity to apply the stonework in a workmanlike manner, and further, that the homeowner relies upon the representation and anticipates suitable goods and services.

There exists another form of risk in the insured-contractor's line of work, that is, injury to people and damage to property caused by faulty workmanship. Unlike business risks of the sort described above, where the tradesman commonly absorbs the cost attendant upon the repair of his faulty work, the accidental injury to property or persons substantially caused by his unworkmanlike performance exposes the contractor to almost limitless liabilities. While it may be true that the same neglectful craftsmanship can be the cause of both a business expense of repair and a loss represented by damage to persons and property, the two consequences are vastly different in relation to sharing the cost of such risks as a matter of insurance underwriting.

In this regard Dean Henderson has remarked:

> The risk intended to be insured is the possibility that the goods, products or work of the insured, once relinquished or completed, will cause bodily injury or damage to property other than to the product or completed work itself, and for which the insured may be found liable. The insured, as a source of goods or services, may be liable as a matter of contract law to make good on products or work which is defective or otherwise unsuitable because it is lacking in some capacity. This may even extend to an obligation to completely replace or rebuild the deficient product or work. This liability, however, is not what the coverages in question are designed to protect against. The coverage is for tort liability for physical damages to others and not for contractual liability of the insured for economic loss because the product or completed work is not that for which the damaged person bargained.

An illustration of this fundamental point may serve to mark the boundaries between "business risks" and occurrences giving rise to insurable liability. When a craftsman applies stucco to an exterior wall of a home in a faulty manner and discoloration, peeling and chipping result, the poorly-performed work will perforce have to be replaced or repaired by the tradesman or by a surety. On the other hand, should the stucco peel and fall from the wall, and thereby cause injury to the homeowner or his neighbor standing below or to a passing automobile, an occurrence of harm arises which is the proper subject of risk-sharing as provided by the type of policy before us in this case. The happenstance and extent of the latter liability is entirely unpredictable. The neighbor could suffer a scratched arm or a fatal blow to the skull from the peeling stonework. Whether the liability of the businessman is predicated upon warranty theory or, preferably and more accurately, upon tort concepts, injury to persons and damage to other property constitute the risks intended to be covered under the CGL.

The standardized provisions in the CGL intended to convey this concept include, *inter alia*, the very exclusion clauses at issue herein. These exclusions "insured products" (exclusion "(n)") and "work performed" (exclusion "(o)") are as follows:

* * * *

This insurance does not apply

(n) to property damage to the named insured's products arising out of such products or any part of such products;

(o) to property damage to work performed by or on behalf of the named insured arising out of the work or any portion thereof, or out of materials, parts or equipment furnished in connection therewith.

We agree with Pennsylvania National that, given the precise and limited form of damages which form the basis of the claims against the insured, either exclusion is, or both are, applicable to exclude coverage. In short, the indemnity sought is not for "property damage to which this insurance applies."

The *Weedo* decision is among the most frequently cited of all decisions involving liability insurance, with good reason. Even though its decision is set out in terms of contract exclusions, that is, provisions in the insurance policy that the insurer does not agree to cover, those principles illustrate the idea of internal and external risk that are central to insurance. Stone-E-Brick was able to exercise virtually complete control over the quality of its work and the products. It could choose what kind of stucco to apply, how to mix the stucco, how to apply it, how long to let it cure, and even who did the work. So long as any problem was entirely limited to what Stone-E-Brick could control, its risk was entirely "internal" and not insurable. Any other conclusion would turn insurance into a device by which a business could get someone else to make good its defective work or products.

By contrast, when Stone-E-Brick stucco fell off of the wall and hit someone below, the risk was not entirely within Stone-E-Brick's control. The harm to someone else was not entirely within Stone-E-Brick's control. Who would know that to stucco piece would fall off at just the right moment to harm a passer by on the street below? It is this kind of external risk—in essence, harm that is dependent upon something beyond the insured's control—that is the core idea of a fortuitous event from an insurance perspective. Again, the idea is a deep one, dependent not only on the insured's actions but upon the harm that follows and potentially some objective or subjective perception of whether that harm is the kind that should reasonably be expected by the insured to follow from its acts.

The issue continues to trouble courts and practitioners alike, but this at least is a first approach to understanding it.

Finally, of course, there are those who simply wish to hurt others or cause problems. They pose no real problem; their acts are not fortuitous or accidental, and for them, there is no coverage.[8]

Tort Cases Arising from Insurance

This, then, is some of the *theory* behind insurance as it may have an impact on the study of torts. Now let us look at the impact of insurance on the ins and outs of litigation as it is likely to affect you.

A typical liability policy — usually one providing for commercial general liability coverage, liability coverage for homeowners, or automotive liability coverage — obligates insurer and insured to do or not do certain things.

The insured generally is obligated to report claims and suits to the insurance company in a timely fashion, to cooperate with the insurance company as it proceeds with its defense, and to refrain from conduct that will prejudice the insurer's conduct of the insured's defense.

The insurer is obligated to provide the insured with a defense to claims that may be covered under the policy (warning: this is not always true — some policies do not contain such an obligation!), and to make appropriate efforts to settle claims against its insure within policy limits. Now let's see how these duties play out in "real life."

Interaction Between Insurer and Insured

Notifying the Insured of the Claim

Interaction between insured and liability insurer usually begins when the insured becomes aware that a claim may be made against it. Sometimes awareness is as obvious as being involved in an automobile collision, but in other cases, the first awareness of a problem arises when a demand letter arrives in the insured's mail or a process server shows up at the door.

In any case, the insured is obligated by the policy to provide notification of the claim, any demand letters or suit papers and other relevant information to the insurance company as promptly as possible. In most situations, this is done by calling one's insurance agent or broker, but some policies contain specific directions that must be followed.

What happens if the insured does not provide notice as promptly as possible? In the past, courts rather rigidly held that this omission voided coverage. The rule still applies in some states and situations, but many jurisdictions generally require that the insurer be prejudiced in some fashion by the late notice. Entry of a default judgment against the insured is a good example of such prejudice, but there definitely can be others.

Businesses that would flirt with giving late notice should remember that courts tend to be less sympathetic to forgetful businesses than forgetful people. Still, late notice rarely is an insuperable problem between insured and insurer.

Insurer's Receiving the Claim

The next stop in the relationship between insurer and insured comes when the insurer receives the claim. If its policy obligates the insurer to defend the insured by providing counsel and paying costs associated with the defense (and most policies do contain such a provision) the insurer must decide whether the claim being asserted is such that a defense should be provided.

Analysis of the Factual Allegations

Courts in various states apply a variety of different rules to this process, but there are a number of common threads. First, with respect to the suit papers themselves, the insurer generally must focus upon the factual allegations rather than upon the legal theories of recovery in making its decision whether a defense must be provided.

If any of those allegations are such that there might be (or would be in some states) coverage under the policy if they are proven, the insurer must defend.

In suits or claims where there are multiple counts or issues, the insurer generally must defend the whole package if any of the counts or factual allegations meet the foregoing test. Some states affirmatively require the insurer to base its decision to defend solely on the text of the suit papers. Others require the insurer to conduct a reasonable investigation of the events surrounding the claim or suit before it decides what to do.[9]

The logic behind these rules becomes clear with a little thought. The requirement that facts, rather than theories, be the basis for the insurer's decision helps prevent unscrupulous attorneys from manipulating suit papers that attempt to bring an otherwise uncovered claim within the terms of the defendant's insurance.[10] Also, requiring the insurer to defend the entire lawsuit against the insured if any part may be covered protects insureds and avoids possible problems when two different lawyers later try to represent the insured on parts of the same suit.

The states that require an investigation generally do so on the principle that the reality of the situation should form the basis for an insurer's decision to defend.

Insurer's Decision

Whatever rules apply, however, there comes that moment when the insurer must make a decision as to what it is going to do. It has three basic choices:

1. It may **accept the defense of the matter unreservedly**.

2. At the other end of the spectrum, it may **decline to defend** because it perceives that there is no coverage for the matter under the policy.

3. It may take a middle ground, **offering a defense under some kind of reservation of its rights to decline coverage later**.

Accept Defense

Although there are those who believe otherwise, most insurers accept the defense of most claims unreservedly. By so doing the insurer tacitly agrees that the claim or suit is covered under its policy and that it will provide a defense and pay judgments or settlements up to the policy limits. This decision sometimes can change as suit papers are amended or as new information becomes available, but not often.

The insurer has the right to choose counsel for its insureds, and generally has relationships with lawyers who will undertake such representation when called upon to do so by an insurer. Some insurers use "house counsel," lawyers who are employees of the insurer, to defend insureds in certain kinds of claims. A number of state bar ethics and disciplinary bodies have attacked this practice, but "house counsel" operations can be effective and economical if properly run.

Deny Defense

An insurer's decision to deny a defense often is both contentious and risky. In some cases, it is not difficult. The policy may have expired or been canceled. Sometimes the injury or damage clearly has taken place outside of the policy period. In most cases, however, the insurer's decision rests upon its perception that the allegations in the suit papers are not covered.

If the insurer is wrong, its refusal to honor its obligations can lead to lawsuits against it for breaching its contract with its insured and, in some states, for violating provisions of state insurance or consumer protection statutes. For this reason, at the same time that they decline to defend a lawsuit or claim, many insurance companies file lawsuits for declaratory judgments seeking a ruling from a court that the insurance policy did not in fact obligate the insurer to defend. These often proceed while the original lawsuit against the insured is underway, and the interplay between lawsuits can be challenging.

Defense with Reservations of Rights

In the middle are situations in which the insurer believes that it may have grounds to decline coverage but does not wish to decline a defense immediately. Here the general practice is to defend the insured "under a reservation of rights." This reservation generally takes the form of a letter from the insurer to the insured in which the insurer sets forth those bases it believes would relieve it of any obligation with respect to the matter.

If the insured accepts the defense offered by the insurer, it generally is held to have agreed that the insurer can raise the coverage defenses set forth in the letter at some future point. Sometimes the insurer asks the insured to sign a "**non-waiver agreement**," a contract that allows the defense to continue without waiver of the insurer's right to contest coverage later.

Response by the Insured to Reservations of Rights

In some cases, insureds do not accept the insurer's reservation of rights. Older decisions often held that the insurer had two choices in such a situation: (1) abandon its objections and offer an unreserved defense or (2) decline to defend at all.

More recent decisions generally try to steer a middle ground between these alternatives. They permit the insurer to stand upon its reservation of rights and tender a defense even over the insured's objection. Nonetheless, this is an area where the relationship between insured and insurer can be the most uncomfortable.

Responsibility of Counsel

The lawyer who represents the insured but is paid by the insurance company must steer a careful course. Case law universally holds that the insured's attorney must make the interests of the insured paramount. The attorney cannot represent the insured at the same time he or she also represents the insurer in trying to avoid its coverage obligations.

By corollary, it is inappropriate for the insured's lawyer to feed information to the insurer that will be used to defeat coverage.[11] The lawyer must also avoid trying to steer the insured's case into an uncovered area. At the same time, it is inappropriate for the insured's lawyer to represent the insured in a lawsuit against the insurance company over the very case in which the attorney serves as the insured's counsel.[12]

In practice, there are several ways to avoid these problems. The first and most important is for the team appointed to represent the insured to remember what its obligations are and to live up to them at all points. The next is to try to avoid problems by ensuring that insured and insurer agree on the path to be followed if at all possible. Communicating fully, equally, and promptly with both insurer and insured, and simply suggesting the best[13] course of action consistent with one's obligations as counsel generally is a very good way to avoid problems.

Settlement Questions

At some point, usually around the time that the case against the insured is set for mediation, there will be interaction and possible conflict between insurer and insured as to whether the case should be settled, and if so for how much. More often than not, insureds want the cases against them to be settled within the limits of their policy without regard to how much is spent. Insurers, on the other hand, have the right to control the settlement process by the terms of most insurance policies,[14] and they may not be as willing as the insured to settle at any price or even to settle at all.

Courts have taken two overlapping approaches in dealing with this conflict and how the insurer—who has the money—should resolve it. The first line of authority reasons that, because the insurer has exclusive control over the settlement process, it must place the insured's interest first in deciding whether to accept a settlement offer or even whether to initiate negotiations. The general phrase used in such states is that the insurer must give at least **equal consideration** to the interests of the insured in deciding whether or not to accept a settlement offer.

The second line of cases imposes what amounts to a negligence standard. As phrased in Texas, one of the leading states adhering to this doctrine, the insurer must use **reasonable care** in deciding whether to accept a settlement offer within policy limits.

In practice, the two doctrines have identical consequences for insurers who fail to meet their obligations. The insurer becomes liable for the entire amount of any verdict against the insured, even if it exceeds policy limits by a substantial amount. In some states, other damages can be imposed, including damages for mental distress or anguish, loss of profits or financial problems caused by the presence of an adverse judgment, and punitive damages. In some states, failure to engage in good faith settlement negotiations can also be a violation of state insurance or consumer protection statutes.

Mediation and similar forms of alternative dispute resolution have eased some of the potential for conflict at the time of settlement. Most jurisdictions require both insurer and insured representatives to be present at the mediation, and good mediators often can resolve any coverage disputes at the same time they resolve the original lawsuit against the plaintiff.

A variation on this theme can arise when some causes of action in a lawsuit are covered by insurance and others are not. A similar situation can arise when a large self-insured retention or deductible exists, that is, an amount that the insured must pay itself before the insurer's obligations arise. The law is clear that an insurer does not have a duty to pay judgments or settlements that are not covered; compare this with its duty to defend, which generally is considerably broader. You and the other members of the defense team must try to effect a settlement of the whole case. In such situations, the best that the defense team can do is communicate to insured and insurer its best estimate of what the various causes of action are worth and encourage each side to be an active participant. If one or both does not see reason, all the defense team can do is the best it can with what it has.

That, in a nutshell, is a first peek at how liability insurance works in the "real world." The picture is complicated by an increasing number of states and situations in which liability insurance is mandatory as a device for satisfying a financial responsibility requirement to drive a car, practice in a profession, or even operate a waste disposal area. And as experience with asbestos and other mass tort litigation shows, insurance can be a key — sometimes the only — on which a mass tort or class action settlement can be fashioned.

These are difficult issues, and many involve difficult questions of public policy. There are many ways to meet such problems, but they do inevitably change the role of insurance as it was initially conceived from a voluntary form of risk management to a mandatory form of loss distribution.

Key Words and Phrases

equal consideration
external risk
fortuity
insurable interest
loss in progress
non-waiver agreement
reasonable care
sharing a risk
sharing an event
sharing expenses

Review Questions

1.   Do you have 30 persons in your class? Even if you don't, try the same-birthday check. Don't forget to include your instructor. He/she has a birthday too.

2.   If you're using this textbook as part of a paralegal studies course, you are probably aware that tort and personal injury law provide career cases for paralegals. Check Internet resources listed at www.lexisone.com/ html/legal_guide/ general_practice_areas_NEW/ personal_injury_tort_law.htm.

---

[1] For those who are interested, it is not the number of people that counts but the number of possible combinations. The first person compares birthdays with 29 others (you don't compare with yourself), the second with 28 (he or she already has compared with person 1), the third with 27, and so on. The total number of chances for a birthday to match equals 29+28+27+26+25 ... +1 or 435 combinations of people to check for a common birthday. Since there are only

365 days in a year, you can see why it is so nearly certain that at least two will have the same birthday.

[2] Please do not be afraid. This is not going to morph into a statistics textbook.

[3] There are, of course, other kinds of relationships that do not constitute insurance. Among the most famous is a tontine, an arrangement in which a group of people contribute money to a fund. The last survivor receives the proceeds. You may recall a particularly poignant episode of *M*A*S*H* in which Colonel Potter received the proceeds of a unique tontine—several bottles of fine old wine.

[4] Insurance on ships was the first modern insurance, and Lloyd's coffee house in London was the place where shipowners and charterers went to buy it as far back as the late 17th century. Of course, Lloyd's still exists as one of the greatest of all insurance markets, and its history and workings are stories far too rich to set forth in this book. For those interested, a study of Lloyd's is legally, historically, and economically fascinating.

[5] There are problems, however. It is easy (well, sort of) to determine many of the issues associated with life insurance. After all, the mortality tables are really quite accurate, and since the amount to be paid under a life policy is determined in advance, the insurer's maximum exposure can be determined with relative precision. It would take a truly catastrophic epidemic to overtake these calculations.

With liability insurance, however, the kinds of risks insured are much broader, and sometimes they are not even in existence at the time the policy is written. CERCLA, the federal environmental statute, is a prime example. This law, which was not passed until 1980, imposed strict liability on those who had dumped toxic waste improperly. After the courts held that the statute applied retroactively, conservative estimates put the total cost of cleaning up CERCLA sites at well into the tens or hundreds of billions of dollars. Obviously, those charged with CERCLA liability looked to their insurers for coverage. Insurers responded that the policies had not provided such coverage or that coverage was excluded under various pollution exclusions that had been added to policies from 1968 onward. We need not decide in this endnote who was right; the point is simply that neither CERCLA liability nor the magnitude of costs that could be imposed under it had been rationally measured when the earlier policies had been written.

[6] If you haven't, you should view it. It's a wonderful detective film about insurance fraud with Barbara Stanwyck, Fred MacMurray as the bad guy, and Edward G. Robinson as a dogged insurance claims adjuster.

[7] Actually, these are much deeper waters than this very quick introduction may lead you to believe. Is the conduct to be judged subjectively, that is, by looking at the actual person's actual conduct and expectation, or objectively, using a reasonable person standard? If a bad intent exists, is the harm still an accident if it is not the kind that ordinarily would follow from the intent? ("I meant to burn down the building, but I didn't know anyone was inside who could be hurt.") Remember also that insurance involves a contract, so many of these decisions will depend upon contract language.

[8] Again, there are problems here that this blanket statement tends to mask. At what point does a decision to dump waste into pits (for example) turn into non-fortuitous and uninsured conduct if the waste leaks out and pollutes another's property? Is it when the waste goes in the pits? When the dumper discovers the leakage? When the dumper discovers the harmful nature of what's in there? Or is it when the dumper discovers that some amount of pollution has occurred, really the equivalent of the no-insurance-for-flood-when-water's-in-the-living-room idea? There is no bright line, just a series of shades of gray.

[9] This is the broadest of outlines. There are many other issues. Examples: is participation in a government ordered investigation of pollution at a clean-up site a "suit"? What about an administrative proceeding? Suppose the letter is just a notice of a claim. Is that something that has to be defended? If it later turns out that there was no obligation to defend, may the insurer recover the amounts it has expended? Another deceptively simple area!

[10] This sort of thing happens and, up to a point, it is not inappropriate. But there are cases where the plaintiff's lawyer goes overboard. In one case, the lawyer for a plaintiff attempted to characterize a minister's lewd sexual conduct as being "negligent." The Court of Appeals quite properly and summarily rejected such a characterization.

[11] Clearly, though there must be an exchange of information because the insurer will need to know enough about the case to set aside a sum of money sufficient to provide for defense costs and possible settlements. This being so, once the information is in the insurer's hands, there can always be the perception that it

will be misused. To minimize this possibility in cases where there exists a serious coverage issue, many insurers "split their files." They assign the coverage issues associated with a particular matter to one adjuster and the liability issues (the issues associated with the original lawsuit against the insured) to another. This "ethical wall" approach is not entirely effective, but it does work in most cases.

[12] This is not to say that counsel is prohibited from advising the insurance company that it should settle or even from demanding that it do so. But it is incongruous and inappropriate for the insurer to have to pay a lawyer to sue it! Additionally, since the lawyer is likely to be a key witness in any insured vs. insurer litigation, there is an obvious ethical problem in continuing to represent one side or the other.

[13] Meaning "the right thing to do" without regard to who did the hiring.

[14] Some insurance policies (usually providing coverage for professional malpractice) contain a "consent to settle" clause that prohibits the insurer from settling a claim against the insured without first obtaining the insured's consent. If the insured improperly refuses to settle, the insurer is protected because these provisions generally provide that the insurer is liable for no more than what the case could have been settled for if the settlement offer had been accepted.

Chapter Seventeen

A FEW CLOSING THOUGHTS

As the new century unfurls and we pause to ponder the most important developments in law during the last thousand years, keep in mind the critical one that underlies what we have studied in this book: that legal duties to an unseen and future public do exist.

Contract duties arose in face-to-face transactions. The parties knew with whom they were dealing and what was at stake. At the other end of the spectrum, criminal law — the obligation to the sovereign — was as immediate as the sheriff. You might get away with breaking the law, but there was no doubt of the consequences.

In both cases, the demands of the law were specific and personal. Even the earliest torts — trespass, conversion, and battery — had deep roots in property rights or in face-to-face interaction. Battery was, after all, the first legal codification of "being in someone's face"!

The Concept of General Duty

Imagine, then, the changes that we have more or less taken for granted in this book. First the idea of a **general duty**, something defined only in terms of what would be reasonable in the community at large. No longer could one look to a contract or a code of conduct for specific guidance. Suddenly there was just an amorphous floor, a minimum standard that could result in liability.

And to whom? As the debate in *Palsgraf* makes clear, as late as 1929 it was difficult for many to accept the idea that a legal duty could run from an individual to the entire world, that chance encounter with perfect strangers could result in legal liability.

The second change that followed from the first was as revolutionary, if not more so. With the decline of privity, **duty could exist to people in the future**, unknown and possibly not even born yet. The architect of a building that collapsed years after it was built from a latent defect ... the manufacturer of a drug that caused cancer in the daughters of the mothers who took it ... these and other breaches of duty "to the future" would have been unthinkable without privity first having gone by the wayside.

Once the idea of duty was decoupled from privity — face-to-face relationships — much else could, and did, follow. Responsibility for defective products could only exist comfortably as a doctrine once the idea of privity was no longer necessary to the idea of a sale or commercial transaction. Mass torts — asbestos, cigarettes, and silicone gel implants are examples — need both the ideas developed in individual tort cases *and* the idea of mass duty and obligation to survive.

Future Torts

Looking ahead, we can see a rich future flowing from this idea. Recent efforts at "tort reform" have by no means diminished the substantive richness of the concepts in this field. Growth of the Internet is even now prompting discussions about "e-torts," the next likely area of growth in this fertile field.

As gene therapy and genetically engineered material becomes more common, we can easily envision expansion or change in existing doctrines to meet the rush of technology. It isn't even all that farfetched to think about a law of torts in space. Remember that the seeds of our current law were planted at a time when steam power was revolutionary and the computer would have been thought witchcraft by all but a very, very few.

To paraphrase the recent song, if we can dream it, sooner or later we will need principles of law to help guide it. Tort law is a likely candidate to provide such guidance, since it offers flexible principles that can be applied consistently. If the history of the field is any prediction, generations of legal professionals to come will find it a fertile and rewarding field in which to work.

burden of proof
 defined · 124
 generally · 352
burden of testing
 generally · 223
Burk Royalty Co. v. Walls · 202

C

*Callahan v. Cardinal Glennon
 Hospital* · 111
 multiple proximate cause discussion
 · 114
Cardozo, Justice · 57, 102, 104,
 219, 226, 246, 338
causation
 defined · 102
cause of action
 element
  defined · 28
caveat emptor
 defined · 218
 generally · 245
chattels
 defined · 179
City of Tyler v. Likes · 192
Clardy v. Cowles Publishing Co. ·
 277
comparative negligence
 percentage of fault
  generally · 136
comparative negligence doctrine ·
 130
comparative negligence systems
 49% comparative fault · 134
 50% comparative fault · 134
 pure comparative fault · 134
 slight gross comparative fault · 134
 state-by-state · 134
compensatory damages
 defined · 174
concept of warning
 effect on legal team · 232
 generally · 232

concurrent causation
 defined · 117
*Connors v. University Associates in
 Obstetrics and Gynecology, Inc.*
 · 93
consent
 as defense to assault or battery · 43
consequences
 limiting · 12
consideration
 defined · 10
 detriment · 10
 forbearance · 10
contract
 defined · 10
contract law
 concept of implied warranty · 218
 concept of transparency · 218
 evolution to tort law · 219
 mass-produced products · 217
contracts
 distinguished from torts · 20
 elements · 19
 overlap with torts and crime · 20
contractual duties
 elements · 12
contributory negligence
 generally · 128
contributory negligence rule · 130
conversion
 contract to trespass to chattels · 37
 defenses · 38
 defined · 35
 elements · 35
 generally · 34
 money · 36
Coyne v. Taber Partners I · 145,
 147
crime
 defined · 17
 elements · 19
 overlap with torts and contracts · 20
criminal law
 keeping the peace as foundation · 17
 similarity to torts · 18
Cudahy, Justice · 265

sharing of common risk by group ·
372
sharing of event · 372
sharing of expenses · 372
tort cases · 385
intent
defined · 18
intervening cause
defined · 147
invitee
generally · 155

J

jury instructions
punitive damages · 213
sample for negligence and
proximate cause · 135
sample on assault · 39
sample on battery · 40
sample on trespass · 29

K

*Keener v. Dayton Electric
Manufacturing Co.* · 227, 231,
232
King v. Williams · 69, 81, 84

L

lack of intent
as defense to assault or battery · 43
as defense to assault or battery · 43
Lake v. Wal-Mart Stores, Inc. · 286,
291, 306, 307
landowner duty towards child
trespassers
generally · 161
last clear chance
affirmative defense · 124
lay witness

defined · 80
legal cause
defined · 105
Leventhal, Judge Harold · 291
liability for defective products
defense of contributory fault · 231
generally · 231
misuse as reasonably anticipated use
· 231
quality v. quantity · 231
user negligence · 231
liability insurance
generally · 375
libel
generally · 249
licensee
generally · 155
life expectancy tables
generally · 371
linkage
generally · 101
Little v. Morris · 336
loss in progress
defined · 380
loss of use
generally · 180

M

*M.L. Lee Acquisition Fund L.P. v.
Deloitte & Touche* · 341
Maisel v. Gelhaus · 177
malice
defined · 209
malicious prosecution
advice of counsel as defense · 318
defined · 312
elements · 317
probable cause contrasted to malice ·
318
malicious proseuction
probable cause element · 318
McIntyre v. Balentine · 128, 132
contributory negligence discussion ·
129

U

V

W

Z